Teaching Without Disruption in Secondary School

D1586319

A model for managing
pupil behaviour

Roland Chaplain

Routledge
Taylor & Francis Group
LONDON AND NEW YORK

First published 2003
by RoutledgeFalmer
11 New Fetter Lane, London EC4P 4EE

Simultaneously published in the USA and Canada
by RoutledgeFalmer
29 West 35th Street, New York, NY 10001

RoutledgeFalmer is an imprint of the Taylor & Francis Group

© 2003 Roland Chaplain

Typeset in 10/12pt Times NR by
Graphicraft Limited, Hong Kong
Printed and bound in Great Britain by
MPG Books Ltd, Bodmin

British Library Cataloguing in Publication Data
A catalogue record for this book is available
from the British Library

Library of Congress Cataloging-in-Publication Data
Chaplain, Roland.
  Teaching without disruption : a multilevel model for managing
behaviour in the secondary schools / Roland Chaplain.
    p. cm.
  Includes bibliographical references and index.
  ISBN 0-415-24834-5 (pbk.)
  1. School discipline—Great Britain. 2. High school students—
Great Britain—Discipline. I. Title.

LB3012.4.G7C53 2003
373.1102′4—dc21   2003040930

A catalogue record has been requested

For Sandra
who makes it all worthwhile

Contents

List of Illustrations   ix
Acknowledgements   xi

Introduction   1

PART I
Managing yourself   7

1   Stress coping and effective teaching   9

2   Teacher thinking and pupil behaviour   34

3   Professional social skills: controlling social
    communication   56

PART II
The school as an organisation   81

4   Whole school influences on behaviour management ✓   83

5   The role of senior management in facilitating positive
    behaviour ✓   103

PART III
Classroom management   119

6   Classroom environment and climate ✓   121

7   Classroom structures: the role of rules, routines and
    rituals in behaviour management ✓   140

PART IV
Coping with emotional and behavioural difficulties   159

8   Managing students with emotional and behavioural
    difficulties: when the going gets tough   161

    Bibliography   185
    Author index   197
    Subject index   201

Illustrations

Figures

I.1	The multilevel model of behaviour management	2
I.2	Layered questions about behaviour management	3
1.1	An interactive model of stress and coping	17
1.2	The architecture of BOSS and EMPLOYEE systems	19
1.3	Individual coping analysis ICAN	29
2.1	A simplified model of the teacher expectancy-confirmation process	38
3.1	Information loss in classroom communication	62
3.2	A hierarchy of social skills used in teaching	65
3.3	Facial code	66
3.4	The business gaze	69
3.5	The social gaze	69
3.6	A model for developing assertive behaviour	77
4.1	A simple systems model	90
4.2	Communication networks	96
4.3	Person–environment fit	100
6.1	Potential influences of classroom environment and atmosphere on the thinking, emotions and behaviour of students	122
6.2	Traditional classroom	126
6.3	Lecture theatre	127
6.4	Coffee bar	129
6.5	Nightclub	130
6.6	Committee table	130
6.7	Open circle	131
7.1	Developmental perspective on classroom management comparing early and later encounters	146
8.1	Behaviour change cycle	173
8.2	An A-B-C model of behaviour	174
8.3	Frequency graph showing number of occurrences of negative and positive behaviours recorded by day of the week	175

Tables

1.1	Everyday coping in school	20
1.2	Functions of social support	26
1.3	Coping styles	31
1.4	Individual coping analysis (ICAN)	32
2.1	Implying personality from limited information	47
2.2	Explanations for Lee's misbehaviour	52
3.1	A simplified social script for a lesson	62
3.2	Some examples of professional social skills used by teachers	63
4.1	A simple systems analysis of inputs, processes and outputs	92
6.1	Explaining success and failure	134
7.1	Evaluating classroom routines	156
8.1	Comparison of the key differences between three approaches to intervening with behavioural difficulties	171
8.2	Relative seriousness of antisocial behaviours	175

Acknowledgements

In writing this book I am indebted to a cast of thousands. I will start by thanking the many pupils I have worked with over the past twenty-seven years, who taught me so much about schools and schooling. Thanks also to the hundreds of headteachers, teachers and trainee teachers I have taught, interviewed and spent time with, and who also had much to say about schools and schooling. Thank you to my colleagues and friends with whom I have worked, exchanged many thoughts and shared the occasional beer along the way!

In various places throughout this book I have included quotes from a number of the above. Some were happy to be named, others were not, so I decided to stick with pseudonyms for the sake of consistency.

I would also like to thank the staff at Papworth Hospital, for making sure I stayed around long enough to finish it.

On a personal note, there are a few others to whom I also owe much. My mother for teaching me the power of reflection, my father for teaching me the need for detailed analysis and my sister, Gloria, for her support and insight.

Last, but certainly not least, my wife, for reading endless revisions and for translating my scribbled hieroglyphics, often written on the backs of envelopes and serviettes, into a manuscript.

Introduction

Behaviour management has always, of course, been of interest to teachers and managers in schools. There are many approaches suggested for improving the ways in which teachers 'control' students' behaviour, and each has its own strengths and limitations. Which approach is considered most appropriate by an individual teacher or school depends on a range of interlinked organisational and individual factors (school ethos, relationships and the personal characteristics of those who work and study there). There is no single right way of doing things.

This is very much a point-of-view book in which I have used an integrative multilevel model of behaviour management (see Figure I.1) as a basis for understanding and developing the management of behaviour. The model represents a top-down approach, advocating progressive focusing, moving from organisational to individual strategies. If a behaviour policy is working correctly and is well thought out, supported and operated by all staff, it should eliminate many of the low-level disruptive behaviours, making life easier for teachers and providing them with more time to teach. The behaviour policy, or discipline plan, should also provide the fundamental principles for managing individual classrooms and supporting teachers when dealing with extreme behaviour. However, this does not mean that teachers should not enjoy distinctiveness in how they operate their classrooms. Far from it: the whole school framework provides the continuity, which combines with the idiosyncrasies of different teachers and departments, to construct the school's identity. Obviously, there has to be some balance between the three levels in order to minimise confusion for students and staff, so a monitoring and evaluation process is recommended (see Figure I.1).

Before I proceed to describe the contents of the chapters, you may welcome some orienting comments. Much advice on managing behaviour focuses on teacher–student relationships in the classroom and this book is no exception in that respect. However, whilst classroom relationships are central to the learning process, there are many other factors which are also influential and, I argue, essential to effective behaviour management. These issues should be viewed alongside classroom activity as opposed to being seen as something to be kept separate.

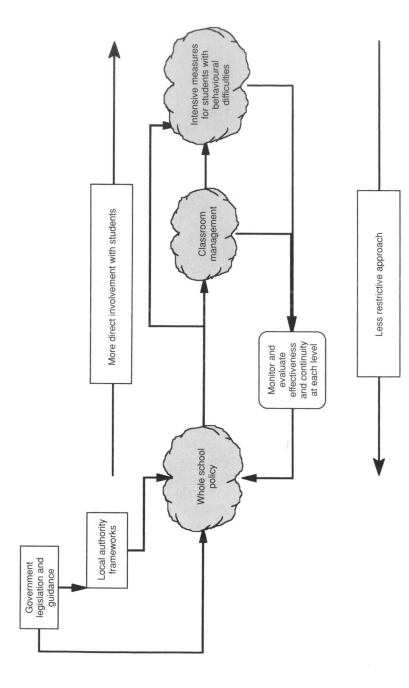

Figure 1.1 The multilevel model of behaviour management. The whole school policy is the reference value or standard against which both classroom management and intensive strategies are compared. As the management function moves from left to right so does the level of intrusiveness or direct control over student behaviour.

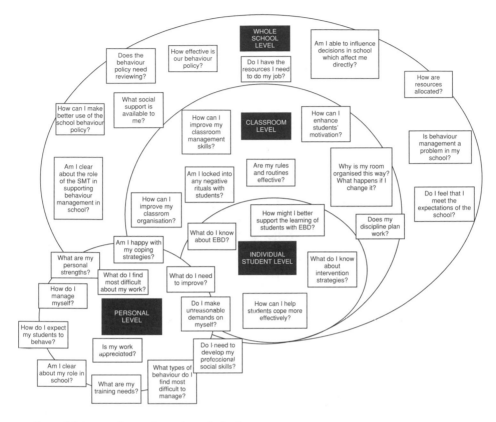

Figure I.2 Layered questions about behaviour management

Taking on board this wide brief, from whole school to individual issues, inevitably limits the depth of coverage that can be given to each topic. I have therefore included a large number of references throughout to enable you to follow up any areas you might wish to develop, or find interesting. There is a strong practical theme running throughout represented through a series of focused questions and activities within the various chapters. I opted to build them into the text rather than putting them at the ends of chapters, so you could engage with them at the relevant point in the text. Some can be used for private reflection or with colleagues and some with your students in order to gain their perspective and enhance your knowledge of how they function. They are predominantly questions to help to provide focus for you to reflect on your own practice and context, rather than trying to offer rigid prescriptive direction.

Figure I.2 provides an overview of the types of questions this book seeks to answer; these are nested in the various layers of the multilevel model.

A brief examination of Figure I.2 reveals interrelatedness and overlaps between the various levels. Whole school activity is shown as encompassing classroom management and individual work with difficult students, the behaviour policy providing the framework and direction for behaviour management at these levels. The personal level questions refer to the teacher; this level is shown as overlapping the other three levels, highlighting the centrality of the teacher in the overall plan.

I have used the term 'classroom managers' to describe teachers, since I wanted to highlight the multiplicity of tasks and decision-making that teachers have to perform, under pressure, in order to achieve their everyday objective – educating children. Unlike administrators, who are bound by procedures and have the luxury of being pedestrian in following them, teachers and managers have to make continual decisions whilst 'on the hoof' – the luxury of taking time to marshal the evidence, consider alternative strategies before acting is not always readily available. However, this does not prevent the proactive or anticipatory planning of behaviour management and the practising of different strategies and procedures outside the classroom, in order to be prepared for what might happen when teaching. Clearly, as any experienced teacher will be aware, it is impossible to prepare for every eventuality when interacting with several hundred young people in a day, so you will not be able to plan for every conceivable problem – meaning you will inevitably have to use deflective and reactive strategies as well. Deflection activities provide a breathing space whilst the situation is occurring, allowing you to regroup your thoughts and think of the most effective way to respond. Reactive strategies are used after the event. The advantage of using anticipatory strategies (e.g. seating arrangements, removing temptation, clear rules) as opposed to deflection tactics (e.g. deliberately ignoring behaviour, praising peers, invading personal space) or reactive strategies (e.g. warnings, sanctions, exclusion) is that the first are far lower profile than the other two and therefore less damaging to teacher–pupil relationships.

Behaviour management can be considered in a multiplicity of ways; despite this, the psychological level is, I suggest, the crossroads where all these influences meet. It is an individual's appraisal and interpretation of themselves and their situation that hold the key to understanding why they behave the way they do, and why they think others think and behave the way they do. I am a firm believer that teachers will be more effective in managing behaviour if they are reflective, analytical and critical in thinking about their practice and that these processes should be informed by high quality empirical research.

The plan of the book is to start with the teacher as the focus, move on to organisational and interpersonal issues and finish by looking at individual students – a roller-coaster ride through the different levels of activity!

Part 1 considers the personal level or how the individual teacher thinks, feels and behaves. Chapter 1 explores the stress and coping process. Various illustrations are used to explain why we might become stressed and, more importantly, how we might improve our coping. The ways in which we think about students and the process by which this thinking might unwittingly influence their behaviour are the concerns of Chapter 2. The final topic in Part I relates to professional social skills. Chapter 3 addresses the complexities of nonverbal behaviour and how such behaviours influence what we think about ourselves, and how we interpret the behaviour of others.

In Part II the emphasis shifts to looking at the school as an organisation. The relationship between the behaviour policy, school climate and communication and how each connects to school effectiveness are highlighted in Chapter 4. The importance of achieving balance between organisational needs and individual goals is also taken on board. In Chapter 5 I discuss the role of the head and senior management team (SMT) in leading development of behaviour management and ask a series of questions about what style of leadership is most supportive to teachers in this respect.

Having discussed organisational climate in Part II, Part III focuses on the impact of the classroom climate on student behaviour. How to manipulate the physical environment to create the desired conditions for learning and positive behaviour is the starting point for Chapter 6. In the latter part of this chapter I consider the psychological effects of classroom climate on students' motivation, how they value themselves and disruptive behaviour. The final chapter of Part III (Chapter 7) examines the use of simple rules, routines and rituals in the effective management of student behaviour. The thesis is to take up as much of the management task as possible, using limit-setting structures which students learn and which become routinised, minimising the need for the teacher to be continually engaged in thinking about and actively directing behaviour.

Part IV takes on board the difficult issue of coping with and helping students who have emotional and behavioural difficulties (EBD). How to define, identify and intervene with this group of students is a complex activity. I suggest engaging in personal reflection alongside official guidelines before deciding how to go about assessing what the difficulty might be and where it might be located. Again recognising the importance of, taking account of the multiplicity of potential influences, as well as the multiple levels involved, should be included in the reflection process. The chapter ends with consideration of three different approaches to supporting emotional and behavioural difficulties, which relate to different understandings and beliefs about the causes and control of human behaviour.

Despite the interconnectedness of the four parts, they are designed to stand alone if required. Thus, the book can be read from cover to cover or alternatively you could follow the topics in your own preferred order, concentrating first on those aspects of behaviour management you most wish to develop.

Part I

Managing yourself

Chapter 1

Stress coping and effective teaching

The aim of this chapter is to help you better understand the causes of stress and how to improve your coping. It is based on the premise that it is possible to improve how you manage behaviour through positive action. Furthermore, it sets the scene for how the rest of the book is organised by examining stress and coping at multiple levels, that is, personal, interpersonal and organisational levels.

Stress has become a buzzword in recent years surrounded by an ever-growing industry offering advice on how to avoid and/or cope with it. It is generally accepted that stress is on the increase due, in part, to accelerated social and technological change. In British schools the pace and rate of change over recent years have been dramatic and coping with it has proved difficult for many teachers (Travers and Cooper 1996).

A commonly held belief is that stress is to be avoided at all costs since it results in bad health. Whilst there is evidence to demonstrate a relationship between stress and ill health (Bartlett 1998), this does not mean that all stress is invariably bad for you. Being under too much pressure and unable to cope can make you ill, but stress can also be a motivator – the spice of life! Whether or not events are pathological or inspirational depends on how stress is being defined together with how an individual perceives and deals with it. Some individuals plan things down to the last letter before proceeding and then pace themselves throughout. Others wait until the last minute and when the pressure is on leap into action to complete a task. Neither tactic is right or wrong; they just represent different ways of coping and are fine – provided they get the job done and no one suffers as a result.

Considerable research evidence has demonstrated a correlation between teacher stress and pupil behaviour (Kyriacou 1998) that is, high levels of stress are associated with high levels of disruptive behaviour. Again, establishing a *causal* link between the two is more difficult. Are students badly behaved because teachers are coping with too much pressure from other sources? Or do badly behaved students cause teacher stress? The 'answer' could include either or both and the relationship is not necessarily linear since other factors can intervene. One important psychological factor in understanding this relationship concerns how what we *think* might happen can influence outcomes. For example, all teachers are likely to perceive some students or groups of students as potentially difficult. This perception can lead to those teachers feeling anxious and exhibiting behaviour (often unwittingly), which reflects this anxiety to which the students reciprocate – often negatively. This student behaviour reinforces what the teacher expected which creates further anxiety and hence the cycle continues.

Teaching in schools makes fairly unique demands on teachers compared with other professionals. They are required to be knowledgeable about a number of subjects and ensure their students' success. At the same time they are required to control and guide the social behaviour of young people, some of whom have little desire to be in school. Furthermore, teachers are expected to empower young people to make their *own* decisions, whilst making sure they behave in a way that adults have determined. Remarkably, many teachers balance all these demands on a daily basis, some with notable ease. Examining the causes of these pressures, how teachers achieve balance and signalling ways of setting about improving coping are the subject of the following sections.

Stress in schools

Armchair conjecture suggests that teaching *per se* is a stressful occupation. That teachers are stressed is often unchallenged and needs little elaboration since many are. However, overall there seems little clear evidence that teaching is likely to damage your health. Undoubtedly, most teachers will experience some stress at some point during their career. There is also a minority of teachers who are extremely stressed and fall ill and others who are denied appropriate help and support.

In the early 1980s the International Labour Organisation (1982) highlighted teacher stress as a 'steadily growing problem', a problem that, according to the National Union of Teachers (NUT 2000), remains unchanged: 'Stress is one of the biggest problems facing teachers today'. Workplace stress has been recognised as a health-related issue by the Health and Safety Executive (HSE 2001), who issued guidance to employers informing managers that they have a duty to ensure that employees' health is not harmed by work-related stress. In recent years stress has attracted the interest of many research and professional communities with thousands of articles appearing in journals for teachers, educationalists, psychologists and health professionals who often disagree about what stress is and how it should be measured, leading to 'confusion, controversy and inconsistency' (Elliot and Eisdorfer 1982: 5).

Labelling teaching as a stress-ridden profession can be destructive for both practitioners and those thinking of entering the profession. Doing so can create self-fulfilling prophecies since 'teachers read frequent reports that teaching is stressful and start to believe it. As a result, perhaps normal upsets that are part of most jobs become mislabelled as chronic, inherent stressors, and a vicious circle begins that results in a higher incidence of self-reported stress' (Hiebet and Farber 1984: 20).

In his review of research into teacher stress Kyriacou (1998) listed five categories of stressors which have repeatedly been identified as major contributors, four of which were concerned with organisational issues and the fifth with student behaviour. However, it is important to recognise that the bulk of the studies adopted a particular method of collecting data (self-report questionnaires) and as Kyriacou (1998: 6) points out, 'given the subjectivity involved in self report, one must be very cautious about its use in providing information about a particular teacher's level of stress'. Using alternative methods to collect data is likely to produce different results.

Possible causes of stress in schools are multilevel in nature. Stress at the organisational and structural level can result from: ineffective management (Torrington and Weightman 1989); lack of communication; poor working environment; excessive workloads (Johnstone 1989); staffing levels; lack of administrative support; time pressures and lack of resources; job demands; role strain, role ambiguity and role conflict (Bacharach *et al.* 1986); or, in more global terms, through negative organisational culture and climate. Most of these stressors are not peculiar to schools and can be found in any organisation (see also Chapters 4 and 5).

At the interpersonal level, lack of *perceived* support from colleagues can make coping more difficult, since social support correlates negatively with stress. The higher the level of perceived social support, the lower the level of stress (Sarason *et al.* 1990). Believing your colleagues are there and prepared to offer help in the form of materials, cover or just an adult to have a chat with can combat feelings of isolation and uncertainty. It is long established fact that social support operates as a buffer to stress (e.g. Cobb 1976) but the relationship is not a simple one. Social support is multidimensional in terms of structure, function and also changes over time (Kahn and Antonucci 1980) and therefore differs in its power to alleviate stress.

Relationships with students, both individually and in groups, can be both the source of greatest job satisfaction and a major source of stress. Where feedback from students is positive, it raises levels of job satisfaction but where it is negative, it can make excessive demands on coping, notably when having to spend time managing disruptive students at the expense of teaching (Kalker 1984).

Many studies of occupational stress fail to acknowledge pressures beyond school, which can significantly influence overall coping. Galloway *et al.* (1985) for instance, reported that one in six New Zealand teachers questioned said they suffered extreme stress from their families, and one in seven reported stress from financial worries. The interplay between home and work was shown in a study by Syrotuik and D'Arcy (1984), who found levels of social support from spouses were inversely related to stress among individuals with high-pressure jobs. Despite the stressful nature of their jobs social support from spouses could buffer their negative effects. This is not to suggest that teachers are unique in experiencing stress from their personal lives and interpersonal relationships. However, expectations of teachers in terms of commitment, preparation and marking outside school hours, which encroaches on personal lives, along with poor career and salary structures, have the potential to create disharmony in some households and leave people feeling unsupported.

Personal resources or vulnerabilities either facilitate or impede coping. An individual with appropriate resources and weak constraints develops adaptive coping strategies, which results in being healthier psychologically and physically (Jerusalem 1993). As teachers progress through their careers, factors considered responsible for stress change. It is often assumed that new entrants to the profession will experience more stress than their older and/or more experienced colleagues (Coates and Thoresen 1976). Whilst new entrants are likely to experience some anxiety as they attempt to adjust to the demands of work, more experienced teachers have been found to experience stress in relation to their career and perceived obsolescence (Laughlin 1984). At the beginning of their careers, teachers' concerns are directed inward, to issues concerned with survival and protecting the self, which has been linked with stress (Chaplain and Freeman 1996). In contrast experienced teachers tend to be more student-focused, concerned with empowering and developing them holistically (Fuller 1969). Smilansky (1984), however, found that *more* competent teachers reported higher levels of stress since they felt more pressured to ensure higher levels of performance, which could be difficult to live up to. Hence, just as concerns change with age and experience, so do potential causes of stress.

At the personal level a range of dispositional characteristics have been shown to influence levels of stress and well-being. For example: type A personality (Cinelli and Ziegler 1990); self-efficacy (Schwarzer 1992); locus of control (Steptoe and Appels 1989); extraversion (Hills and Norvell 1991); self-esteem (Brockner 1988); sense of humour (Martin and Dobbin 1988); assertiveness (Braun 1989); and hardiness (Funk 1992). However, their ability to predict coping has been challenged because accurately isolating and measuring single characteristics and controlling for the effects of overlaps between some of the constructs is problematic (Burchfield 1985; Schaubroeck and Ganster 1991). It is well established that people differ and that individual differences can affect how they approach or cope with stress but there is no complete explanation of the stress and coping process.

In conclusion, stress cannot be explained just in terms of organisational effects, although certain organisations do generate stressful conditions. Similarly, stress cannot be explained purely in terms of individual characteristics but certain 'types' of individuals appear more prone to stress than others.

Separating individual differences from context is unwise because of the dynamic nature of stress.

What is stress?

In seeking to understand what causes stress it is necessary to first understand what stress is.

Early accounts of stress focused on stimulus or response models and were based on behaviourist or biological accounts. The first group, stimulus models, explained stress in terms of how stressors exist in the environment, a school organisation for instance, to which we respond. Individuals are viewed as having elastic limits (like an expansion spring) in respect of how much stress they can tolerate before being stretched beyond those limits. Some events are identified as fairly constant but low level or daily hassles (Kanner and Feldman 1991). Others are more extreme life events; Holmes and Rahe (1967) produced a scale to quantify the various events people might encounter (e.g. death of a spouse, or divorce). However, criticisms of this approach highlight how the same event can be perceived as significantly more or less painful to one individual than it is to another (Schroeder and Costa 1984).

The second group of definitions focus on physiological reactions to stressors in the environment and as such focus on individual qualities. Hans Selye (1956), the so-called 'father' of stress, offered a biomedical explanation of stress. In his account individuals respond to all stressors (food deprivation, heat and so on) in a similar way. As the body attempts to maintain homeostasis (balance), it goes through a common sequence of events, which he called the general adaptation syndrome (GAS). The sequence has three components. First is the initial shock where resistance to the stressor is lowered. In the second phase there is resistance of varying level to the stressor, which continues up to maximum. Third, if the stressors continue, the individual is exhausted and ultimately dies. Selye offers no psychological aspects of stress, for example, people's ability to cope, so has limited value in contemporary accounts of stress.

Whilst early accounts provided valuable foundations for more recent explanations, they failed to account for individual differences and the human capacity to cope. What is mildly stressful to one person, is interpreted by another as chronic. Being asked to teach thirty, sometimes reluctant, adolescents whilst managing their social behaviour would horrify most people yet many readers of this book probably do so everyday without too much apprehension.

My reason for including the above models is that as explanations they are often favoured by the popular press – you will no doubt be familiar with the questionnaires so popular in magazines and newspapers where you 'add up' your stressors and are then offered simple explanations. Whilst they may be fun, they offer little to people wanting to develop effective coping strategies.

Most recent explanations of stress highlight the centrality of a psychological dimension to stress and coping. In doing so, account is taken of how individuals are capable of mentally representing their worlds which affects their experience of stress and how they cope. Within most psychologically based definitions, cognitive appraisal is seen as an important element. Hence, the degree to which something in our lives is stressful or not depends on how we perceive or interpret it; to what extent we consider it a potential or actual threat; and what resources we perceive are available to help us to cope with it. An imbalance between perceived stress and resources determines whether we consider ourselves stressed or coping.

To understand the relationship between stress, coping and pupil behaviour many psychologists refer to an interactive or transactional model of stress. Lazarus (1966) is credited as the founding father of the stress and coping paradigm – arguing that an event could only be considered stressful if perceived as such by an individual. In other words stress arises as a result of how the individual perceives and interprets events which occur in their environment. Lazarus emphasises the importance of mental activity (cognition) in what he refers to as transactions with the environment – individuals both *influence* and *respond* to their environments. Stress is experienced when the magnitude of stressors exceeds the person's ability to resist them. Coping individuals then change themselves or their environment in order to counter or prevent this from occurring. This relationship is interdependent, dynamic and reciprocal.

A number of developments and changes have been made to Lazarus's original model both in terms of stress generally and more specifically in respect of teaching (e.g. Sutherland and Cooper 1991) took place. It is to a cognitive model of stress and coping, developed by Freeman and myself (Freeman 1987; Chaplain and Freeman 1996) that I now turn to explore stress and coping in schools.

Thinking, feelings and behaviour

Stress is about thinking (cognition), feelings (emotions) and behaviour. Someone who is stressed will have thought about and interpreted an event, experienced some emotion and will probably behave differently from normal. In his explanation of stress Lazarus emphasised the role of thinking (cognition) and its 'transaction' with the environment. Kyriacou (1997: 156) highlights the emotional component of the process: 'The experience by a teacher of unpleasant emotions such as frustration, anxiety, anger and depression, resulting from aspects of his or her work as a teacher.' However, Chaplain and Freeman (1996: 10) incorporated all three elements, highlighting the role of individual differences: 'Stress is a negative feeling state which has both psychological and physical components. It is experienced as an assault on "self". Stress is not consistent between individuals, nor stable over time.'

What constitutes an assault on the self is down to the interpretation of the individual teacher. It could be the social self – being made to look stupid in front of others – or professional self – feeling that your teaching competence is being questioned and so on. The self comprises of, in part, a set of goals which are apparent in ongoing behaviour, many of which are experienced socially and stress results from these shared experiences being interrupted (Millar *et al.* 1988). An example of this occurs when disruptive students disturb the shared goals of teachers and on task students, increasing coping demands on both.

Cognition, emotion and behaviour are not mutually exclusive. They are interlinked. For example, a male student disrupts a lesson, preventing a teacher from managing the behaviour or learning of the class, and the teacher *interprets* his behaviour as deliberate and directed towards her, then she may feel anger toward the student which is likely to be mediated through body position, facial expression and language. Anger is described as a moral emotion, that is, a response to personal offence and usually results from attributing blame to a person for a wrongdoing (Power and Dalgleish 1997). If the teacher had attributed responsibility to herself instead, because she had not prepared the lesson correctly, she is more likely to experience guilt or shame. These are social emotions which again are likely to be mediated verbally and nonverbally. Cognition and emotion are not the only mental activities to consider in relation to stress, as there is another member of the psychological trilogy – motivation. Attributing blame (see Chapter 2) in particular directions affects the degree to which we are subsequently prepared to persevere with a task (Hewstone 1994). If a teacher attributes a student's misbehaviour to internal, unchangeable and uncontrollable causes, the teacher is unlikely to see any value in persevering to try and change that student's behaviour.

Levels of coping

How we cope depends on how we appraise and interpret potential stressors and how that appraisal makes us feel. Alternatively, how we feel can affect what we select to appraise and give attention to in the first place. If we are feeling sad or depressed, we are likely to attend to negative behaviours and if we are feeling happy, we attend to positive behaviours (Calder and Gruder 1988).

Not all coping results from deliberate attention (conscious activity), some is carried out automatically or unconsciously (Kihlstrom 1999). One measure of the competent individual or expert learner is the degree to which they can cope or solve problems with minimal conscious attention, that is 'automatically' (Power and Brewin 1991). Automaticity is demonstrated by competent individuals who, with seemingly little effort, solve problems or cope with difficult situations. In contrast, less competent individuals would need to engage more deliberately with a problem in order to find a solution.

Coping teachers are similarly able to integrate cognitive, emotional and physical activity to manage a class apparently without effort. Their body language, what they say and how they say it project confidence and authority. Expressing appropriate emotions, interacting with students, focusing primarily on positive features but quickly perceptive to changes such as signs of off-task or unacceptable behaviour and responding with a little fine-tuning here and there to keep students on task. Yet in the same school there may be colleagues who seem to have to work flat out, are hurried and overwhelmed and who struggle to maintain a reasonable level of order. How might we explain these differences, given that they share a similar environment? Can it be put down to personal qualities and are these qualities inherent or learned? Some people have attributes more suited to particular activities, build or attractiveness or manual dexterity, for instance. Others appear able to organise and reflect on their thinking more easily than others. Some seem to flourish in environments that others feel sick even thinking about. These and other differences highlight the multiplicity of factors involved in trying to unravel how people differ in their response to pressure.

However, people can improve their coping skills by redefining the way in which they view the world and how they interact with it. By analysing their resources, seeking appropriate support and reflecting upon how they perceive and solve problems, they can extend their repertoire of coping skills. If these skills are then practised (overlearned), they can become automatic, reducing the amount of mental energy required to use them.

A number of cognitive and motor skills, initially carried out deliberately, can be made automatic through overlearning, after which we have no direct introspective access, such as driving a car. In other words, we cannot reflect *directly* on the procedures (introspect) or operations involved. An example might be asking competent teachers how they manage their class so easily and effortlessly, only to find that they find it hard to explain, which people often put down to intrinsic characteristics. However, it is more likely they will have spent considerable time planning and carrying out various tasks. They will have learnt, memorised, redefined and modified strategies, incorporating what they have been taught and observed, initially in a very deliberate and planned way before it later became automatic. The process is similar to an athlete who trains continually to develop muscle memory and coordination. Understanding the learning experiences and identifying how they influenced the final outcome becomes extremely difficult if not impossible.

In their model of coping Chaplain and Freeman (1996) offer an architecture which explains how coping occurs at two levels; coping teachers differ from those who are not coping and the various personal, situational and organisational and interpersonal dimensions might influence the coping process (see Figure 1.1). In this model, understanding how levels of thinking interact with the different mediating factors is the key to understanding stress and coping. The remainder of this chapter will discuss some of these issues.

The *two levels of thinking* reflect different systems and are explained by reference to a metaphor of the functional relationship between executives and workers in an organisation referred to as BOSS and EMPLOYEE. These terms were adopted from work carried out by Morris and Hampson (see Morris 1981; Hampson and Morris 1989 for a fuller discussion). In simple terms, some low-level mental activity is carried out at the *non-conscious* level, for example, perception, memory, learning and thought. They are automatic, routine processes whose operation we find hard to explain but carry out them out continuously throughout our lives. The non-conscious processes in this model are referred to as EMPLOYEE systems and include a range of actions developed by teachers over time and carried out by them without having to think about them. Standing in a particular position in the classroom to get attention, using ritualised behaviours to gain attention (e.g. clapping, coughing), setting up routines which occur with simple prompts, using peripheral vision to monitor off task behaviour and so on.

In contrast, higher level cognitive activities (e.g. planning) are controlled by BOSS systems which require *conscious* intentional activity, are flexible and responsive to novelty (see Figure 1.2). For example, if I decide to move house I would go through a procedure that would demand considerable problem solving and emotional control.

Whether or not a person becomes consciously aware of an event depends on the level of attention that BOSS systems pay to particular incoming information, their active knowledge of that information and their current state. In the classroom, whether or not we choose to respond to the behaviour of a particular student amongst the mass of information reaching our ears, eyes and nose will be influenced largely by how we are feeling, which behaviours we are generally sensitised to, specifically in respect of this student, plus any other things demanding our attention. We may be conscious of a wide range of activities going on around us, such as smell, taste, images, language and associations (for example, awareness of being happy at hearing a friend's voice). It is also possible to close our eyes and concentrate on sounds and smells, bodily sensations, the flow of thoughts and feelings, even though these thoughts and sensations usually encroach minimally on conscious awareness. When the executive system (BOSS) takes in information it restructures and reorganises it and decides whether to process it further or discard it. This manipulation of information occurs at many levels, from

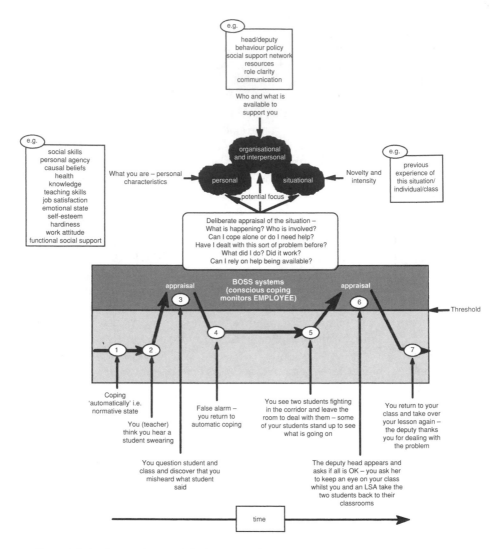

Figure 1.1 An interactive model of stress and coping.
Also included is an example of how automatic and conscious coping might interact over a period of time. Mental activity in the dark box is carried out deliberately, i.e. you are aware of having to solve the problem and able to identify why you may be experiencing particular emotions (e.g. anger or fear). In the lighter coloured box the teacher is coping with managing the class without having to deliberately think about it, leaving BOSS systems free to concentrate on the lesson content. The three resource boxes represent potential supports – within the teacher (knowledge, experience, personal disposition) and from other people or organisational structures.

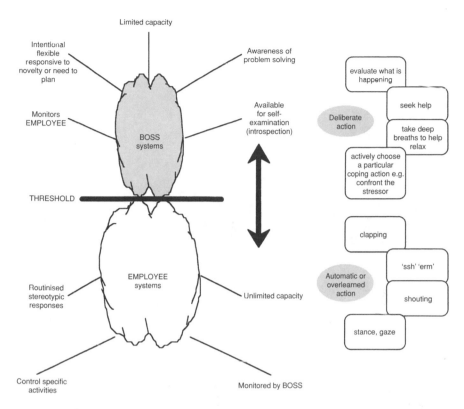

Figure 1.2 The architecture of BOSS and EMPLOYEE systems.
    The size of the two components symbolises the relative capacity of each:
    EMPLOYEE has the more extensive capacity but deals only with routinised
    behaviour. The threshold distinguishes the two different types of coping and
    changes depending on internal and external conditions. If you are feeling
    unwell (internal) for instance, you may be preoccupied with your health,
    which takes up some of BOSS processing capacity, limiting its availability for
    other problem-solving activity.

simple images to how we represent the world. The point at which coping
changes from BOSS to EMPLOYEE and vice versa is called the *threshold*
(Freeman 1987). The coping teacher has a large repertoire of automatic
coping responses so has a high threshold, hence the longer it takes before
having to engage in conscious coping, minimising demands on BOSS.
Teachers who are poor copers have low thresholds requiring them to make
more regular demands on BOSS in order to cope.

    The threshold is dynamic for both effective and poor copers. Various
issues can influence its upward or downward movement. Consider the
example of a teacher's working day in Table 1.1.

Table 1.1 Everyday coping in school

Time	Event	Appraisal	Coping or not coping	Emotional state
08.00	Start the day on a high, having just received a tax rebate.	Life is great: now I can afford a new stereo – will take my husband out this evening for a meal!	Coping.	Happy.
11.30	Have a great morning teaching combined science to Years 9 and 10. One or two students clowning around but I deal with them quickly.	Teaching is really satisfying, the kids are enthusiastic and this is a subject I enjoy.	Normal coping mainly automatic (EMPLOYEE).	Happy.
13.15	During lunch find a group of students smoking outside school gates, which leads to a confrontation and a threatening outburst by one of them in the street.	Not acceptable behaviour, especially doing it outside school gates as it shows a lack of respect. Arguing and threatening when caught is pushing the limits and especially embarrassing in public.	Coping but requiring more BOSS level thinking to resolve conflict and deal with aggression, feeling a little stressed.	Irritated and angry.
14.00	Report incident to Head, who arranges to meet with the students and myself at 4.00 p.m. to discuss situation.	Could have done without meeting then as I have to pick up my husband from work.	Coping (still using BOSS) with student problem but have to negotiate with my husband for later pick up. Head is likely to keep me there until turned 5.00: not normally a problem, and I could tell him about my date, but I am applying for promotion.	Frustrated.
14.30	The Head of Year asking me (again) to cover for a regularly absent colleague, stopping me from completing my GCSE marking, which needs to be completed for tomorrow.	Getting sick of covering for Joan, who is always off 'sick' after the weekend – she has no consideration for others. Tonight's date looks like being a disaster.	Struggling a little to cope (still using BOSS) quite annoyed at students, colleagues and Head of Year – I feel really put upon.	Angry.
15.30	Boys involved in incident come to the classroom and apologise. I give them a detention, which they accept without an argument.	Feeling a little better, don't need to go through drawn-out discussion with the Head. Just need to avoid him or he will end up telling me his life story if I tell him I have dealt with the situation. I will send him a message.	Can get back to thinking about winding up this lesson (using EMPLOYEE). I can now go back to thinking about spending my windfall and start smiling again.	Relieved and happy.

The table illustrates how levels of coping can fluctuate over even short periods of time and may be accompanied by emotions which have their own logic. Feeling good in your personal life is no guarantee of feeling likewise at work and vice versa, but each can influence the other quite markedly.

BOSS is also responsible for monitoring EMPLOYEE systems – to make sure everything is working OK. If you thought you saw your partner in the street and asked the person what he or she fancied for lunch, only to discover it was a complete stranger, you might decide a visit to the optician is called for, as one of your EMPLOYEE systems is not functioning correctly. In the present model, stress is experienced when our BOSS systems decide we are *not* coping, usually when overlearned non-conscious coping strategies have been identified as unsuccessful (an example was provided in Figure 1.1).

Automatic coping is the norm, since most people cope with a range of difficulties with little or no apparent conscious regard for them. To ensure they cope, people tend to select (where possible) activities which they enjoy and in which they are usually successful. However, it usually becomes painfully obvious if our strategies and actions are not working once we are alerted to feeling stressed (not coping). We often pause, and select carefully what we say, take deep breaths to control our heart rate, and look for support from others. In this way, coping becomes an intention, of which we are fully conscious (i.e. at BOSS level). BOSS, however, has limited processing capacity and so is more restricted in the number of procedures it can carry out at any one time. Try multiplying 5467 by 13 in your head whilst reading this page to see what I mean! However, you could almost certainly recite your two times table whilst reading the page since you probably overlearned the two times table as a child. Overuse of BOSS to cope with trivia leaves people feeling unable to think about other important issues. The best copers tend to have a large repertoire of automatic coping strategies (EMPLOYEE) relieving pressure on BOSS. Poor copers are more aware of having to make an effort to cope. Because they have a limited number of effective overlearned strategies, they frequently need to think about coping with problems and control their emotions i.e. extensively use BOSS. As a result their preoccupation with having to make an effort to cope and find ways to 'survive' minor disruption reduces available processing capacity in BOSS. In the classroom poor copers are aware that they are not managing their students' behaviour and make effort to solve more 'crises', limiting attention to thinking about teaching, making lessons less interesting and making matters worse.

Whilst poor copers do have automatic responses, they are usually ineffective such as overuse of avoidance or withdrawal which become less and less helpful over time. Many of the latter responses, developed in childhood, continue into adulthood but remain unchanged and immature, for example, shouting, bullying, running away and sulking, which creates difficulties for everyone. Since they are activated automatically people are unaware they are using them unless they take time to consciously reflect, appraise and modify them.

I have, on a number of occasions, observed teachers trying to reduce the noise level in their classes by repeatedly using commonly recognised instructions such as 'be quiet' or 'stop talking' but seemingly unaware that the pupils are not taking a blind bit of notice. Despite this being the case they carry on often increasing the frequency and/or volume to little or no avail. When told about this they often do not believe it until they see themselves on videotape. There is a range of similar expressions and behaviours which result in similar outcomes such as shouting, clapping, folding arms and so on. This is not to say that such techniques do not work for many teachers, nor am I questioning the use of triggers to signal routines or responses from students, provided you are sure they are working – which means making sure you monitor what is going on. Many behaviours and expressions that come naturally and which are used automatically often work well; however, they may become inappropriate or redundant. Examining such behaviours can be enlightening and provide information helpful to developing new ways of working (see Chapter 3).

Amongst a large staff group it is probable that some will, at times, use immature ineffective strategies in order to cope but until they become aware of doing so, alternative effective strategies will not be forthcoming. For some, this will occur only after they have become angry or dealt with a situation badly. Hence some overlearned coping strategies create more stress and upset, *not* because we intended to use them *but* because they were activated before we became aware of them.

In summary, a lack of coping at EMPLOYEE level usually comes to BOSS's attention through cognitive appraisal or feedback from others. Therefore coping precedes stress, since stress is awareness of not coping. At that point BOSS systems take over and plan how to deal with the problem and to monitor/control emotional functioning. EMPLOYEE functions continue to be monitored by BOSS as long as overload is not being experienced. New ways of dealing with novel situations if practised can become EMPLOYEE strategies.

BOSS is responsible for appraising the nature and intensity of the event which EMPLOYEE has failed to cope with; for controlling emotions and for deciding what actions will solve the problem. A teacher would carry out this process by appraising:

- *The current situation*: what's happening? Is this a threat to me? Do I understand what is going on? Am I coping? If not, why not?
- *Personal resources*: how can I gain control of what is happening using my previous experience, personality or bluff? How am I feeling?

- *Interpersonal resources*: who can help me? Are they available? What sort of help do I need?
- *Organisational resources*: what does the school policy say about how to deal with this problem? What resources are available to support me?

Appraising a stressful event

Appraisal seeks to answer three questions:

- What is happening to me and is it a threat?
- Have I got resources to cope with it?
- Did I cope effectively and how might it help me in future?

What is actually appraised will vary from event to event and from individual to individual, for example what constitutes a threat will differ from class to class, student to student and indeed where in school the event is taking place. Dealing with an aggressive Year 11 student in a hidden area of the school car park whilst surrounded by a group of his friends *may* be perceived as more threatening than dealing with him in a corridor with colleagues nearby.

Figure 1.1 showed the three principal sources of stress, perceived personal inadequacy, external impediments and situational threats, that are the usual targets for appraisal. Within these three areas the range of possibilities is almost limitless because of the interplay between individual and context. What follows are just some examples of the potential influence different factors may have but it is not presented as exhaustive.

Situational variables

The first response to becoming aware that you are not coping is usually to consider the immediate situation to confirm whether you have read and understood it correctly and to what extent it poses a threat, and second, the degree to which it is novel or familiar to you. If it is novel then you may, at first, be alarmed or shocked as to why it has occurred and the initial emotional reaction may require you to consider how to react. Coping with the unexpected can result in people reacting inappropriately when emotions are running high, because they have not previously considered or rehearsed how to cope with it. However, it is also possible to mishandle the familiar since a teacher and student(s) may have fallen into a ritualised negative cycle, which is reinforcing the undesired behaviour. Always sending particular students to a senior member of staff when they carry out a particular act may in fact be something which the students quite enjoy so they have an incentive for misbehaving! The message here is twofold: on the one hand anticipating possible changes and being proactive in preparing for how to deal with them and on the other reviewing the strategies you are currently using which may be unwittingly creating problems for you. In a nutshell, evaluate, plan and monitor how you manage your students.

Organisational and interpersonal variables

Organisational and interpersonal support can provide a framework for helping teachers to deal with difficulties often in a fairly routinised and predictable way. For example, a teacher is more likely to cope effectively if he or she:

- believes that effective sanctions and rewards are available in school and he or she can draw upon them
- perceives the management team as supportive, available and committed to professional development in respect of behaviour management and minimising unnecessary pressure on teachers
- considers communication systems are appropriate, accessible and effective (see also Chapters 4 and 5)
- works at a school which encourages open discussion of stress and behaviour management, as opposed to viewing stress as a personal weakness on the part of a teacher
- receives interpersonal reciprocity – an expectation of positive feedback for their efforts from the organisation for doing a good job and from students in respect of teacher–learner relationships.

Social support has been shown to be a buffer to stress (Cohen and Wills 1985). Having colleagues and friends whom you perceive as supportive alleviates feelings of isolation and having to cope with everything yourself. However, what constitutes appropriate social support is not always straightforward. There is evidence to suggest that having a social network is less important than functional social support (Cassidy 1999). Teaching in a large comprehensive school may provide a large social network of professional colleagues (structure) but who an individual teacher perceives as providing little functional support. Schools usually have people officially designated to provide support with special educational needs (SEN) or curriculum for instance, who genuinely (if sometimes mistakenly) believe that they do provide appropriate functional support. However, thinking that you are being supportive without regard to how your intended recipients perceive it can make for inefficient working practices and dysfunctional relationships. It is the appraisal and representation of social support networks by individuals that hold the key to the buffering effects of social support. Social support can reduce vulnerability to depression in a number of ways by supporters providing examples of how to manage difficult situations, the value of per-

Table 1.2 Functions of social support

Category of social support	Function	Type of stress buffered
Emotional	Someone to turn to for comfort	Unexpected events which are usually emotionally charged
Instrumental	Practical advice and tangible support	Expected events e.g. preparing to teach a difficult class where availability of resources is known and is accessible
Esteem	Recognition of effort or competence being valued by others	As an ongoing buffer to prolonged heavy workload or after a particularly stressful period
Inter-group	Colleagues with shared professional interests	Sharing teaching methods, developing new initiatives to support teachers and students

sistence as well as providing resources to help deal with difficulties (Major *et al.* 1990).

Also, a number of different types of social support have been identified including emotional, instrumental or practical, esteem and inter-group or informational (Cohen and Wills 1985) which are specific to cushioning particular types of stress (see Table 1.2).

At the organisational level social support is strongly related to social identity. Where people feel there is a strong sense of social identity in a school they are more resilient to the negative effects of stress (Cassidy 1999).

Within schools where the emphasis is on shared values and expectations, teamwork and mutual trust, a single individual's stress affects many others.

A useful exercise is to make a list of people in your social network in both your personal and professional life. Alongside each name identify what function you think they should fulfil and alongside that the type of support they actually provide (emotional, practical, esteem and informational). Is there a balance or are there gaps? What type of support do you feel you need more of to cope more effectively?

Personal variables

Personal characteristics are often seen as the key to effective coping; indeed much advice on stress is how to develop a healthy lifestyle, how to become more assertive, developing skills and knowledge, enhancing self-esteem and the like, a number of which are discussed elsewhere in this text. However, whilst the value of individual strengths are clear, it is equally important to remember that a teacher exists within a complex hierarchy of nested systems (Bronfenbrenner 1979), some of which he or she has direct influence over whilst others are more abstract. A wide variety of personal characteristics have been found to relate to levels of stress including those referred to above and others shown in Figure 1.1. Some of these are discussed in more detail in other chapters; for example, causal beliefs are covered in Chapter 2 and social skills in Chapter 3. The remainder of this section will expand on personal agency and social support.

Personal agency refers to the power an individual believes they have to bring about consequences intentionally. Psychologists maintain that people make causal contributions to their functioning through mechanisms of personal agency, a central feature of which is self-efficacy. Bandura (1981: 200) referred to self-efficacy as 'individuals' beliefs about their abilities to execute and regulate important actions in their lives, and these self-perceived competencies affect the person's choice of what they undertake (or) avoid'. If individuals believe they do not have the ability or power to bring about a particular result, then why bother trying in the first place? If two people had the same ability levels but differed in self-efficacy, the one with the higher self-efficacy would persist longer when faced with a problem.

The development of self-efficacy is complex and begins in childhood through self-appraisal skills which inform self-knowledge and self-regulation. As an individual gets older, self-efficacy continues to be influential in how he or she copes with various life transitions (for instance, home to school, school to work, job to job and so on) and feedback from significant others. Self-efficacy can be generalised or specific to particular activities (such as professional self-efficacy) and is also changeable. In respect of stress and coping, Maier et al. (1985) argued that it is not stressful life conditions that determine whether an experience will be detrimental but the degree to which individuals believe they are capable of coping with them. People experience lower levels of anxiety from threats they believe they can control. High self-efficacy then acts as a buffer to negative stress and fosters positive appraisals of difficult situations (Carver and Scheier 1988).

Efficacy operates at the personal and institutional level in schools and the effects on teachers' performance and well-being are well documented. As Bandura (1995) points out in his summary of the literature:

> Many teachers find themselves beleaguered day in and day out by disruptive and non-achieving students. Eventually their low sense of efficacy to fulfil academic demands takes a stressful toll. Teachers who lack a secure sense of institutional efficacy show weak commitment to teaching, spend less time in subject matters in their areas of perceived inefficacy, and devote less overall time to academic matters. . . . They are especially prone to occupational burnout . . . a syndrome of reactions to chronic occupational stressors that include physical and emotional

exhaustion, depersonalisation of the people one is serving and feelings of futility concerning personal accomplishments.

(Bandura 1995: 20)

Organisational conditions which undermine teachers' professional self-efficacy include limited professional development, heavy workloads, poor prospects and an unsatisfying imbalance between their work life and personal life (McAteer-Early 1992), features which have an unwelcome resemblance to those highlighted by research into teacher stress reported above.

Teachers with a low sense of self-efficacy are vulnerable to difficult situations because they worry about their level of competence, experience strong negative emotional reactions, feel criticism is directed at their self-worth and tend to accept criticism for failure more readily than praise for success. They are also likely to affect their students in a similar way, creating an overall negative classroom environment. Gibson and Dembo (1984) found that teachers who have high instructional efficacy empower their students to master their learning whereas those with low efficacy undermine their students' efficacy and cognitive development.

Low self-efficacy can be improved by attention to issues at personal, interpersonal and institutional levels. For example, try forcing yourself to take recuperative breaks from emotionally taxing work by not taking work home all the time and stopping ruminative thinking. Bandura (1997) and Rosenthal and Rosenthal (1985) suggest that such advice is not usually welcomed by those who work this way and who convince themselves that there is no time to rest or they are too tired after work to engage in leisure pursuits. Bandura (1997) recommends a guided mastery programme to help them gain control of their lives to alleviate pressure. However, this is not likely to be sufficient since the difficulties are not just at the individual level (as previously discussed), and so intervention is also required to prevent organisational demands undermining teachers' efficacy. Teachers need some control over matters which affect their working lives and ownership of schooling as well as classroom process. In appraising their effectiveness teachers should focus on those features over which they have control. Other areas of empowering staff efficacy are discussed in Chapter 4.

Think of a recent occasion where you felt stressed. Write down what had happened prior to the event and how you coped. Did you take some direct action or try and forget about it? Was the event something which occurs regularly or was it a novel occurrence? Was it something that you feel you had control over? Could you change things to stop it occurring again or to improve the way you coped with it? Did you think you coped with it effectively? If not, how could you prevent it occurring again or cope more effectively with it next time?

The above analysis offers a simple means of appraising a stressor and quite often the very process of carrying out such activity helps improve

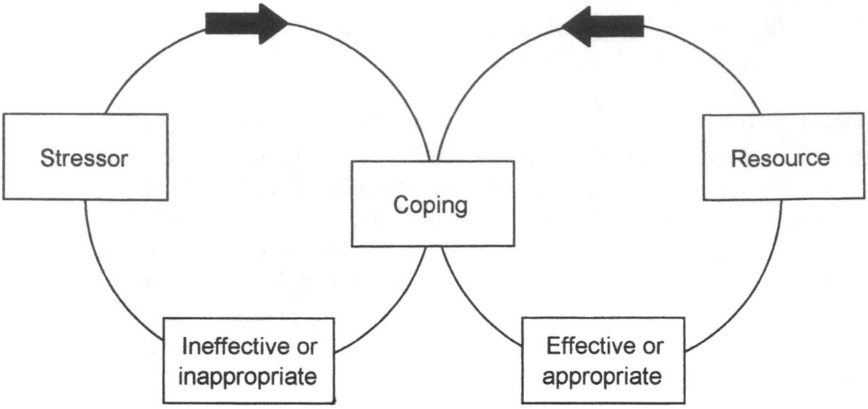

Figure 1.3 Individual coping analysis ICAN

coping. There are some events, however, which are so horrendous that we avoid thinking about them because they are too painful and this is OK under extreme conditions, but not a good general coping mechanism.

Balancing stressors and resources

In order to monitor and evaluate existing coping and develop new ways of dealing with potential stressors, Chaplain and Freeman (1996) developed a simple model; the individual coping analysis (ICAN) is organised around identifying and developing new coping strategies (see Figure 1.3). It is used to analyse the (im)balance between stressors and resources to provide a basis for developing new ways of doing things. The analysis is intended to be ongoing and not just as a one-off activity since, in some instances, stressors and resources change roles over time, stressors becoming resources and vice versa because of changes to our environment and ourselves. One example of this might be professional commitment or enthusiasm. Most people would agree that teachers are expected to be committed to their work and indeed many interviewers are looking for evidence of this when making appointments. In practice, demonstrating one's commitment or enthusiasm often includes completing administrative tasks outside official hours (e.g. marking, preparation), supplementing equipment from personal funds, supporting trips and sports activities outside the working week. If this commitment leads to success in gaining a job or promotion then it could clearly be viewed as a resource. However, if this commitment leads to a teacher (or headteacher) spending more and more time at work or engaged in work-related activities and less and less time at home with his or her friends and family, it can lead to difficulties at either the personal and/or interpersonal levels, becoming a source of stress. In the case of the latter, if those close to you feel marginalised and neglected, then there is a danger of losing valuable social support.

Frank had enjoyed considerable success in his teaching career from the beginning. He entered the profession in his early thirties having previously been in the merchant navy. He was appointed as a mathematics teacher at a local comprehensive school with a reputation for being good at teaching difficult students and made an immediate impact. He was popular amongst staff and students both as a teacher and because of his interest and skill in football. Frank always seemed to be in school preparing lessons and marking or organising, coaching or refereeing football matches.

After a year or so in post his wife, who had supported him through his professional training and career, expressed her concern about the amount of time he was spending at school. Frank said it was a short-term strategy so he could get promoted after which he would be able to ease off a little with some of the extracurricular activity.

Not long after he was promoted to Head of Maths. As his predecessor had been in post for twenty years, there was some expectation from both management and other maths teachers that some change was needed to the way in which the department was run. Frank made it clear at interview that he had a number of ideas which he would like to implement.

Over the following year he worked with his (sometimes reluctant) colleagues to develop the department with some degree of success. He found it increasingly difficult to run the sports activities as well but as no one else was prepared to do it or 'thought he was the best man for the job', he felt obliged to continue for the sake of the students. His wife became increasing irritated that, despite promising to spend more time at home, he was now spending less. Furthermore, when he was at home he was usually catching up on marking and preparation.

Frank felt increasingly overwhelmed with the pressure from home and work and discussed the situation with the deputy, who said she knew how he felt as she was made to 'feel guilty by her husband – who also didn't understand what teaching was about'. She suggested trying to get someone else to take on board the football coaching – but no one came forward.

Frank's experience is not uncommon. Whilst self-esteem enhancement from colleagues and management can be a positive component of social support ('you're the best person for the job – no one else could do it as well as you'), it can be interpreted as taking advantage.

Having a colleague or manager saying they empathise with your situation is a form of support; however, in Frank's situation what was perhaps needed was some instrumental support – the deputy involving herself by getting volunteers to assist with the football or some other way of easing Frank's workload. The price to the organisation of not doing so may be the eventual loss of a competent member of staff.

Disruption in one's personal life can add to difficulties coping at school and vice versa, hence the need to keep one's personal and professional lives in balance should not be underestimated. As with other aspects of our lives it is not difficult to find yourself in a ritual of behaviour in which we fail to acknowledge the thoughts and feelings of others. We need to find time to stand back and evaluate our situation.

Returning to the model, the point at which the two circles meet in Figure 1.3 represents where coping takes place. One might argue that coping invariably occurs (pretending there is no problem, for instance) but some forms of coping are more effective than others (or acceptable/unacceptable) in certain contexts and at certain points in time, but not necessarily in others. For example, an event may be so painful to take on board that initially you ignore it or pretend everything is OK. However, doing so as a long-term or regular strategy is unlikely to work and is likely to lead to further problems. At the same time engaging with and confronting all your problems head on and immediately can also be counterproductive since it is likely to prove exhausting and lead to other difficulties, such as being seen as aggressive (see Table 1.3 for examples of different coping styles). Some forms of coping have their own logic, such as initially deflecting a problem with a view to making space and time to solve it more directly later. A simple example might be overhearing a student swearing and opting not to intervene until the situation is more easily dealt with, perhaps when there is no audience. There is no right or wrong way of coping effectively (beyond legal and professional requirements), it depends on the individual and the social context. To improve your coping requires reviewing and monitoring what strategies you are using, identifying the balance between them and being proactive in

Table 1.3 Coping styles

	Active	Passive
Direct	Confront the problem	Avoid the problem
Indirect	Seek advice on how to deal with the problem	Smoke or drink more

Note: All four coping styles can be effective, but over-reliance on one type can lead to problems. Always confronting the problem may be seen as aggressive; always seeking advice as overly dependent; avoiding a problem as being weak; smoking and drinking too much is unhealthy.

developing new ones to cope with future potential stressors; Lazarus and Folkman (1984) called this 'anticipatory coping'.

You will no doubt be familiar with preparing for particular social encounters, for example preparing for an interview, trying to anticipate what is likely to be asked and how you will respond, and rehearsing what to say. However, rehearsing coping strategies should go beyond what to say to include how to say it along with nonverbal communication, something which we are often less aware of.

Coping is not simply a matter of whether we cope or we do not. In some instances, for example, we might use a coping strategy which is initially effective and subsequently disastrous. There can also be unintended consequences.

Using the individual coping analysis (ICAN) for personal development

To use this model effectively requires the completion of four elements:

- identification and description of stressors and resources
- evaluation of stressors, resources and coping effectiveness in order to provide further understanding
- planning and practising alternative coping strategies
- monitoring and evaluating alternative strategies.

The stages of the analysis are as follows:

- Using the headings in Table 1.4 make two lists. One list should contain factors which you perceive as supportive, and the second lists those factors which you perceive as stressful. The lists are likely to contain aspects of both your personal and professional life. It doesn't matter what order you place them in.
- Examine your two lists. Which is the longer? It is important to have more resources than stressors in order to cope effectively. Where stressors outnumber resources, effective coping is less likely.
- Look at the lists again and decide which stressors and resources are long term and which are more recent. If they have changed recently, try to identify explanations (e.g. change of job, responsibilities, lifestyle, time of the year, ageing, how you feel today/this week). Are you aware of any imminent changes (curriculum, class groupings, organisation)? If so, list possible ways of being proactive in controlling the effects of these changes (e.g. additional training/reading, reorganising your classroom to improve control of movement). Planning for future development is central to this process.
- Consider which stressors you have or could gain control over (e.g. change your lifestyle) and those you cannot (ageing). How might you change

Table 1.4 Individual coping analysis (ICAN)

Resource (support)		Difficulty (stressor)
I am a good teacher and I enjoy teaching	**Self**	I do not feel confident of my knowledge of the subject I am currently teaching
They are always prepared to listen to my problems	**Friends**	They want me to go out every night and I can't
I find teaching students with SEN very rewarding	**Students**	I find some of the GCSE groups difficult to motivate
Most are happy to share lesson ideas	**Colleagues**	Some members of my department are inconsistent in managing students which makes problems for me
She really knows her stuff and offers lots of different ideas	**Head of department**	She is hard to get hold of because of all her extra duties around school
The school is fortunate in having lots of good resources	**School organisation**	There is a lack of structure
The head is an excellent teacher and very supportive	**Management**	The deputy undermines my authority by coming into my room and disciplining students when it isn't necessary

Note: Suggested headings and examples of how to start your personal analysis. The headings should be made to fit your context, so may well be different from those suggested here.

the way you cope with each by, for example, putting things in perspective or remodelling them to make them a resource? A perceived weakness in teaching a particular subject could result in your deciding to attend a course which revitalises your interest in professional development.

Since all behaviour can be expressed in terms of the interaction between ourselves, stressors and resources, it follows that the evaluation of our coping strategies is central to understanding whether or not we are dealing with our stressors in the most effective way. Using the layout shown in Table 1.4, you can carry out a number of evaluations, for example if you are concerned about the behaviour of a particular class or student you could analyse:

* how the behaviour which is causing you concern, is influenced by the stressors and resources of the students
* how you normally cope with their behaviour and how this may affect their coping strategies and stressors
* how others cope with this group
* how whole school policies interact with what is going on in your classroom.

It is not sufficient merely to list stressors and resources. It is essential that you take time to examine the interaction between you and the various factors involved. You and other colleagues may all be aware of particular difficulties but cope with them in very different ways despite seemingly having similar resources (training, lifestyle and working in the same organisation).

Suggested further reading

Chaplain, R. and Freeman, A. (1996) *Stress and Coping*, Cambridge: Pearson.

Chapter 2

Teacher thinking and pupil behaviour

Much of what is written about classroom control focuses on observable behaviours. Less is said about the thinking processes which are fundamental influences on that behaviour.

There is a popular belief that having high expectations of students academically and socially will necessarily result in better behaviour and performance in school. However, just as with a number of other popular beliefs, this is an oversimplification of a complex process. Reducing the relationship between teacher expectancy and student outcomes is at best naive, at worst an insult to the professionals involved. It is hard to imagine any teachers not wanting their students to behave well and be successful in their studies, either for their own or their students' benefit. The teacher is a significant other in a student's life, who, having been a student earlier in life, will no doubt recognise the importance of feeling 'valued' by teachers. Few teachers, if any, would deny wanting to have positive relationships with *all* their students or to treat them all equally.

This chapter looks in detail at the social psychology of interpersonal behaviours in the classroom and how these behaviours can mediate unintended messages to students and, most importantly, the effects they can have on the thinking, feeling and behaviour of those students. Ways of preventing and overcoming potential difficulties, and enhancing the behaviour and motivation of students giving concern, will also be discussed.

The central argument of this chapter is:

- Teachers categorise students based on perceptions and expectations of how they behave rather than the behaviour itself.
- Teachers respond to students in qualitatively different ways and can unintentionally influence student behaviour negatively.
- These differences are controlled largely by impressions formed in early encounters interacting with previous experiences to form positive and negative expectations of behaviour.
- Perceived differences are linked to both individual student qualities and cultural variations.

• Teachers' expectations can be mediated to students and can result in unintended consequences for both student and teacher.

It is hardly a novel concept that the way in which teachers think about and act toward their students has the potential to influence their behaviour; after all, if they could not, they would not be doing their job. The concern is how normal everyday thinking processes (cognition) can bring about unintended negative consequences for students and negative teacher–student(s) relationships. To understand the processes involved, it is necessary to consider not only the isolated elements (teacher, student), but also the total situation (the classroom, the school, the organisation of the curriculum). As Lewin (1951: 36) put it, 'a person exists in a psychological field that is a "configuration of forces"'. To consider just the student, the teacher or the situation alone is only part of the configuration and insufficient to understand behaviour. Both student and teacher have needs, abilities, beliefs and expectations, which differ and are influenced by their socio-cultural context.

Central to classroom management is the relationship between teacher and students. Whilst it is commonplace to talk of effective behaviour management being based on 'good relationships' with students, it is not always made clear what this means; like most aspects of interpersonal relations, it is subject to individual interpretation. It is probably true to say that all teachers seek positive relationships in their classrooms and want to have a pleasant environment where students can learn. It is also true to say that most students, even those who are difficult to manage, would, given the choice, prefer to have a positive and friendly atmosphere in their classrooms – despite their behaviour suggesting otherwise. No one enjoys going to school every day to face unpleasantness – that may be what they experience, but not what they desire. So where do things go wrong and how might they be explained?

Teacher expectations: turning thoughts into action

The expectancy confirmation cycle or self-fulfilling prophecy (Cooper 1979) as applied to education settings has been the topic of considerable interest since the 1960s. The central tenet of this phenomenon is that merely by having particular expectations of someone can influence that person's behaviour. Where this influence might disadvantage a student either through leading to academic underachievement or disruptive behaviour, it is unacceptable.

The expectancy confirmation cycle links how social perception leads to social behaviour, and the process can operate at different levels:

• *Cognitive confirmation effect:* expectancy confirmation effects occur in the absence of any interaction between perceiver and perceived. The perceiver interprets the behaviour, attributes causes or recalls actions in ways that confirm their existing beliefs.

- *Behavioural confirmation effect* or self-fulfilling prophecy: the initial erroneous beliefs of the perceiver channel the course of *interaction* to elicit behaviours from another individual or group that confirm the perceiver's original beliefs.

The latter effect is the subject of the following discussion.

Perhaps the most famous experiment to test the expectancy effect in schools was carried out by Rosenthal and Jacobson (1968). Rosenthal had demonstrated how researchers could act in ways that resulted in subjects (animal and human) behaving in ways that confirmed their original hypotheses. Rosenthal and Jacobson decided to test empirically whether a similar effect might occur in school. They selected an elementary school with predominantly lower socio-economic students, and administered a test which they told teachers would identify 'late bloomers' (20 per cent of the class) i.e. students with latent ability that would 'bloom' later – in fact they had been picked at random. The idea, however, had now been put into the mind of the teacher. The results confirmed that *generally* the 'late bloomers' showed greater improvement than the students not labelled. Additionally, teachers considered the 'late bloomers' were 'better adjusted and more intellectually alive' than their peers. Although the results seemed clear and tantalising to many, there were criticisms of both the method and logic used in the experiment (see Elashoff and Snow 1971).

Nonetheless, despite criticisms the experiment provided the impetus for hundreds of subsequent studies using a range of different methods – some examining effects, others looking at the expectancy processes involved (Harris and Rosenthal 1986). One particularly noteworthy, if disquieting, study was carried out by Rist (1970) who, using an ethnographic approach, observed the behaviour of a kindergarten teacher with a class of ghetto children over a two-year period. Almost immediately after their arrival the teacher placed the children into three separate groups 'cardinals', 'tigers' and 'clowns' (no prizes for guessing the status of the clowns!) giving each group a separate table. As the teacher had no information about the academic performance of these children, they were classified primarily on the basis of their socio-economic status. Rist (1970) argued that the teacher was comparing the children to her perception of the 'ideal' pupil, many features of which bore no relationship to actual academic ability. Children on the first table were cleaner, better dressed and better behaved than the second group, who in turn were 'nicer' than the clowns. The most striking observation was that two years later these pupils were still in the same ability groups.

Good and Brophy (1991) highlighted the conditions under which expectations are likely to have most effect. They argued that, having formed expectations of your students based on your existing knowledge, you naturally expect differences in performance and behaviour from different students. These expectations affect the decisions you make whilst teaching, where students are seated, the type of work given to them, how often you speak to them and how long you wait for them to answer. In this way, your students learn what they are expected to do and behave accordingly. You observe the behaviour that confirms your original expectations and the cycle continues. But what if the student's behaviour does not confirm your original expectations, or the students attempt to change their behaviour, does this result in changing teachers' opinions? Not necessarily, according to the work of Schmuck and Schmuck (1992), or Rogers (1982) who commented:

> the fact that the pupil's behaviour does not shift in the expected direction will not necessarily have the effect of weakening or changing the initial expectation. It will be the teacher's perceptions of events that count and these will not always be accurate.
>
> (Rogers 1982: 59)

The conditions under which unintended consequences are most likely to occur are when teaching large classes with intermittent contact, as is the case in many secondary schools. The more regular contact in primary schools allows closer relationships to form. However, primary-aged children tend to be much more easily influenced (Rogers 1982).

Where teachers work with small groups or individuals, they receive more immediate feedback and have the opportunity to gain greater knowledge of individual students. It provides teachers with more opportunity to observe behaviour changes and disconfirm inaccurate initial impressions. It is not unusual to hear stories of students who have been excluded from mainstream classes who 'become' well behaved and communicative with their new teachers after having been placed in special units with smaller teaching ratios. If the information received about a student is not diagnostically valid for determining dispositions (for example, being told a student comes from a low socio-economic group should not be diagnostically sound as an indicator of intellectual ability), a teacher is likely to avoid using it to draw conclusions about a student. However, they can become hypotheses about likely qualities which they can test against behavioural evidence to make judgements. If the opportunity then arises to acquire behavioural information about someone, people use a 'confirming strategy' to find evidence which supports their original hypothesis by selective attention to particular behaviours whilst ignoring others. In other words, you look for evidence of the expected behaviours, weighting them in favour of those that confirm expectancy-beliefs. Inconsistent behaviour is explained in terms of the situation rather than the student, thus reinterpreting inconsistent behaviour as being consistent with initial expectancy, for example a 'yob' behaving altruistically might be reappraised as disguising his or her *real* motivational intent.

Expectancy research has generally supported the proposition that holding a particular expectation under certain conditions can influence outcomes for

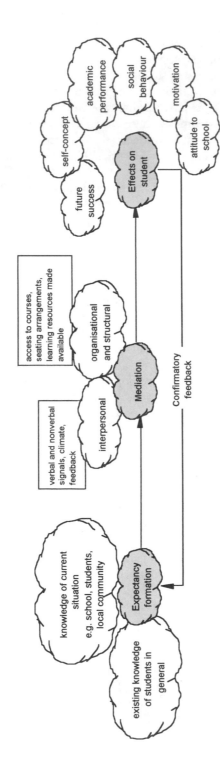

Figure 2.1 A simplified model of the teacher expectancy-confirmation process

others, and that these outcomes can be social and/or academic performance and either positive or negative. One set of questions for those involved with trying to bring about change in schools is as follows:

- How are expectancies formed?
- How are they mediated and under what conditions?
- Why do they persist if known to be inaccurate?
- What are the likely outcomes?
- How can we guard against negative outcomes?

A number of researchers have offered models to explain the teacher expectancy-confirmation process (Rogers 1982; Harris and Rosenthal 1986). Figure 2.1 offers a summary of the salient elements. Essentially the process consists of forming expectations, the mediation of expectations and potential outcomes. I emphasise the potential, since not all expectations are mediated, received or attended to by students; where that happens, they do not inevitably bring about particular outcomes. Nonetheless, the fact remains that, in a significant number of cases, they do (Darley and Fazio 1980; Jussim 1986). Where they result in the Pygmalion effect (i.e. where student performance improves), there is usually less cause for concern. However, where the opposite occurs there is certainly cause for concern. The Golem effect (Babad *et al.* 1982) is the negative effect of *teacher expectancy* and happens when a teacher expects lower performance or problem behaviour from a student, which results in a student behaving in that way. There are difficulties in demonstrating this phenomenon since it is unethical to construct experiments which cause students to underachieve or to behave badly.

There are three stages in the expectancy cycle:

- forming expectations
- the mediation of expectations
- potential outcomes.

Understanding students' behaviour

Expectancy formation is dependent upon social cognition, which is concerned with the acquisition of social knowledge and how we think about and develop understanding of our social worlds. It concerns the processes we use to make sense of other people and also guides our social behaviour (Abrams and Hogg 1999). Put simply, it concerns how we think about people plus and how we *think* we *think* about people.

Social cognition is relevant to the study of thinking, motivation, feelings and behaviour. It includes the study of a wide range of phenomena including social perception (Zebrowitz 1990), impression formation (Brewer 1988), stereotypes and stereotyping (Leyens *et al.* 1994), attribution theory (Hewstone 1994) to name a few. Social cognition has a particular relevance to classrooms and schools, as it provides a link between cognition and social psychology, is orientated towards processes and a concern with real-world issues (Ostrom 1984). Socio-cognitive processes explain interpersonal relationships in school including the expectancy process.

Our social behaviour arises from a combination of how we believe we should act in social situations, how we expect others to behave, our interpretation of the feedback we receive from others, all of which we use to self-regulate our own behaviour. However, we do not interact with the actualities of a situation but rather our perceptions of it (i.e. what we believe to be true). Furthermore, whether we like it or not, we all make assumptions about ourselves, other people, groups and the situations we find ourselves in. Many of these assumptions are functional and we would not be able to go about our daily lives without using them. However, sometimes they can be dramatically inaccurate or overly rigid, thus resistant to change and result in unintended consequences, something which will be discussed in detail later. In well-known situations we rely on typical procedures to direct often complex sequences of behaviour.

Imagine going into a classroom full of Year 9 students for the first time; you will no doubt be able to think of how you might expect them to behave, irrespective of how much you know about the actual students.

List how you would expect such a group to behave on your first encounter in a new school. Consider the sequence of events leading to you starting to teach the lesson.

It is likely that you will have a sequence in mind which will probably be on the lines of, as you enter the room expecting the students to stop talking or messing about, scanning the room, picking out specific individuals, maintaining eye contact, making a mental note of who does and who does not respond to your presence, moving to a 'safe' position in the classroom which gives you a good viewpoint, saying hello, students saying hello, introducing yourself, letting them know how you feel about how they were behaving (if necessary) and so on. This whole process is regulated by what psychologists call a social schema or in this specific case an event schema (Abelson 1981).

To appreciate the salience of event schemas, imagine the following lesson. Mr Allen is teaching a class of Year 10 students. The class has been working quietly. Suddenly Damien shouts out 'bloody' and everyone laughs. Mr Allen sends Damien to see the head teacher. Why do you think Damien was sent to see the head?

A social schema is a generic mental structure (Taylor and Cocker 1981) which contains organised prior knowledge of, for example, people, events, roles and self (NB there are many more possible types and many overlap). Such structures allow people to simplify the storage of knowledge about their social worlds in an inclusive way, often discarding some data to give an overall impression – as opposed to sorting the data in an elemental way with every bit of knowledge being kept in a 'raw' form. Schema influence social information processing in three different ways: perception and encoding of new information, memory of old information and inferences about people where information is missing. A social schema is a rough and ready but organised framework, which allows the quick processing of information. For instance, the event schema for entering a classroom is probably unremarkable and familiar rather than novel and would be generally identifiable (with minor tweaks) in all schools. It is worth noting that the ritualised behaviour of event scripts can, in some conditions, undermine classroom relations. Where the 'script' for the first meeting with a group is negatively evaluated and the messages in both directions confirm expectations, this can result in a negative cycle, which continues if unchecked.

During the initial interactions with students or whole classes you will automatically make rapid assessments of them. If you couldn't make assessments of your students you wouldn't be doing your job. In the example of a script, you would probably note who was first to respond to your arrival, who seemed to ignore you, who needed reminding about how they should behave, any possible troublemakers and the like. What you attend to will be influenced by a whole range of factors, including individual features of the students (e.g. physical attractiveness, sex, volume of speech, dress) and cultural features (ethnicity, social class) as well as the situation and your own characteristics. Your assessments are based on a combination of what you know about schools and students which you have acquired over many years through experiences as a pupil, student and later a teacher. Added to these data is what you know about the current situation from official briefing by colleagues or managers, staffroom gossip, the school's and the class's reputation, what you know of the local community and its residents. This information will influence your expectations, modify how you behave toward the group and regulate what you say and how you say it. If the school has a reputation for good behaviour and this class appears noisy, you may start with 'I don't expect to hear this sort of noise from a group of students in this school!' (i.e. emphasis on the behaviour being unacceptable to the social identity of the school or the group). If, on the other hand, the school or class has a reputation for bad behaviour you may start with 'This level of noise is not acceptable in my classroom!' (i.e. emphasis on a less abstract level – the behaviour being unacceptable to your personal standards or new standards being expected).

If your answer to the earlier question about Damien being sent to the head was because you think he misbehaved (swearing or shouting out), then your classroom 'script' probably made you assume (quite reasonably) that Damien had disrupted the class and had been sent to the head for his misbehaviour. You were not, however, given this information originally, so your explanation results from your own schema in action. Damien may have been referring to having cut his finger – 'bloody' being his response to you asking how bad it was, everyone laughing may have been in response to you making a joke with Damien, and being sent to the head may have been to organise for him to be driven to the hospital. Event schemas are not just limited to classroom behaviour; people have scripts for social events in general and all act to provide expectations about the likely sequence of events.

This process is normal and used to make life predictable and is based on how people reason about probabilities. Social psychologists have directed considerable attention to weaknesses in this process – our biases and our lack of understanding of the rules that govern probabilities of events, along with how we reason. But just how does this process work? What are its strengths and weaknesses?

Impressions of people are not based on the actual behavioural acts of the individual to whom we respond, but our impression of the person carrying them out. If a student comes into class and greets you in a warm and friendly way and your existing knowledge of the student suggests that he or she is generally a friendly, helpful student, you will accept it in the spirit you perceived it to have been offered. On the other hand, if the student has, on previous encounters, proved to be devious and calculating and he or she suddenly acts in a warm and friendly way, then you are likely to be suspicious and detect some underlying motive. The ability to understand underlying motives is a component of social competence (see Chapter 3) – competent, that is, if we read the situation correctly!

Before we can apply our existing schema to a person or situation, we have to assign them to a particular category. The process of social categorisation is less about accurately matching an individual's attributes to a category than it is an inference process. A category may be invoked when it is *sufficiently related* to a person rather than when it matches a person's attributes. This means that when encountering another person, we rely on a vast range of categories and can even generate categories on demand.

As soon as you assign someone to a particular category (e.g. disruptive student) based on particular attributes (probably male, perhaps not wearing school uniform, continuing talking when you entered the room, having his feet up on the desk), you can apply your existing knowledge of students in this category (e.g. troublemaker). Social psychologists are interested in what the necessary and sufficient qualities are that define the boundaries of a particular category. How do we decide an individual belongs to one category (e.g. disruptive student) and not another (high spirits) or a set of behaviours to one situation (e.g. students talking whilst working) and not another? Whilst accurate determination of categories might be possible in mathematics and science, it is less so in the social world. Here people and situations are categorised by their membership of 'fuzzy sets' (Fiske and Taylor 1991) so it is sometimes not always clear that someone belongs to a particular category, nor which attributes are being attended to by the perceiver.

Think of a student you consider disruptive. What behaviour led you to place him in that category (e.g. answers back) and how does he differ from other students who might answer back but do not belong to that category? An example might be the student who is very good at academic work but who often behaves in a way that, were he or she not so academically talented, would be considered disruptive.

Social perception leads us to decide that some group members are more typical than others and that there is a prototypical member around which the group is centred. The prototype is generated from a number of examples. Think of the range of students you might identify as disruptive. How are they similar and how do they differ? When someone new is encountered they are classified on the basis of their similarity to the prototype for that group (e.g. bright or dull, naughty or nice). What is encoded may be altered to fit existing elements in memory. However, given that the prototype is the *central tendency*, it follows that there will be individuals at both extremes of typicality and atypicality who also 'belong' to that category. So, a category may consist of students from the extremely bright but naughty student to the extremely dull but well-behaved student. Categories are believed to be organised hierarchically and have different levels of abstraction (Cantor and Mischel 1979).

Disruptive students can be categorised at the classroom level (least abstract) but also belong to a larger category of misbehaving young people which might include those with emotional and behavioural difficulties who, in turn, belong to an even bigger group of young people which might include young criminals and so on. We use all of these different categories for varying purposes. In encounters with students, we are likely to draw out category-consistent information and miss that which does not fit the prototype. Furthermore, along with allocation to a social category, we like to think we can predict other people's behaviour even when, strictly speaking, people rarely do the *same* thing twice. Behaviour is subject to constant change as people adapt to the changing world around them, so it is important that we modify our social perceptions in line with changes to their behaviour. Those of you with children of your own will recognise the difficulties we sometimes have adjusting our perceptions as they move from child to teenager (argh!) to adult.

In the classroom, social perception is multifaceted. Teacher perceives student, students perceives teacher, teacher perceives how the students are perceiving the teacher and the students perceive how the teacher perceives them. This perception of perceptions, referred to as metaperception, influences the value each party places on the other.

If a student feels that a teacher did not pay sufficient attention to him or her and believes that this is because the teacher does not like him or her, the student may reciprocate, showing lack of interest in the teacher. The teacher, on the other hand, may merely have been preoccupied with something else, but interprets the student's behaviour as lack of interest in the subject. This misinterpretation of one another does not nurture a good working relationship. How they came to these conclusions about each other is clearly of interest. How the student perceives the teacher perceives him or her will influence how the student then responds to a whole range of teacher behaviour and vice versa. This perception of one another does not usually take place without other input. Each party will have a prior expectation and/or knowledge of the other. There is a likely imbalance in how much information each will have access to. The teacher is likely to have access to more official information about the background of a student than a student will have about the teacher. Knowledge of teachers is often in the form of myth and rumour: 'I wouldn't cross him if I were you, he'll knock your head off (not that he ever has of course)' or 'He's a right Wally'. Myth, rumour and folklore about teachers are the stuff of school playgrounds and provide much information for the teacher schema that students carry.

Effects on students may be short and long term, both in terms of motivation towards schoolwork and attitude towards teachers. Some feeling for this can be gained from the following quote taken from an interview with a Year 11 student who was talking about school, work and her future:

> I really loved history when I started secondary school. I had done lots of history projects at my primary school. In Year 7 we had this right snobby bitch teaching us. I don't think she liked the class or the school, I think she was just here 'cos her husband moved to the area to get a job. She said I hadn't done the work on my project but I had spent hours on it so I didn't bother after that, why should I? My mum said I was the only one who would suffer but she wasn't being taught by her. I didn't start enjoying history until Year 10 after that. Mr T [Year 10 history teacher] was great and he really encouraged you to do extra

work and he marked it as well. I might do it for my A levels now – no thanks to that snobby cow!

(Melissa, Year 11)

Where the two sets of perceptions fail to synchronise or are distorted, there is potential to undermine the relationship. The ability to read what others are likely to be thinking about us is a complex socio-cognitive skill and has a developmental dimension. Younger and older students differ in the way they understand and interpret the behaviour of others.

In addition to categorisation, social perception includes a diverse range of other processes, which are concerned with how we perceive and judge human attributes (see Zebrowitz 1990). Examples of these processes include person perception, judging emotions from facial expression, impression formation and causal attribution. It is to the latter two areas we now turn.

Impression formation

The processes involved in forming impressions about others, whether in a bar in Ibiza or a classroom in Manchester, are similar. These impressions are based on a combination of our wider (distal) knowledge of people and their membership of a particular 'category' alongside the individual knowledge we have about them and the immediate situation (proximal).

So how does this operate in practice? Here's how one student determined the personality of his new teacher before and after meeting him:

> I was dreading going to his school. I'd heard from his son and others that he was really strict. Someone said he was a nutter – he apparently threw one kid across the room whilst the kid was still sitting in a chair! When I first met him he frightened me to death. He seemed to look right through me. He said he didn't appreciate people who messed about in his class and we knew what that meant! But most of us enjoyed being in his class – except the idiots who always messed about with other teachers but he wasn't frightened of them – not hitting 'em or anything – but they didn't mess about in his class. After a while I thought, 'He's all right really – he's a good laugh', I even joined his fishing club. I still wouldn't want to cross him though. When he looks angry, you just get on with your work.

(Barry, Year 10)

So, how did Barry form his initial impressions of his new teacher and decide how he would behave toward him? Would he attend to different attributes weighing up the potential value of each before deciding? Or did he view the person as a whole, assigning them to the nearest reference group with which he was familiar and ignoring some of the details – papering over the cracks, as it were? Does the nature of the encounter or the context make a difference? Barry's early data came from a third party, the teacher's son, and at that stage he appeared to categorise him negatively. Later, having spent time observing this teacher, his perceptions changed and he added new, more positive, data to his theory about this teacher. Was the initial emphasis on understanding his teacher or was it self-serving?

There are two broad approaches to the impression formation process:

* theory-driven (inferential)
* data-driven (evaluative).

Supporters of the theory-driven approach (Asch 1946; Heider 1958) argue that we do not experience other people as a sum or average of their traits or 'ingredients', but rather as a complete psychological unit, fitting them into an underlying theme or theory. We combine the various components of a person's make-up to produce an overall impression. In a famous series of experiments Asch (1946) showed how people infer a whole range of traits about a non-existent person, based on limited information about specific traits. In one experiment he gave two groups of people two almost identical lists of seven words (see Table 2.1a); the only difference between the two lists was that one contained the word 'warm' and the other the word 'cold'. He then gave each group a second longer list of additional qualities and asked them to identify further traits to describe this imaginary person; some of the results are shown in Table 2.1b. Asch argued that the presence of the words warm and cold had disproportionate effects on the overall impression that the groups formed, since they were central traits. It is important to note that the two people 'described' by these seven words did not exist; however, despite this the groups were able to differentiate readily between them.

Supporters of the structural or data-driven approach posit the perceiver as attending to individual characteristics of a person (intelligent, industrious, cold) and evaluating these qualities individually in terms of their positive and negative qualities (Anderson 1981). These individual qualities are differentially weighted and the resultant average determines the impression formed. Thus, whilst being intelligent is positive, being cold is strongly negative resulting in a negative evaluation.

More recent research has suggested that on their own, neither of the two models offers a satisfactory explanation of how we form impressions. As a result, combination models were developed, in which theory- or data-driven models are shown to operate under different conditions depending on the decision made by the perceiver (Brewer 1988; Fiske and Neuberg 1990). In these models, initial theory-driven impressions are formed using pre-existing schema about categories of people. The person-based (data-driven) impressions are activated only if the target cannot be fitted to an existing category or is of interest or personal relevance to the perceiver. Whether or not you

Table 2.1 Implying personality from limited information

Table 2.1a	Imaginary person	
	A	B
Adjectives used to describe two imaginary people	Intelligent	Intelligent
	Industrious	Industrious
	Skilful	Skilful
	Determined	Determined
	Warm	Cold
	Practical	Practical
	Cautious	Cautious

Table 2.1b	Ratings of additional descriptors	
Additional descriptors	Person A 'Warm' (%)	Person B 'Cold' (%)
Generous	91	8
Wise	65	25
Happy	90	34
Good-natured	94	17
Humorous	77	13
Sociable	91	38
Popular	84	28
Humane	86	31
Altruistic	69	31
Imaginative	51	19

Note: Table 2.1a shows the initial information given to two separate groups of people. Each received five adjectives that described an imaginary person and which were the same, except for the words 'warm' and 'cold'. Table 2.1b shows a sample of the ratings made by the two groups of further characteristics, which show clear differences, despite the fact that assessment by the two groups was based on minimal information.

change that initial impression depends on whether or not you move on to using data-driven information.

In addition to expecting disruptive students to have particular traits, you are also likely to have expectations about how such students are likely to look, dress, the sorts of things they are likely to say, their attitude to school and life in general. So, how and when does the second model come into play? As mentioned previously, you will resort to identifying personal qualities only if the individual or group is of interest or importance to you and/or you are motivated to do so.

Having expected a problematic group, you are more likely to go into your first lesson intent on keeping a lid on things and not letting the group take control. This may involve being more formal than informal; your concerns make you smile less and you are more sensitive to off-task behaviour or potential disruption in order to nip it in the bud. Your attention is more likely to be biased towards picking up on negative behaviour (in a sense justifiably) but your actions may in fact encourage it.

Similarly students have their theories about teachers. Barry had categor-ised his new teacher as very austere, almost dangerous, 'not to be messed with, very strict'. Having made contact and initially treating him gingerly, over time he became more aware of those qualities in this teacher that he admired. Yes, he was strict and didn't stand any messing, but he was like that with any student large or small, so was seen as fair and in control; on top of that he had a sense of humour. Barry integrated the individual characteristics (data driven) with his theory-driven impression concluding that overall, the teacher was an all right guy. However, as is often the case, he still had the 'slight' reservation that there might be a grain of truth in the myth of the flying student, no matter how improbable, and wouldn't want to join him! Barry went on to say that he perpetuated the myth with newcomers to the school, perhaps for devilment or as a badge of courage, since he considered himself close to this teacher whom *he* admired.

Research suggests that impression formation is a twofold process. The first is 'automatic' – putting someone into an appropriate social category and, if you then have no further involvement leaving them there, with all the inferred qualities – positive and/or negative – attached to that category. The second involves taking on board individuating information, of having time to engage in learning about a person's individual characteristics and gaining understanding of why they behave the way they do. The problems for many secondary teachers are how to do this when you work with a whole class for maybe one or two periods per week and seldom, if ever, get any quality time with individuals? How do you set about revising your opinions of individuals?

Causal attribution: explaining the causes of behaviour

Causal attribution is an everyday, normal activity carried out by everyone. Heider (1958), the reputed father of attribution theory, suggested that people act like naive scientists forming hypotheses about what or who causes things to happen in their world, to help make life predictable. Attribution theory is concerned with the answer to three questions:

• What are the perceived causes of an event?
• What information influenced this causal inference?
• What are the consequences of ascribing these causes?

An example will help to explain. Imagine you are walking through the school grounds and are hit on the back of the head with a conker. You are likely to want to find out who or what is responsible. You turn round and see a group of students, whom you had recently reprimanded for misbehaving in class, standing under a horse chestnut tree with handfuls of conkers, looking your way and laughing. You might consider the likely cause to be one of this group, based on the evidence described. The consequence might be that you further reprimand them. If, however, you turned round and saw no one, then heard a 'meow', looked up and saw a stranded cat in the horse chestnut tree above your head, struggling to balance and knocking leaves off in the process, you might infer a different cause and hence react differently. Neither example may in fact be the real cause – but it is the perceived cause that really matters in people's understanding of causality.

According to attribution theorists, people seek to identify general causal principles which they use to predict the future, control events and guide their own behaviour (Fosterling and Rudolph 1988). People have causal explanations for their own behaviour (intrapersonal attributions), for other people's behaviour (interpersonal attributions), and others are shared with groups (inter-group attributions). An example of the latter might be the shared understanding amongst a group of teachers in a particular school as to why students misbehave in class. Whilst there may appear to be a shared understanding when with the group or even at the interpersonal level, individual teachers may not personally hold that view but do so in the group situation.

There are a number of attribution theories which, although different, share a number of qualities. As to deciding which one is right, it really depends on the conditions and the situation being analysed. As Fiske and Taylor put it:

> all of them have some validity, but under different circumstances and for different phenomena. The theories cannot be pitted against each other in the usual scientific manner. Rather, each outlines a series of processes that can be used to infer attributions if the appropriate circumstances are present.
>
> (1991: 40)

Two prominent contributions to our understanding of how people make inferences about other people's attributes and behaviour were Jones and Davis's (1965) correspondent inference model and Kelley's (1967) two interpretations – causal schemas and the covariation model. The latter will be used to demonstrate the relevance of attribution theory to the teacher expectancy-confirmation cycle. Kelley (1967) argued that our knowledge of the social world is often limited and ambiguous. Whilst under normal circumstances we have sufficient information to enable us to cope, there are other times when we have difficulty doing so. For example, if we experience an assault on our 'self' (knowledge, social, esteem and so on) or instances where our coping levels are exceeded, or where information is ambiguous, we are likely to engage in causal analysis by searching for an explanation for our predicament. If faced with a group of students who are proving more difficult to manage than we have experienced in the past, we are likely to look for a causal explanation. Am I not up to the job? Are these students so disturbed that no one could manage them? Am I being expected to teach extreme children with insufficient resources? Clearly, the answers to these different possible explanations call for different responses. If I feel I am no longer up to the job, then I could get another job or go on a training course to develop my behaviour management skills. If I consider the students to be disturbed, I could ask for assessment and/or support from other professionals. If I consider the lack of resources unacceptable, I could ask for more support. This all sounds very logical and common sense – hence Heider (1958) referred to it as commonsense psychology. However, it has been shown that we make errors in some of our causal explanations.

Three types of attribution errors have been identified:

*   The first is a tendency – notably in western society – to overemphasise personality, as opposed to situational attributes, as causes of behaviour. In other words, if a student misbehaves, we are more likely to blame him or her than the situation.
*   Second, in interpersonal situations there tends to be a difference between how the person in a situation explains the causes, compared with how an observer sees things. A teacher having difficulty managing a student is more likely to blame the situation or the student for what is happening, whereas an observer is more likely to blame the teacher for not being in control.
*   Third, egocentric attributions refer to the tendency to attribute successes to ourselves and failures to others. If an event at school was heralded a great success, we are likely to claim credit whereas, if it is a flop, we blame others.

Attributing causality in these three ways serves to protect an individual's self-worth. Even though they may be incorrect, the perception that we can justify our behaviour to ourselves and others by generating 'plausible' explanations or excuses is an important coping mechanism. The effects of doing so on others might not be so useful. In his search to identify what information people use to arrive at causal explanations, Kelley developed two models: causal schema and covariation models. Which one a perceiver uses to explain events depends on the amount of information available. As most teachers have access to information about students and see them usually more than once, I will concentrate on his covariation model.

In this model the perceiver has access to information about the behaviour and intent of others from multiple events and can perceive the covariation of possible causes with what they are observing. A secondary teacher, after a relatively short period of time, will have taught similar topics to many different groups. Under such circumstances the teacher will utilise the covariation model to conclude the causes of events. Covariance refers to two events happening together. If your class is badly behaved only whenever a particular student is present, then there is a high covariance. You may attribute the disruptive behaviour to this student's influence. If your class is sometimes badly behaved when the student is present and sometimes when he or she is not, there is a low covariance. The student may not be the sole reason for the disruption. Kelley reasoned that to conclude a causal explanation for someone's behaviour, people measure covariation across three dimensions:

- *Distinctiveness:* does the behaviour occur only when this student is present but does not when the student is absent?
- *Consistency:* has this behaviour occurred when I have taught them in the past?
- *Consensus:* do other teachers have the same problem when the student is present?

Where high distinctiveness, high consistency and high consensus occur together, people are able to make attributions with confidence. Of the three dimensions, consistency is the most preferred dimension for determining causality. Causation would be directed to a student if, whenever he or she is present in class, with any teacher, there is a problem which does not happen in the student's absence. If, on the other hand, the student was problematic only when you were teaching the class and this had happened before with you, but not with other teachers, you are likely to come to a different conclusion! Table 2.2 shows three alternative causal explanations resulting from different assessments of the three variables.

The casual analyses suggest attribution of blame to one of three explanations – the student, the teacher or the environment (problems at home or Lee being bullied, for example). Which of the three explanations is selected will result in different consequences. If Lee is seen as being the cause, then Mrs Black is likely to feel less inclined to want to teach him, since she expects the same behaviour in the future. If she is seen as the problem, then a different set of responses are required, for example, attending a behaviour management course, mentoring, in-class support, different responsibilities. If the situation is seen as the cause, Mrs Black may decide to talk to Lee and ask him if there is anything bothering him or speak with his form tutor.

This description may imply that causal attribution is done in a rational, logical and just way when in fact that is not always the case. The self-serving bias and tendency to attribute causes to personality rather than the situations discussed mean that Mrs Black is *less* likely to attribute responsibility to herself.

Table 2.2 Explanations for Lee's misbehaviour

Distinctiveness	Consistency	Consensus	Likely attribution
Low Lee is cheeky to most teachers.	High Lee is always cheeky to Mrs Black.	Low Other students are not cheeky to Mrs Black.	It is Lee's fault.
High Lee is not usually cheeky to teachers.	High Lee is always cheeky to Mrs Black.	High Other students are cheeky to Mrs Black.	It is Mrs Black's fault.
High Lee is not usually cheeky to teachers.	Low Lee has not been cheeky to Mrs Black before.	Low Other students are not cheeky to Mrs Black.	There is something different about the situation.

Note: The table shows three possible causal explanations in answer to the question: Why is Lee being cheeky to Mrs Black?
In Row 1 the problem appears to be with Lee since he is *consistently* cheeky to most teachers, including Mrs Black, but other students are not.
In Row 2 the problem appears to be with Mrs Black, since Lee is not usually cheeky to other teachers but is to Mrs Black, as are most other students.
In Row 3 the problem appears to be something beyond the two individuals since Lee is not usually cheeky to any teacher, including Mrs Black, and nor are any other students.

Attributing causality may involve deliberate and time-consuming logical analyses or may result from rapid cognitive processing to make a quick decision about what is happening and how you should react. If causality is regularly attributed in a particular direction, it can reach a point where it is done automatically or scripted, becoming difficult to break. Where the perceived cause has been attributed incorrectly, it may continue unchallenged.

Getting the message across: mediating expectations

Forming an impression (false or otherwise), categorising and attributing your students' behaviour as disruptive do not mean you will necessarily communicate those thoughts to students and, even if you do, that they will take them on board and fulfil your expectations. In order for this to happen you need to mediate them further for the student to recognise, encode and accept the messages.

Expectations are mediated in a variety of ways including:

• *verbal:* supportive, encouraging comments versus non-supportive, discouraging comments
• *nonverbal:* posture, gesture, social distance, eye contact
• *organisational:* ranging from being placed in particular ability groups which limits/empowers access to particular courses/exams, to where

students are seated in relation to teacher and peers, or whether they have access to equipment and particular areas of the school.

I will repeat one of my opening comments: I do not believe any teacher would intentionally make their students fail but, given the evidence that teachers treat students in quantitatively and qualitatively different ways, and that these are related to social and academic outcomes, it is essential to ask why it happens and how does it happen?

In the search to find what student features most influence teachers' expectations, a number of single variables have been investigated with varying and sometimes surprising results. Stereotypical expectations of students were found to have some influence. While sex differences proved insignificant, race and physical attractiveness were shown to have modest influences (Gage and Berliner 1988). The largest influences were found in respect of students' past performance and social class (Darley and Gross 1983).

If working-class boys are expected to be more disruptive than other students, then any information the teacher takes in, from interactions with this group, will be sifted through this belief. The level of influence such a belief might have will depend on how his, or her impressions are organised.

Harris and Rosenthal (1986), in their metanalysis of over 400 studies of teacher expectancy, identified four teacher factors which were central to, and most influential in, the mediation of expectancies and resultant student behaviour. These factors were climate, input, output and feedback – climate is the most influential and feedback the least. The following examples relate to the treatment of students for whom a teacher has high expectations:

- *climate* (and emotional support): communication style and warmth towards students, nonverbal messages (especially eye contact)
- *input:* the amount and level of difficulty of material, plus time and attention given
- *output:* frequency of questions and interactions initiated by students, opportunities to perform and learn more difficult material
- *feedback:* clarity and quality of information given to students about their performance; type and amount of praise; acceptance of pupils' ideas.

A number of factors have been identified as being most likely to facilitate the expectancy-confirmation cycle (see Snyder 1992 for a review). These factors include those attributable to the perceiver (teacher), others to the target (student) and a third group related to situational variables (school):

- Teachers whose goals include getting along in a friendly way with their students and who are motivated to develop an accurate data-driven view of their students, are less likely to produce self-fulfilling prophecies than those who are motivated to arrive at a stable and predictable view of their students.

- Students who are uncertain of their self-worth, or who have unclear self-perceptions regarding their ability and their self-efficacy are more susceptible to social influences, including teachers' self-fulfilling prophecies. Where a student's self-perceptions are clear, they are more likely to convince others to view them as positively as they view themselves. Furthermore, if the motivational goals of the student can be facilitated by the teacher (e.g. help with a project, a good mark), then they are more likely to conform to the teacher's expectations.
- Students moving into new situations (such as going to a new school, or transition through school years) are more susceptible to the influences of teachers' expectations as they attempt to develop a social identity, cope with their new surroundings, goals and demands, so are likely to be less clear and confident in their self-perceptions. The timing of the mediation of expectancy effects is also an important factor. Experiments have shown that, where a false expectancy has been introduced in the early stages of a teacher forming impressions about students, expectancy effects were found more often. When similar experiments were carried out after the teachers' impressions had crystallised, the effects were not found as regularly, reaffirming the early discussion about the impression formation process.
- Finally, effects seldom occur separately in social contexts (e.g. the classroom) since it is the cumulative effects or their interaction with each other, which usually results in expectancy effects. Cumulative effects can include: cognitive (learning, self-efficacy), social (peer group relations) emotional (motivational style, joy, depression) and behavioural (disruptive versus conforming behaviour) factors.

Ways to avoid sending the wrong messages

There are a number of ways in which teachers can help to avoid negative expectancy effects:

- actively monitor the type, amount and quality of interactions (questions, feedback) to try to ensure equal treatment of students
- avoid using disruptive students as messengers or monitors, sitting them at the back of the room or praising them for marginal or below average performance
- use the same sanctions for all students – whatever their ability
- contact parents of disruptive students for academic reasons not just behavioural ones
- monitor your explanations of the causes of disruption with different students and classes

- examine the *actual*, not perceived, behaviour of students especially those who have been difficult in the past to make sure your impressions are accurate
- focus on learning strategies, not just outcomes
- refrain from grouping, which conveys ability as the sole source of success
- determine students' perspectives on learning and behaviour
- promote cooperation over competition
- teach students realistic goal setting.

Suggested further reading

Rogers, C.G. (1982) *A Social Psychology of Schooling: The Expectancy Effect*, London: Routledge & Kegan Paul.

Chapter 3

Professional social skills

Controlling social communication

When people use the expression 'she's a born teacher', what do they mean and what are the implications for those teachers who are not? No one is born with knowledge of the National Curriculum nor of administration skills; however, some people are extremely effective in communicating with and influencing others, in some cases from an early age. Such individuals are usually socially active and find it easy to make and keep friends, can communicate effectively, listen to others, negotiate, help resolve conflicts, manipulate the behaviour of others and are able to read social situations quickly and accurately. Put simply, they are socially intelligent or socially competent – but what are the characteristics of social competence and are they inherited or learned? Like most areas of social science, there are a number of competing and often conflicting explanations, many of which accept that it is a combination of both.

Social competence

Greenspan (1981) offered a model of personal competence which included physical (gross and fine motor coordination, strength and speed), emotional (character and temperament) and intellectual (multiple intelligences) dimensions. The intellectual dimension he further divided into conceptual, practical and social intelligences. Conceptual intelligence includes the ability to solve problems (e.g. mathematical), practical intelligence includes skills (e.g. wiring a plug) and social intelligence (e.g. understanding and communicating with others). He provides a framework for understanding social competence, which Greenspan argues, comprises three components:

- temperament
- character
- social intelligence.

Of the three, temperament and character are identifiable in neonates and are most stable and are the hardest to change. Some babies, for instance, are very socially active. They respond positively to the presence of others and enjoy interacting with them. Others are less gregarious, preferring the company of one or two familiar faces. The third component, social intelligence, tends to develop over time. It is more malleable and responsive to cultural and other environmental influences. What is considered socially acceptable in one culture is considered offensive in others. For instance, turning your backside towards someone and slapping it is considered offensive in some parts of the world. In England, it is used to demonstrate value for money at a well-known supermarket! This malleability is a positive feature, since it means that where an individual has difficulties or is ineffective, change is possible – people can be taught alternative strategies. However, change can be difficult because it is not always easy to monitor exactly how we are behaving, since we cannot see ourselves in action, relying instead on our interpretation of feedback we receive from others to measure our effectiveness.

It is often 'assumed' that those choosing to become teachers, will enjoy communicating with others and be effective doing so. Given the fundamental requirement of having high quality people skills, one might expect significant parts of teachers' training to be spent developing them, particularly as they represent the bread and butter of the job (Argyle 1981). In practice, few, if any, courses provide structured developmental programmes for these essential skills, reinforcing the belief that good teachers are born not made.

However, we are continually reminded of the problems that some teachers face on a daily basis when attempting to manage students. Managing students' behaviour requires competence in complex interpersonal skills including negotiation, conflict resolution, questioning and assertiveness. The fact that many teachers achieve this, despite not receiving specific training, is praiseworthy but needs to be considered alongside the high levels of reported stress and numbers leaving the profession prematurely because of difficulties coping (Travers and Cooper 1996).

Being socially competent requires a large repertoire of social skills, the ability to read and interpret social cues and being able to respond appropriately to particular contexts. However, social encounters can be affected negatively by emotions, which can undermine social competence. An example will help to qualify this.

Jasmin, a bright, young and newly qualified teacher, is meeting her new class for the first time. She is well prepared for her lesson, in terms of having a detailed lesson plan, considered classroom layout, appropriate resources and background information on the students. She has thought about where to stand in the classroom to establish authority, how to stand and what to say. However, when she asks for quiet, the students seem slow to respond, then some start laughing. Just then the Head of Department sticks her head around the door and asks if everything is OK and Jasmin says 'Yes, thanks' – the students laugh again. She smiles to the Head of Department trying to suggest that she is in control. The situation makes her feel uncomfortable. She feels hot. Her mouth feels dry and she has butterflies in her stomach. She is not sure why at this stage. Everything *ought* to be all right, after all when she was on professional placement she had coped extremely well. However, she is now feeling stressed, anxious, uncertain and unhappy that things are not going the way they should.

Jasmin's feelings (e.g. anxiety, guilt) represent a reaction to the conflict between what she thinks 'must', 'should' or 'ought' to be happening in order for her to be considered a competent teacher and what she perceives is actually happening. Being preoccupied with what 'ought' or 'must' is irrational and can result in strong emotional reactions and is the subject of cognitive behavioural theorists (Meichenbaum 1977; Ellis and Dryden 1987). These theories are discussed in more detail in Chapter 8.

Feeling anxious leads to a preoccupation with the self and survival. Some of the symptoms result in our experiencing one of the three Fs – fight, flight or freeze. What Jasmin is thinking and feeling will be communicated through her behaviour. These behaviours include facial expression, eye contact, body posture, gesture, voice (pitch, speed and frequency), paralanguage, moving to a defensible space, hanging on to something solid, increasing social distance, attempting to get out of the 'spotlight'. Facial expression is likely to signal fear by being more tense than normal, making it difficult to smile. This expression will suggest to the students that she is frightened, through the positioning of the eyebrows and mouth. Eye contact becomes less likely. Body posture and gesture become protective and 'closed', rather than open and confident. Tension in the muscles and having a dry mouth may raise the pitch of the voice, making it sound 'squeaky'. She may retreat to a safer position such as moving away from the group or moving behind her desk – a physical barrier, again signalling fear. Finally, the need to 'get out of the spotlight' often results in a tendency not to take time to explain what is expected of the class or individual student, instead wanting them 'just to get on with it'. Unfortunately, the hurried instructions mean that some students don't know what is expected of them, so do nothing. Those that do try to participate, ask what they are supposed to be doing, which may be interpreted by the teacher as them not having paid attention. The students become increasingly aware that the signals seem wrong, and will often respond negatively, exacerbating the teacher's anxiety and leading to further ineffective messages perpetuating the cycle.

Social interaction is self-regulated by ongoing assessment, comparison, verification and discrepancy management. An individual behaves in particular ways in order to elicit responses from others, which confirm that they think he is the person he wants them to think he is. We are attracted to people who confirm what we believe about ourselves and avoid, or are less receptive to, those who do not (Swann *et al.* 1989). People use feedback to monitor if how they see themselves matches how they believe other people see them.

Assess your feedback to students by videotaping some lessons and observe:

- who you allow to ask most questions and the quality of your responses to them
- what you say and how you say it
- whether or not you smile
- what posture and gestures you use
- the amount of 'banter' (humorous chat) you engage in with students
- who they were and under what circumstances?

Banter is, for many teachers, a valuable part of interacting with students, especially at the secondary level, but some students are more restricted in what they are allowed to say. The level of tolerance is usually related to a teacher's perceptions of a student's ability to know where to draw the line. Students are aware of this, especially when a teacher's authority is not being sustained.

As one of our respondents informed us:

> she starts joking with this group of boys, like if they pass some comment or something, then gets upset when they won't get on with their work – then she gets annoyed and refuses to teach the class. It's well out of order because we want to learn and we haven't done anything wrong.
>
> (Lisa, Year 11)

A central theme of this book is self-awareness and self-regulation through feedback loops and how we are not always consciously aware of all the messages that we transmit. Whilst you may think you are interacting with all the group members equally, this often is not the case.

The structure of social skills

Social skills refer to those behaviours used in social encounters. Often used interchangeably, albeit inaccurately, with social competence, social adequacy and sometimes 'assertiveness'. Social skills include a wide range of behaviours ranging from simple micro skills (e.g. eye contact) to the more complex (e.g. interview skills) and fall into two main categories:

- verbal communication (VC)
- nonverbal communication (NVC)

Verbal communication includes speaking clearly at the appropriate volume and using appropriate language and paralanguage; nonverbal communication includes everything else. However, exactly what is included under the heading of NVC is not always clear. Given that essentially nonverbal behaviour can include everything except words, there are endless possibilities. Apart from obvious behaviours, such as eye contact, posture and gesture, NVC can also include smell, taste, touch, dress, choice of setting and so on. Many social psychologists (e.g. Argyle 1975) have focused on more obvious aspects of bodily communication for their frame of reference. It is also widely acknowledged that nonverbal behaviours include both biologically determined characteristics (e.g. physical attractiveness) and socially constructed and rule-governed behaviours (e.g. standing up at assemblies). Failure to observe, or not understanding these rules, draws (often unwanted) attention, since communication is hampered.

Whilst we are usually aware of what we say, the same is not always the case with NVC. In other words, our mouths say one thing whilst our bodies communicate, or are interpreted as communicating something else – sometimes despite our efforts to avoid doing so. Nonverbal communication is not always intended in the manner in which the receiver interprets it. Pupils in your class may be paying attention, but cannot control a stray yawn which you may interpret as being bored and respond with 'Am I keeping you awake?', which may be treated as a joke or may be resented and stimulate a cycle of negative behaviour between you and the student.

Emotions can interfere with NVC, leading to conflicting messages. For example, a teacher who retreats from an argumentative or aggressive pupil to a position behind the desk, and then points and shouts at the student from this position, is in danger of escalating the situation. 'Hiding' behind the desk and increasing the social distance suggest fear, whilst finger pointing is an aggressive gesture often encouraging an aggressive response from the student. The increased social distance effectively draws in other students, distracting the teacher and providing the student with an audience.

On some occasions we can sense something is not quite right in a social interaction but do so non-consciously – you have a 'gut' feeling that something is amiss, but cannot put your finger on exactly what it is. This is usually because you are not continuously aware of all the cues you are perceiving. One simple example of such perception is that of (eye) pupil size – experiments have demonstrated that when you are attracted to someone your pupils tend to dilate (Hess 1972) and they become smaller when you are angry. It is unlikely, however, that you will be consciously aware of this – but you might be from now on.

Observing nonverbal behaviour

Rather than trying to superimpose a universal set of principles on what is a very idiosyncratic process, the best starting point is to audit your own nonverbal behaviours and identify the areas for improvement.

Using a video camera or an observer are two ways of doing this. Feedback from observers whom you feel comfortable with and whose opinion you respect is useful, but having them present in the classroom specifically for that purpose can generate different behaviour from normal. Asking other adults to interpret what you believed you were communicating is potentially problematic in itself. This is not to suggest that having a video camera in class is necessarily an easy alternative, since initially it will distract both you and the students. It can, however, be used over a sustained period (unlike observers), is more readily concealed and hence likely to capture a more natural record of what happened.

The main advantage is that sequences can be played over and over again, helping to identify who did what and how others reacted. When I have used this technique with teachers, they are often surprised to find that they had not said what they thought they had said, that they were standing awkwardly, or used 'novel' gestures and projected other unintended nonverbal messages. Their voices sounded unfamiliar, with accents and different pronunciation from what they had expected. Figure 3.1 shows where information can be lost during transmission.

Plan one or two lessons or micro situations (e.g. introducing a topic, issuing instructions) and video tape them:

* Write down what you plan to say (but don't read it out aloud or it defeats the object).
* Compare what you had planned to say, thought you were saying and doing with what actually happened – you might be surprised!
* You might also test how much the students took in relative to your output.

People seldom deliberately monitor or practise verbal and nonverbal skills, assuming they go on naturally and that they are OK – unless they become painfully aware that they are not working, for example, having difficulty managing a situation. Even then they tend to look for an explanation that is self-serving (see Chapter 2) such as blaming the situation. Social psychologists argue that, in most social encounters, people rely on what is known as a script which provides them with a typical sequence of events for familiar situations to aid understanding of a range of social phenomena (Lallgee et al. 1992). Our scripts help us to plan our behaviour, since they specify the behavioural steps that lead to effective interpersonal relationships. Think

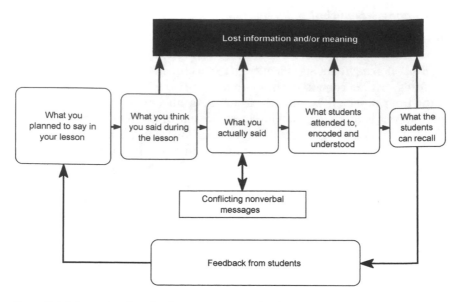

Figure 3.1 Information loss in classroom communication

Table 3.1 A simplified social script for a lesson

Activity	Behaviour
Greeting	Saying hello
Establishing relationships	Getting attention, assessing receptiveness of students, outlining objectives, giving instructions
Completing the tasks	Students learning, monitoring their understanding and behaviour, controlling off-task behaviour
Re-establishing relationships	Regaining class attention, pulling group together, summarising the lesson
Parting	Saying goodbye

of any social encounter, a single lesson for instance, which can simply be divided into a sequence of events, as shown in Table 3.1.

Over time these social scripts become ritualised and assumptions are made about what is being said or done without conscious attention and so, even when we are not being effective, the ritual continues. Ritualised behaviour can lead to us being insensitive to change within individuals, groups, relationships and contexts and can occur in any social institution. It is not uncommon for people in intimate relationships to speak of being taken for granted or their partners not making an effort to notice them or how they have changed. If this occurs with intimate relationships, it is hardly surprising

Table 3.2 Some examples of professional social skills used by teachers

Listening skills
Assertiveness
Proposing ideas
Expressing dissatisfaction
Expressing emotion
Expressing authority
Supporting students having difficulty expressing themselves
Questioning
Disagreeing and criticising
Negotiating
Scaffolding students' ideas
Offering explanations, reasons and difficulties
Seeking clarification, explanation and information
Managing discussion
Encouraging the reluctant to speak
Tempering the over-enthusiastic
Interpreting students' ideas
Consolidating learning
Admitting difficulty
Managing aggression
Defending
Scanning whole class whilst working with individuals
Deflecting challenges

that it should happen with individuals who meet for one or two forty-minute periods each week.

Professional social skills

Professional social skills include a wide range of possibilities. Table 3.2 offers a few examples of some of those regularly used by teachers. I will not discuss all of them in detail but will highlight some, raise a number of questions and provide pointers for personal development, one of which is taking things for granted. When people talk of someone being an effective negotiator, what does this mean, and how might it be quantified? Social effectiveness can be explained in terms of input, process or outcomes. Should successful negotiators be defined in terms of specific social skills, such as being confident, speaking well, making appropriate eye contact, posture and gesture; or on their ability to maintain the flow of the process, for instance keeping people focused and on task, not being distracted and maintaining the interest of their audience; or is it individuals' ability to get what they wanted? The three are not the same. Individuals getting what they want may be effective negotiators, but if done in an aggressive way, this is less socially desirable. Alternatively, some people may have the requisite social skills but have difficulty applying them in some contexts because they are anxious.

Social perception and social influence

Two key components of social competence are social perception and social influence. *Social perception* (see also Chapter 2) concerns how we form general impressions about people, perceive motivational intent and emotions in others and explain *why* they behave the way they do and is clearly central to everyday classroom interaction. Teachers hold psychological models of what causes them to behave the way they do and the reasons for doing so; this helps us to make sense of our world. This influences how we *perceive*, categorise and predict how others are likely to behave, as well as how we should respond to them. Having perceived an individual, we go on to categorise them (social categorisation). Using categories allows us to make quick decisions about people but it can have negative or unintended consequences if we either misclassify someone and fail to modify our original assessment, or fail to recognise when an individual has changed which, in a classroom, can result in deteriorating relationships.

Social influence concerns how we guide the behaviour and thinking of others. In the classroom this refers to establishing and maintaining authority, persuasion, negotiation and compliance.

Interpreting nonverbal behaviour

Social skills are arranged hierarchically in terms of their complexity (see Figure 3.2). The more complex skills (conveying authority, enthusiasm or assertiveness) can be broken down into strategies (scanning, questioning, listening or resolving disputes) or, further still, into basic skills (such as eye contact, facial expression or posture). Whilst we don't usually communicate using single micro skills, they are nonetheless triggers for behaviour in others. Eye gaze or facial expression alone can be powerful methods of communicating what you are thinking and feeling about someone.

We usually look for combinations of nonverbal signals (macro skills) rather than individual micro skills when communicating. However, it is possible to identify those micro skills that are preventing effective communication and learn alternatives to improve performance. The next section will examine a selection of social skills relevant to the classroom in more detail, focusing on:

- the face
- eye movement
- eye contact
- posture
- gesture.

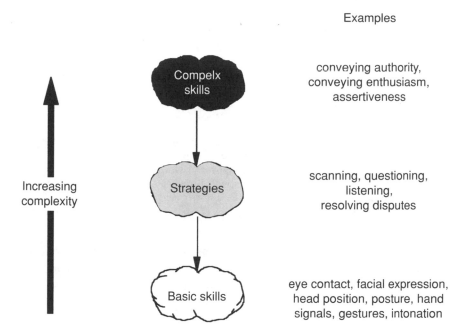

Examples

conveying authority,
conveying enthusiasm,
assertiveness

scanning, questioning,
listening,
resolving disputes

eye contact, facial expression,
head position, posture, hand
signals, gestures, intonation

Figure 3.2 A hierarchy of social skills used in teaching

The face

The face is probably our most powerful nonverbal communicator and research has demonstrated that facial communication has deep evolutionary meanings (Harrison 1976). It frames communication in developing infants (Vine 1973) as well as in adults (Ekman and Friesen 1975). Argyle (1975: 212) suggests that the face conveys 'the main interpersonal relationships – dominant, submissive, threatening, sexual, parental, playful etc.' Facial expression has also been linked to emotional feedback, in terms of not only the more familiar interpretation of the emotions of others by their expression, but also how we interpret our own emotional state. The suggestion that your expression can influence the way you feel (proprioceptive feedback) has long been recognised (James 1884). More recently Laird (1974) and Ekman *et al.* (1983) found that holding a particular facial expression intensified an emotional experience. However, whether it is the facial expression *per se* that influences the emotional experience or whether it is the associated muscle tension or respirational changes is questionable – it appears to do so in some circumstances and not others (Buck 1988). Feedback from facial expression appears to contribute to emotional experience if, and only if, it complements an emotional state – it has a confirmatory role.

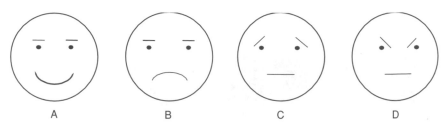

Figure 3.3 Facial code – simplified pictures which show how emotion is signalled and how it can be changed by the alteration of one simple feature. Whilst A looks happy and satisfied, B looks unhappy and worried merely by inverting the mouth. Picture C shares qualities with B (unhappy, worried) but additionally signals fear and anxiety. Picture D is a menacing expression, signalling anger and disapproval.

Interest in facial expressions led researchers (particularly those working with children) to develop a facial code (Ekman and Friesen 1978), a simplistic pictorial representation of the layout and dynamics of the face (see Figure 3.3), which is quickly recognised and interpreted, dependent on the direction of the eyebrows, mouth and diameter of the eyes. It is used to indicate the main influences in making judgements about socio-emotional states.

Eye contact

Ask people what they understand by the term nonverbal communication and most will make reference to eye contact. This is hardly surprising, given that almost 90 per cent of information passed to the brain comes from the eyes, with a further 9 per cent from the ears and the remainder from other sources (Pease 1997).

Gaze and mutual gaze are another central component of interpersonal relationships. However, Argyle (1975) highlights that, whilst gaze is frequently engaged in by young children, it is less prominent amongst adolescents when young people become more self-conscious, often avoiding eye contact and gaze before returning to and maximising its use in adulthood – an observation of particular relevance to teachers.

In the classroom there are clear advantages for maximising gaze and mutual gaze between teachers and students. As repeated elsewhere, the principal objective in managing behaviour is to keep students focused on legitimate learning goals. Motivating students to pay attention is an obvious requisite to learning; Pease (1997) highlights the importance of matching the content of what you say to what you are displaying visually. Take, for example, a lesson in which you are using an overhead transparency and where students are required to observe its content whilst you are speaking.

If the spoken content does not relate *directly* to the content of the visual aid, then less than 10 per cent of the information is likely to be absorbed by the students. In contrast, where the content of the overhead is directly related to the speech, then between 25 and 30 per cent is likely to be absorbed. Communication can be further enhanced by using a 'pointer' to gain and hold control of students' gaze whilst talking through what is being highlighted. When you need to move attention from the slide to speech alone, take the pointer from the overhead and hold it on an imaginary line between the students' eyes and your own. This has the effect of drawing the students' attention to what you are saying, re-establishing eye contact and achieving a more concentrated communication of your message (Pease 1997).

Eyes are used primarily to see rather than transmit messages but, as Argyle (1975) points out, they transmit two types of information during social encounters. First, they indicate that you are prepared to receive information by showing that the lines of communication are open. Second, they demonstrate your interest in the other person or persons. The amount of time you spend looking at someone is one indicator of the degree to which you are 'interested' in them or what they have to say. There is also interplay between conscious and non-conscious activity in respect of eye contact. For instance, some people might make a conscious effort and practise looking people in the eyes but find that when a particular encounter takes place, they look away, despite making a determined effort to maintain eye contact.

Eye contact acts as a measure of dominance or submissiveness and as an indicator of sincerity. People often assume (inaccurately) that liars tend to look away. When lying, they are 'shifty eyed', hence the saying 'look me in the eyes and say that!' In reality, experienced liars are more likely to look you in the eye for longer periods than someone telling the truth. Furthermore, and perhaps surprisingly, people (including teachers) are generally not very accurate at detecting liars (Zuckerman *et al.* 1981).

There are a number of references in everyday language to the power of eye contact in interpersonal relationships. For example, giving someone the 'evil eye', 'looking daggers', being 'gooey eyed'. Most of these references are concerned with the size of an individual's pupils (whilst recognising the influence of eyebrow and eyelid position). Emotions such as excitement, anger or fear can be signalled through the size of an individual's pupils. When you are attracted to someone, your pupils dilate up to three times their normal size. In contrast, the pupils of someone who is angry or irritated will contract, hence the expression 'beady little eyes'. Detecting the size of someone's pupils is done without conscious awareness – you seldom walk around with a ruler measuring them. The subtle nature of reading people's thoughts and feelings through their eyes was demonstrated through experiments involving expert card players. Researchers found that experts won fewer games when their opponents wore sunglasses, than when they could see their eyes or pupil signals. Whilst these signals are monitored subconsciously, it is possible to influence the process consciously. Chinese and Arab traders, for example, were known to spend time studying the pupils of their buyers when negotiating prices, identifying their customers' level of interest in different products. Some military and law enforcement agencies use low-peaked hats, dark or reflective sunglasses to hide the eyes and prevent messages being transmitted by them. Holding a steady gaze with an individual can be very difficult, since it intensifies communication and can prove uncomfortable and intimidating.

Teachers wishing to improve their ability to influence student behaviour will benefit from knowing how to use and develop gaze to improve their interpersonal skills. Practising a neutral gaze with a friend or colleague is one way of developing this skill. See how long you can hold it for. Deciding where to look to maximise intended effects when talking to a student depends on the nature of the encounter, whether it is a formal or informal meeting, and how well you know the student along with the person's age, sex and ethnicity.

Eye movement

There is evidence to demonstrate that we tend to look more often and for longer periods at people we find 'attractive'. If the recipient of our gaze registers this signal, they are likely to reciprocate positively (assuming they find us attractive also). In contrast, and unfortunately, the anxious, timid or embarrassed individual is less likely to engage in mutual gaze and tends to blink more when anxious (Argyle 1975), thus is perceived as shifty and therefore not to be trusted.

Pease (1997) suggests consciously developing different gaze patterns to suit specific types of social interactions. He identifies three distinct gaze patterns: business, social and intimate. The first two are relevant for teacher-student interaction.

Pease (1997) recommends the business gaze (see Figure 3.4) for more serious encounters – letting people know that you mean business. Here, focus is maintained on an imaginary triangle, the base of which is a horizontal line joining the two pupils and the peak is the centre point between the eyebrows. Pease (1997) argues that, provided an individual's gaze does not drop below eye level, you can maintain control of the interaction and so this would be particularly suitable when discussing a serious topic with a student.

The second type or social gaze is used for more informal encounters. Here the focus of the gazer moves in a downward triangle, from the eyes to the mouth (see Figure 3.5).

The third type or intimate gaze extends the downward gaze from the eyes to the chest, and is not suitable for encounters between teacher and student.

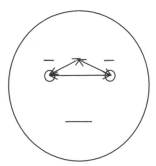

Figure 3.4 The business gaze

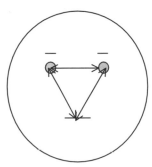

Figure 3.5 The social gaze

Posture

Body posture transmits a whole range of messages – both intended and unintended – and is usually related to the type of activity being pursued. According to Argyle (1975) there are three key human postures – standing; sitting, squatting or kneeling; and lying down. Within each category are a series of sub-categories, each with its own combinations of arm and leg positions as well as body angles. These combinations can indicate authority, submissiveness or neutrality. Clearly, in the classroom a teacher is concerned with demonstrating authority, so awareness of stance and positioning the arms and legs are important if you wish to avoid unwittingly undermining your authority.

Children are able to interpret the meaning of posture from an early age. It is also important to note that not all postures are used or, where they are used, mean the same in different cultures.

A useful way of gaining insight into what your students perceive and infer from posture and other social cues can be done by using social skills materials (e.g. Spence 1979) which include photographs from which they identify what is being communicated.

Standing with your arms folded and legs crossed is generally seen as a defensive position, usually observed in first encounters when people are unsure of one another. In contrast, the open-handed gesture coupled with uncrossed legs suggests being relaxed. Standing when addressing the class is the norm and communicates your authority to the whole class. However, when working with students at their desks, standing and towering above them whilst trying to help can be offputting to some students. Squatting or sitting to share the same head and eye level is a means of reassuring students that you are attending to what they have to say; this is less intimidating and more motivating (Van Werkhoven 1990).

Sitting or lying on tables or equipment whilst you teach may seem to be projecting a more relaxed persona, but can be problematic if students model the behaviour.

Knowing the effect of particular postures and gestures and deciding to apply them does not necessarily mean you will do so when under pressure, with emotions running high, that is, when they are most needed. Practising and overlearning them (in front of a mirror for instance), when there is no pressure, is a means of being proactive in using body language to its best advantage.

Gesture

People seldom keep their hands still when talking (try it), and there appear to be two distinct types of hand movement. The first, referred to as self-stimulation, includes scratching, fiddling or rubbing the hands, nose and ears. Freedman and Hoffman (1967) called these body-focused movements. Observers often interpret such fumbling or 'preening' movements as indicators of stress or anxiety. In class, students are often quick to identify these signs, as three young people involved in a research project informed us:

> We can always tell when he's getting a stress; he starts rattling his keys in his trouser pockets. It's a right laugh.
>
> (Mike, Year 9)

> She starts fiddling with her clothes and twisting her hair – then everyone starts talking louder and she does it even more. Then we start laughing and she goes to tell the year head.
>
> (Alice, Year 11)

> He takes his specs off and taps them on his desk when he's getting angry. No wonder they're bent!
>
> (John, Year 10)

The other type of hand gesture is related directly to speech; there are two theoretical explanations of these movements. The first is psychoanalytic, and claims that hand gestures indicate a speaker's emotional state (Feldman 1959). The second is that hand gestures represent a communication channel that either supplements speech or replaces it (Baxter *et al.* 1968). However, gestures can undermine communication: overuse of arm gestures, moving your hands all the time and making large sweeping arm movements can be offputting to listeners. The major benefit of gestures is not always easy to demonstrate except, for instance, in communicating ideas about shape. However, it has been shown that changes occur in the quality of speech, notably content, fluency and size of vocabulary, when people are not allowed to use gesture (Graham and Heywood 1975).

Teachers often use hand gestures as a means of control. Pointing at someone or showing them the palm of your hand on an outstretched arm are ways of expressing authority but can have very different meanings. Pointing is perceived as signifying dominance, but more aggressively than using the palm of your hand. The palm acts more as a holding gesture, for example signalling to an eager student to wait until instructed to add his or her contribution to a discussion.

Summary

Verbal and nonverbal behaviours are central to teaching. If you can't get the message across accurately, perceive, interpret and respond to feedback from students or influence the behaviour of others, then you are going to find teaching hard work. However, there is no reason why you cannot improve your existing social skills so as to make your life that much easier. It is important to remember the link between social skills and emotional control since the latter has the potential to undermine your social competence.

Professional social skills: assertiveness and effective listening

Earlier in this chapter we discussed some examples of professional social skills which teachers use in their everyday management of students' behaviour. Assertive behaviour is an effective way of expressing authority in the classroom whilst maintaining respect for students. Listening skills are generally useful in teaching and particularly so when trying to help students who are having difficulty communicating their thoughts and feelings.

Listening skills

Effective listening is a complex skill often taken for granted in everyday teacher–learner situations. Listening is the first social skill we learn; it is the most used but taught less than any form of communication in schools (Steil

1991). Whilst most people are capable of hearing what others say, this is not the same as listening. As a teacher you invariably have to listen to groups and individuals who are distressed, angry or confused. Effective listening requires attention to the motivational intent of the speaker and their non-verbal signals, as well as verbal components, and also being aware of the feedback you are giving to them.

Students become irritated when teachers do not appear to be taking an interest in what they have to say, or worse, those who appear to be pretending to listen by making the right 'noises' by nodding and agreeing, but do not seem interested. A teacher who is an effective listener is able to pick up on changes in the responses of the student(s) during a conversation, which may indicate a cause for concern. Spotting a mismatch between what is being said and the accompanying body language, posture, gesture, eye contact and facial expression requires attention to the task in hand if perception is to be accurate. The effective listener will also be able to encourage and prompt individuals to convey what they are thinking and feeling and self-moderate the conversation according to this feedback.

Sensitivity to physical presentation is also important when interacting with students. Facing the whiteboard whilst teaching is not a good means of helping students to listen to what you have to say, nor for you to obtain feedback about their understanding and interest. Listening to individuals who have important (to them) things to say in a busy corridor or in an office with continual interruptions is not appropriate and does not suggest that you value what they have to say. Physical conditions which result in the listener being distracted, or listeners who check their watches, fiddle with papers, appear to be attending to other 'important' things or seem to be in a hurry (even if they are) are similarly unhelpful. Not providing appropriate conditions for listening or the expected verbal and nonverbal feedback can result in a negative experience for both parties. The student feels undervalued and the teacher does not get the response he or she requires.

The following points describe some qualities of effective listening:

• Making students feel that they have a teacher who is accessible, has time for them, is genuinely concerned about them, enthusiastic, and will listen and take on board their concerns.
• Providing appropriate space – not busy corridors, classrooms or offices where staff wander in and out – and not answering the telephone. It is essential to concentrate on the student even though there may be distractions that appear important.
• Looking and feeling relaxed and unhurried suggests that you are receptive to what is being said and makes the encounter less threatening. Sitting bolt upright, standing with folded arms, slouching on a desk, appearing restless or impatient or fiddling with pens and paper can be stressful and make the student less willing to talk.

- Showing interest by being alert to what is being said can be shown through slight forward lean and being aware of what you and the student consider appropriate social distance.
- Matching the mood and reflecting the feelings of the student.
- Keeping the conversation flowing and gaining more information by using appropriate supportive prompts – including verbal (such as 'Go on . . . Fancy that . . . Yes . . . I see . . .') and nonverbal (such as gentle head nodding, smiling) to convey genuine interest and involvement.

Asserting your authority

Assertive behaviour is when individuals satisfy their own goals whilst maintaining respect for the goals of others. This means tactfully and justly expressing preferences, needs, opinions and feelings. Assertiveness lies somewhere around the midpoint of a continuum that ranges from aggressive behaviour at one extreme, and submissive behaviour at the other. The aggressive person is determined to get what he or she wants, irrespective of the needs and feelings of others. In contrast, the submissive person puts the needs and feelings of others before his or her own. Being assertive in social situations leads to feelings of positive self-worth and is at the heart of effective social communication.

Indecisive, fearful and submissive teachers who cannot communicate what is required or who do not carry out what they threaten feel inadequate, frustrated and resentful of their students (Canter and Canter 1976). Their students feel unsafe, irritated and resentful and likely to reciprocate in a negative way. The aggressive teacher uses harsh sanctions and maintains order at the expense of students, putting them down or humiliating them. Students are then fearful and comply but their self-esteem and confidence suffer. Assertive teachers are able to communicate their dissatisfaction when students do not adhere to the rules but are just as quick to express pleasure when students behave as expected.

Developing assertiveness is not just a method of overcoming immediate problems, it represents a way of life and relates to self-respect, self-confidence, self-regulation and meeting one's own needs and values, but not at the expense of someone else's. Being non-assertive can lead to feeling discomfort, tension, negative self-worth and self-anger and is marked by various behaviours such as:

- saying 'yes' to something when you really mean 'no' and doing so for fear of hurting the other person's feelings
- feeling embarrassed about speaking out in a group in case you appear incompetent
- feeling unhappy or angry about being manipulated by others and feeling incapable of stopping them

- not feeling comfortable expressing a different opinion from that of others
- feeling anxious about asking someone to do something, even though reasonable, in case they refuse
- not saying what you think and feel at the time it needs to be said, if say not satisfied with the behaviour of a student.

Whilst standing up for yourself sounds a fair way to behave, people are often reluctant to do so and make excuses because they worry about making the situation worse (Bower and Bower 1976). Excuses for not being assertive may appear rational but are often just examples of submissive behaviour, for example, procrastination ('Perhaps I am overreacting – I'll give them another chance') or hoping the problem will go away ('It probably won't happen again') or fear of public shame ('I don't want to make an embarrassing scene') or fear of the other party ('He will get angry with me'). The other party may well get angry with you, but the alternative is to get angry with yourself for not doing anything.

Other excuses suggest powerlessness ('Everyone else seems to be prepared to put up with it') or helplessness ('I will not be able to make any difference whatsoever'). Perceived helplessness is a major contributor to submissiveness and is self-deprecating. It externalises control of your life to unchangeable factors such as other people or systems which you cannot directly influence (see Chapter 1).

A person is seldom universally non-assertive; it tends to occur in specific situations:

- Where do you feel most and least assertive?
- Who makes you feel least assertive (managers, colleagues, students) and why?
- What situations make you feel least assertive?

Becoming more assertive

If you consider that you are not assertive in situations important to you – the classroom, the staffroom, departmental meetings or with managers – there are ways of improving your assertiveness. As with most topics in this book, there is no quick fix. You will not become assertive overnight. It requires practice to learn new assertive behaviours, such as negotiation, conflict resolution and persuasion. Be prepared for setbacks along the way; not everyone will respond as you might hope to your new behaviours, as it will upset established routines. Deal with difficulties in a problem-solving way, rehearse more and learn to cope with failure rather than giving up. Not all difficulties can be dealt with directly, so think about possible consequences (intended and unintended) before taking action.

Schimmel (1976) identified a number of behaviours central to expressing assertiveness:

- feeling able to say what you believe and comfortable asking for help from others
- insisting that you are respected as an equal who has rights, including the right to refuse to do things
- expressing negative and positive emotions and feeling comfortable declaring your feelings
- being happy giving and receiving compliments
- questioning and challenging routine and authority which affects control of your life, in order to improve your situation
- feeling comfortable engaging, sustaining and concluding social interactions
- nipping problems in the bud before you become angry and resentful.

Assertive behaviour can be developed using a combination of methods, including feedback from friends and colleagues, exploration of the problem and observing others dealing with similar situations (see Figure 3.6). Talking through problems and testing ways of coping are best done with a trained professional; however, good results can also be achieved using informed colleagues and friends or through self-based methods (reading, mirrors, audio-visual aids).

The following are examples of assertive responses:

1   A colleague spends every break time telling you about problems with people in the department.
- *Assertive response:* you say, 'Every day this week we have spent all break time talking about the conflicts in your department. I enjoy talking with you, but I get fed up hearing about the pettiness, as I see it, of the people in your department. I miss talking about the news, my work, and going to play golf.'
- *Non-assertive response:* you suppress your anger and say nothing or pretend to be really interested.
- *Aggressive response:* you blow your top and tell your colleague how boring and petty he or she is.
2   Your line manager repeatedly asks you to cover lessons in your free period and then often cancels at the last minute.
- *Assertive response:* you say, 'When you ask me to give up my free period to provide cover and you change your mind at the last minute – you've done that three out of the last four times – I feel irritated because it's too late to get on with something else. I also start to think that I am unappreciated and being used as a mug. In the future, I'd like for you to tell me at least one lesson in advance if I am not required. Would you do that?'

- *Non-assertive response:* you just let it go, fearing the manager will get angry.
- *Aggressive response:* you tell the manager how inconsiderate he or she is and how it is amazing that any staff are prepared to give up free periods at all.

Developing your social skills to enhance social competence

Ellis and Whittington (1981) identified three different types of social skills training, each with a different target audience:

- *Remedial social skills training:* primarily intended for people whose general social skills interfere with their everyday life. For example, teaching aggression management or conversation skills to students with behaviour problems.
- *Developmental social skill:* refining and enhancing existing everyday social skills, which are ineffective and inappropriate in some situations. For example, job interview training or managing difficult classes.
- *Specialised social skills training:* developing high level and complex skills for use in particular situations by professionals, forming part of continuing professional development. For example, counselling skills.

Whilst some social skills training is available for teachers, it is usually in response to specific initiatives rather than as part of an individual developmental programme. They can also be introduced as part of continuing professional development (CPD) in schools and worked through with a colleague, group of colleagues or entire staff group. Most specialised skills are usually taught to small groups by specialised trainers. A qualified trainer is preferable (funds permitting) but failing that, good results cam be achieved with someone who has familiarised themselves with an acceptable method. The role of the 'trainer' is to develop a helping relationship in a safe but challenging environment, provide accurate feedback and encourage the development of effective skills that relate specifically to their needs. Social skills teaching involves the use of modelling, role play, homework, video and audio. The object is not to teach a set of fixed skills but rather to tailor them to the specific needs of an individual or group, taking into account their personal dispositions and the context in which they are required to work.

There are a number of established methods for teaching social skills. Behavioural methods (see also Chapter 8) are perhaps the best-known approach and have a successful record in assertiveness training. Here, the individual practises or overlearns a particular micro skill or groups of micro skills in a series of stages. These are practised in different surroundings before being used in the target scenario.

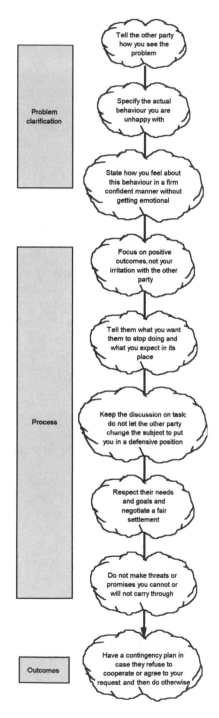

Figure 3.6 A model for developing assertive behaviour

Other examples are more cognitive in their method. Experiential methods focus on the uniqueness of the individual, emphasising definition and development of personal skills though role play and drama. The object being to get the individual to challenge their own thinking and internal (unrealistic) rules about a situation and redefine it and rehearse actions so as to cope more effectively. For example, if a teacher feels anxious teaching a particular class, they might be encouraged to describe the worst lesson they could possibly imagine and to enact it in the form of role play (perhaps using colleagues as surrogate students). The helper then presents even more terrible possibilities at the point when the teacher feels unable to continue. Then the teacher would describe and enact a *normal* encounter with this 'class' which is less painful than the worst case scenario previously experienced. During this enactment the helper highlights how much easier the 'normal' situation is in comparison to the previous one, complimenting the teacher where he or she makes positive decisions. Afterwards, the helper works through the experiences, challenging the teacher's thoughts, beliefs and behaviour to enable him or her to discover ways of coping with the group more effectively, through changing the way the teacher thinks about it and reducing anxiety. From this an action plan can be developed which may well include the helper, team teaching or working with individual students to support the teacher and provide feedback and reinforce successful coping.

A third alternative is a systems approach, which seeks to encourage individuals to think about their coping skills and evaluate how they appraise information about their own and other people's behaviour, which is causing them difficulty. For example, if a student disrupted a lesson and the teacher became upset about it, the teacher may ask, 'What right has this student to insult me in this way?' and 'Was this a threat to my professional self?' The helper seeks to encourage the teacher to consider alternative appraisals of what happened and to explore alternative coping strategies. So, for instance, considering whether the behaviour was a threat or a challenge, whether it reflects personal and interpersonal coping or whether other structural or organisational factors are relevant or to examine the teacher's own behaviours towards the student. The process starts with presenting a rationale for the behaviour, then identifying and disputing irrational beliefs and finally formulating and testing more realistic rules.

The various approaches to social skills training can help teachers to improve their coping skills. However, it is important not to lose sight of the influence that other parts of the system have on these behaviours. It would be naive to suggest that individual skills can overcome all behaviour management issues. Factors beyond the control of individual teachers, departments or even school are more than capable of disrupting or undermining individual performance.

Suggested further reading

Adler, R.B., Rosenfeld, B.L. and Towne, N. (1995) *Interplay: The Process of Interpersonal Communication*, Fort Worth, TX: Harcourt Brace.

Ellis, R.A.F. and Whittington, D. (1981) *A Guide to Social Skill Training*, London: Croom Helm.

Neil, S. and Caswell, C. (1993) *Body Language for Competent Teachers*, London: Routledge.

Part II

The school as an organisation

Whole school influences on behaviour management

Behaviour policies, ethos and school effectiveness

The behaviour policy is the formal representation of a school's vision of how behaviour will be managed. It should reflect expectations, inform practice and contribute to the school's organisational climate. The importance of behaviour policies in developing effective schools has been acknowledged in the Elton Report (Department of Education and Science (DES) 1989) and their necessity is now firmly housed in legislation (Education Act (No. 2) 1986, Education Act, 1996, Education Act, 1997, and School Standards and Framework Act, 1998). In sum, the message is that behaviour policies should specify expectations for the conduct of students, the rewards given for good behaviour and sanctions for unacceptable behaviour.

The School Standards and Framework Act 1998 requires governors to produce and review 'policies designed to promote good behaviour and discipline on the part of its pupils' intended to guide the headteacher in decision-making regarding action in respect of:

(a) promoting, among pupils, self-discipline and proper regard for authority;
(b) encouraging good behaviour and respect for others on the part of pupils and, in particular, preventing all forms of bullying among pupils;
(c) securing that the standard of behaviour of pupils is acceptable; and
(d) otherwise regulating the conduct of pupils.

(61: 4)

A behaviour policy contributes to a school's overall climate, and the importance of getting it right to maximise the use of whole school strategies in managing behaviour cannot be overemphasised. This is not to suggest that activity at the organisational level is superior to, or should replace teacher control, but that they should be mutually supportive.

When the behaviour policy is well thought out, understood and generally accepted by all, it can eliminate or alleviate many minor disruptive behaviours almost 'automatically'. Universal school-wide routines (for example, assemblies, dress, timetable, movement, lining up, reporting, sanctions, rewards) all serve to make visible the expectations and ethos of the school and what it values. The policy should provide the structure for behaviour management at departmental level, in the classroom and for the types of intervention strategies used for students with behaviour difficulties. The principles contained in the behaviour policy must then inform all three levels of activity and be supported by consistent application of what the school community (including teachers, SMT, governors and students) have agreed are appropriate and expected levels of behaviour. Thus, whilst encouraging teachers to have their own style – how they project themselves as individuals or interact at an interpersonal level – the agreed principles of the behaviour policy should be apparent in the classroom management techniques adopted to ensure consistency across all aspects of school life.

Schools, which have a significant discrepancy between the expectations of the behaviour policy and how classrooms are managed, or difficult students supported, are unlikely to function well. Those that share a common negotiated agreement, regularly monitor what is happening and can respond quickly to changing demands are likely to function well. Monitoring includes evaluating both operational activity (what people do) and conceptual shift (movement from agreed principles). Policy development should be informed through evaluation of feedback from the chalkface as well as changes imposed by external bodies.

What is a behaviour policy?

For the purposes of this book a behaviour policy is a statement of aims, values and principles that provides operational guidance on putting these aims into action. It should:

- have respect for persons and human rights and responsibilities as its central tenet
- facilitate effective learning
- make the school community feel safe and secure
- specify behavioural expectations
- encourage contributions from all members of the school community
- make explicit the rewards for acceptable behaviour
- make explicit the consequences of unacceptable behaviour
- include feedback systems to monitor effectiveness and change.

To translate these requirements into a workable document first requires a number of issues to be addressed:

- *Shared meaning:* ensuring that all parties are aware of what is meant by the policy. Do most people in your school agree on what constitutes disruptive behaviour and its causes? Are the behavioural expectations generally considered appropriate and realistic? Are rewards and sanctions generally considered appropriate and hierarchical?

- *Ownership:* behaviour policies belong to the whole school including governors, professional and ancillary staff, students and parents, all of whom should be encouraged to contribute and share ownership and responsibility. Who contributed to the behaviour policy in your school? How were they consulted?
- *Succinctness:* long-winded and complicated policy statements are usually counterproductive and can be the result of weak group decision-making. Where possible, keep the content punchy and to the point to aid clarity. How accessible and easy to follow is your school's policy?
- *Communication:* unless communicated throughout the school community, the policy will not be worth the paper it is written on. Making the policy explicit through a range of media (e.g. in the school handbook, on the back of all official documents, publicly posted, through assemblies and tutorials) on an ongoing basis keeps it in the 'public' eye.

Does your behaviour policy work?

Whilst all schools are required to have a behaviour policy, its effectiveness relies on staff being committed to applying it consistently. Disagreements about its aims and expectations, if it is ill conceived, out of date or there is uncertainty about its usefulness, do not make for an effective policy. Try to complete the following exercise to gain some impression of your existing policy and its application:

- Can you write down four aims or values of your school's behaviour policy?
- List four school rules or routines concerned with pupil behaviour that already exist in the school and which reinforce what the school values.
- List three ways in which students are rewarded for behaving appropriately.
- List three levels of sanctions currently available to deal with a student whose behaviour is getting progressively worse.
- Who has the authority to administer the sanctions you have listed?
- Do you think management of behaviour in your school generally reflects the aims of the behaviour policy?
- How would a new teacher be made formally aware of the school's behavioural expectations?
- Do you think it important to be able to answer any of the above without having to refer to the document?
- What is your school best at?
- What needs improvement?

School effectiveness, school improvement and student voice

School effectiveness and school improvement have taken centre stage in educational debates since the early 1980s. Much energy is being directed towards increasing school accountability and finding ways to enhance quality control and economic efficiency in the statutory education of children and young people. This desire for greater school accountability originates from a number of quarters including government, parents and, indeed, the schools themselves. The primary focus is on identifying characteristics of effective schools and developing strategies to improve ineffective ones. It is nothing new that schools differ in their ability to empower young people to succeed. In the late 1970s Rutter *et al.* (1979) demonstrated that schools produced differential effects in terms of behaviour despite sharing similar catchment areas, staffing and funding. How much difference a school alone can make and in what areas of student development is less clear (Gray and Wilcox 1994).

Although the primary emphasis of much school effectiveness research is on academic performance, a number have demonstrated significant differences in social behaviour (Reynolds 1976; Rutter *et al.* 1979; Mortimore *et al.* 1988). In a study entitled *Improving the Urban High School*, Louis and Miles (1992) examined the long-term outcomes of the 'effective school' programme (introduced in the 1980s). The objectives of these programmes were a focus on strong leadership; a safe and orderly climate; an emphasis on acquiring basic academic skills; high teacher expectations and constant monitoring of students' performance. However, whilst almost half of the schools involved reported improved student attitudes and behaviour, less than one-quarter said there had been similar levels of improvement in student achievement.

The strategy most commonly used to identify school effectiveness is to isolate measurable internal characteristics (e.g. management style, student behaviour, atmosphere, teaching styles, academic performance) and external characteristics (e.g. socio-economic status, funding) as the basis for comparison.

Identifying those characteristics associated with effective schools and superimposing them on to less effective ones would be an attractive approach to school improvement. In practice, this is not as easy as it sounds since, as Gray and Wilcox (1994: 2) argued, 'How an "ineffective" school improves may well differ from the ways in which more effective schools maintain their effectiveness.' The factors required to *change* systems are different from those required to *maintain* them.

School effectiveness and school improvement research, although often discussed together, have different methodological roots. In school effectiveness research the most common approach is quantitative, where comparison is often made using sophisticated statistical analysis of value added to previous academic performance measured between different key stages (see Goldstein 1995).

School improvement studies tend to be more action focused, utilising qualitative approaches. Emphasis here is on developing strategies for change which are grounded in the perspectives of the people involved. A common strategy to studying improvement is to utilise case studies where the emphasis is on detail and 'thick' description. Details of what is actually happening in a school are usually best understood in this way. More recently, there have been encouraging signs of a linking of school effectiveness and school improvement approaches (Hopkins 1996) and towards working with schools to produce a more in-depth understanding of the research and its implications for practice (Stoll 1996). However, this generates further difficulties in expanding the number of variations possible between schools and cannot be limited to simple responses. As Gray et al. (1996) point out, there is a need to obtain a better grasp of each institution's strengths and weaknesses as well as their starting position.

Lists of the characteristics which distinguish successful from less successful ones are not in short supply and many share (unsurprisingly) similar content. Sammons et al. (1994) offer one such list, with a strong commonsense content that provides a baseline for those wishing to investigate their schools functioning under identifiable categories. Wayson et al. (1982) produced a list of characteristics of well-disciplined schools, highlighting the need for whole-school-based proactive and supportive structures. What these and others lack is an indication of how these various categories might be functionally defined, interlinked and quantified.

The role of student voice in school improvement

Gaining a student perspective on school effectiveness and improvement has increasingly been recognised as a potentially valuable contribution. Gray (1990) identified two key indicators in addition to academic performance which require attention to students' perspectives:

- *Pupil satisfaction:* what proportion of pupils in the school are satisfied with their education they receive?
- *Pupil–teacher relationships:* what proportion of pupils in the school have a good or vital relationship with one or more teachers?

I would add a third – what proportion of students feel that the school helps them to cope emotionally and socially? – an area of considerable importance to many students. My work on student stress, for example, highlighted the potential negative effects of school structures and organisation on students' attitude to work and performance (Chaplain 1996b, 2000a).

In *School Improvement: What Can Pupils Tell Us?* (1996b), Rudduck, Chaplain and Wallace argued that too often pupil voice is absent from the literature on school improvement. Those students usually invited to contribute are the most academically or socially competent, whereas other groups who are seen as problematic or difficult, but who often have a valuable contribution to make are marginalised. However, as Rudduck *et al.* point out:

> if teachers have a view that students are adversaries, then it is unlikely that they can unravel the power relationship and convince students that they genuinely want to enter into dialogue with them about learning, to hear and take their views seriously, and to become as Phelan and her colleagues [1992] put it, 'co-conspirators in creating optimal learning situations'.
>
> (1996b: 2)

Students' perspectives offer an essential dimension to the development of behaviour policies – this is not to suggest some romantic notion that they have *the answers* but they can make an important contribution.

In attempting to understand and utilise research on school improvement, it is imperative not to lose sight of the diversity and interrelatedness of the factors involved. Concentrating on one or two initiatives may result in short-term gains, but make little real overall or sustainable difference. Change requires attention to what Fullan (1988: 29) called 'deeper organisational conditions'. Whilst initiatives such as anger control for aggressive individuals, circle time to support withdrawn students or pupil referral units may be effective for those immediately involved, unless the activity is owned, valued and committed to by the whole school, it may stagnate in the hearts, minds and actions of a chosen few. Focusing on behaviour management issues can often be appraised negatively by teachers who really want to teach rather than spend large amounts of time thinking about coping with disruptive behaviour.

Ethos, organisational climate and culture

Research findings have consistently demonstrated a relationship between effective schools, positive climates and 'good' discipline (Sammons 1999). In describing the qualities of a positive climate or ethos, Mortimore *et al.* (1988) concluded:

> 'an effective school has a positive ethos. Overall the atmosphere was more pleasant in the effective schools, for a variety of reasons.'
>
> Both around the school and within the classroom, less emphasis on punishment and critical control, and a greater emphasis on praise and rewarding pupils, had a positive impact. Where teachers actively encouraged self-control on the part of the pupils, rather than emphasising

the negative aspects of their behaviour, progress and development increased. What appeared to be important was firm but fair classroom management.

Outside the classroom evidence of a positive climate included the organisation of lunchtime and afternoon clubs for pupils, teachers eating their lunch at the same tables as the pupils, organisation of trips and visits and the utilisation of the local environment as a learning resource.

The working conditions of teachers contributed to the creation of a positive school climate. Where teachers had non-teaching periods, the impact on pupil progress and development was positive. Thus the climate created by the teachers for the pupils, and by the head for the teachers, was an important aspect of the school's effectiveness. This further appeared to be reflected in effective schools by happy, well-behaved pupils who were friendly towards each other and outsiders, and by the absence of graffiti around the school'.

(Mortimore *et al.* 1988: 122)

Ethos is a popular term within the education community and whilst there are a number of definitions, most refer to the overall atmosphere of the school (see Mortimore *et al.* 1988; Jones 1988) or how a school 'feels'. For Rutter *et al.* (1979) successful schools had pleasant working environments, with an emphasis on learning and encouragement of personal responsibility in students. But beyond artefacts and interpersonal relationships, ethos also includes tacit assumptions about values and purpose.

Ethos or organisational climate differs from 'organisational culture' and is considered more analogous to morale or the quality of the internal environment of the organisation as experienced by its members and which influences their behaviour (Taguiri 1968). It is 'a relatively enduring quality of the school environment that is experienced by participants, affects their behaviour, and is based on their collective perceptions of behaviour in schools' (Hoy and Miskel 1991: 221).

Organisational culture, on the other hand, has anthropological roots and concerns 'shared orientations that hold the unit together and give it a distinct identity' (Hoy and Miskel 1991: 212). However, not everyone agrees that the two concepts are distinct (Furnham 1997).

Much early work on organisational climate was carried out in educational institutions by Stern (1970), who went on to apply his findings to industrial contexts, looking at the relationship between personality and perceptions of the organisational climate.

It is commonly accepted that an effective school needs a positive organisational climate. However, if one takes the trouble to consider in more detail what precisely is meant by positive ethos, a number of questions emerge. Against what criteria should we measure school climate? Should we look at what is put into a school? What they do with it? What the school achieves? On what measurable basis should one school be distinguished from another?

Scales have been developed to measure organisational climate (Halpin and Croft 1963; Brookover *et al.* 1979) from which was developed the concept of loose and tight-coupled school climates. Tight-coupled schools are highly centralised and formal (Hoy *et al.* 1991), a tightly knit and closely related environment focused on organisational goals. In loose-coupled schools there is more independence and less central control, with departments and classrooms preserving their own identity (Weick 1976). Murphy (1992) argued that effective schools are more tightly linked, operating as an organic whole with greater consistency than ineffective schools. Creemers and Reezigt (1996) endorsed this view by identifying four criteria present in effective schools (consistency, cohesion, constancy and control), all features associated with tight-coupled schools.

The Occupational Climate Description Questionnaire (OCDQ: Hoy *et al.* 1991) distinguishes between open and closed climates by rating levels of supportive headteacher behaviour (helpful, concerned); directive headteacher behaviour (rigid and domineering); engaged teacher behaviour (proud of school, support each other); frustrated teacher behaviour (overrun with routine and administration). In open climates issues such as managing behaviour and teacher stress will be discussed, whereas in closed climates they are likely to be ignored. The questionnaire is designed for school self-assessment and for organisational development.

Open systems approaches (Open Systems Group 1981) to organisational behaviour advocate a tight and focused environment committed to the overall purpose of the organisation. They provide a model for analysing the different sub-components of an organisation that contribute to its overall structure. The organisation interacts with its environment taking in information and resources as inputs and transforming them by various processes into outputs into the environment (Nadler and Tushman 1980). In school, *inputs* include students, staff and the buildings, *processes* include the teaching and learning and the *outputs* include educated young people (see Figure 4.1).

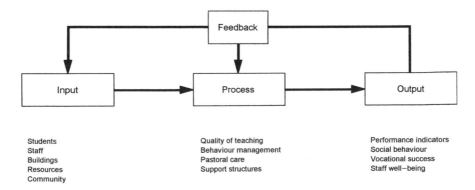

Figure 4.1 A simple systems model

Applying a systems approach to schools raises important questions regarding the purpose of schooling, achievement targets and criteria which indicate success.

Table 4.1 shows in more detail the various types of data which can be collected and used to gain an understanding of strengths and weaknesses of the school generally and in respect of social behaviour in particular.

Breaking down systems in this way enables identification of areas for development and an appreciation of the interrelatedness and interdependency of the various component parts of the organisation. Whilst systems thinking presents schools as rational and predictable organisations, consistency, harmony and cohesion are not always evident between and within various departments and classrooms. Furthermore, measuring some of the different variables can be difficult, so individual schools need to decide how to quantify the quality of relationships or what constitutes acceptable behaviour.

Stern (1970) suggested that climate could be measured by asking what proportion of the organisation agree or disagree with a particular description of a climate to justify describing it in that way, known as the aggregation issue. Obviously, the more people that agree (or disagree), the more accurate the estimate of the climate is likely to be. He argued that 66 per cent was an appropriate level of agreement; others have suggested that it should be significantly more. Clearly, this approach personalises the measurement, grounding it in the population it serves. Irrespective of its critics, recording and analysing the data in this way force discussion and critical thinking about what the school means to those who work there and, in that way, can be very positive:

- How would you describe the climate of your school?
- How many people agree with you?

A further issue in measuring climate arises from differences in perceptions at different levels of the hierarchy. Large schools have many micro climates (departments, teams, interest groups), which may differ from the overall climate. For example, do the SMT agree with junior staff about the climate of your school? Does the mathematics department share the same view as the arts department? Do non-teaching staff share the same view as teachers? Do parents and students and subgroups of both share similar views? Payne (1990) argued that subgroup agreement was only likely where a 'group' shared a common social identity and hence, where agreement was likely to help an individual to be supported by that group. Since subgroups are competing for limited resources in school there is always a potential for intergroup conflict that may undermine consistency in managing behaviour.

A positive climate is also represented through staff having a sense of community in which they enjoy social support and a diffuse role which brings them into contact with other adults in settings outside the classroom

Table 4.1 A simple systems analysis of inputs, processes and outputs

Level of analysis (1)	Focus (2)	General example (3)	Behaviour-related example (4)
Inputs	Staff, students, buildings, curriculum.	Personal qualities of the staff and management (qualifications, personality, training, experience); levels of compatibility and person–environment fit; qualities of the students; quality and care of the buildings.	Students' backgrounds; community stability or change (e.g. large-scale redundancy; SEN provision; industrial/commercial growth; a major influx of socially excluded groups); staff specialist training (e.g. behaviour difficulties); staff cohesiveness; previous successes of the school in managing behaviour; behaviour policy.
Processes	What happens in school.	Teaching methods; classroom organisation, sanctions; teacher and student support systems; extracurricular activity.	Rewards, sanctions; quality of interpersonal relationships between staff and students; departmental practice; level of parental support; discipline measures, rewards; in-school support systems; SEN provision, pastoral system.
Outputs	Short- and long-term effects on the behaviour and development of members of the school.	League tables; social behaviour; value added.	Numbers excluded; parental satisfaction; inspection ratings; exam performance; complaints from the local community; number of police visits; school appearance; students' satisfaction and motivation; staff turnover; job satisfaction and well-being.

Note: Column 3 shows general outcomes and column 4 shows those concerned with behaviour. However, many of the behaviour-related and general outcomes overlap; the above are merely offered as illustrative examples.

(Bryk and Driscoll 1988). A shared commitment to organisational goals, staff well-being and recognition of personal goals and development can be supported through:

- making the work environment stimulating and engaging
- providing opportunities for staff to make their own decisions and show initiative
- encouraging new ideas and suggestions for improving the organisation
- promoting mutual trust
- providing a dynamic but secure atmosphere
- having a sense of humour
- encouraging different perspectives on behaviour
- providing differentiated and appropriate social support
- delegating responsibility and a preparedness to take risks
- recognising effort
- facilitating open and adequate communications between all levels of staff, students and their carers.

Organisational climate and effective communication

The quality of communication in a school and its organisational climate have been described as mutually reinforcing. As Wilkinson and Cave proposed:

> The effectiveness of communication depends to a considerable extent on a favourable climate in the school. . . . Conversely, the climate of the school depends largely on the quality of communication. Good morale, a feeling of confidence and a spirit of cooperation are unlikely to exist if there are continuing and frequent communication barriers and breakdowns. Thus communication both creates and is influenced by the prevailing climate of the school.
>
> (1987: 139)

Too little or too much communication has been shown to be a source of conflict in organisations (Furnham 1997). The method of communicating in a school is an indicator of the quality of interpersonal relationships. Death by a thousand memos usually suggests relationships are not good – people have stopped discussing issues, for whatever reason. We now live in a world where continual bombardment by a range of instant communication is the norm (email, faxes, mobile phones, text messages), all of which discourage talking and listening and seem to demand instant responses. It is probably true to say that, if anything, we receive too much information. Whilst we do not necessarily want to be distracted from whatever we are doing, some forms of communication suggest we should. Being interrupted when you are teaching by a note-wielding student, having just managed to get your class settled, is not relished, means valuable teaching time is lost and is disruptive. Within a school, communication is multi-faceted and it is important to match the type of communication to the issue in focus. In most schools information moves from top-down and (usually less often) bottom-up within the hierarchy as well as sideways among colleagues and within and between departments.

Communication is a repeated concern in this book because of its role in:

- conveying information
- persuading, negotiating and resolving conflict
- ensuring the smooth running of the system
- learning
- managing behaviour.

With regard to behaviour management there are three essential considerations in respect of communication: speed, type and audience:

- *Speed:* some information needs to be communicated rapidly – a serious incident (e.g. physical assault) for instance. Other matters, such as calling a meeting to review behaviour policy, are less urgent but in some schools levels of urgency seem undifferentiated. Being continually interrupted by students sent by colleagues to announce an event or changed agenda can unwittingly create unnecessary management problems for teachers.
- *Type:* what means of communication to use should again be determined by the context. In the event of a serious incident; verbal, face to face (sending someone to get help) or some electronic form (bell, telephone) is probably the most appropriate.
- *Audience:* who needs to know and when and how does the communication need to be recorded? In dealing with behaviour, not necessarily extreme behaviour, it is useful to think about ways of communicating potential problems, or tense situations as well as what to do when things have gone seriously wrong.

Some years ago I was in a school for students with emotional and behavioural difficulties which had alarm buttons fitted in each classroom. No one seemed to know who had decided to have them fitted or was clear about when they should be used. New staff were merely told, 'This is the alarm button which you can use if you have problems controlling the students.' However, a number of staff were keen to tell me the story of a young teacher who, during his first week, was having problems with a group of students and had pressed the button. To his horror his actions triggered off a series of alarms, following which an army of teachers and a cook, complete with utensils, arrived at his classroom door. The humiliation of the poor unsuspecting teacher, who thought pressing the bell merely alerted the senior teacher, was complete when he had to explain to the assembled rescue battalion that the emergency was little more than a group of students being cheeky and refusing to work.

As a system of communication it was quick and effective in getting attention; whether it was appropriate is more questionable and the audience was certainly not who he had expected and slightly larger than he intended! The main problem arose from an initial lack of information during induction where staff should have been made aware of under what circumstances it should be used, and how it would be responded to if activated. It later emerged that, far from being a planned response, staff had merely followed each other.

Getting the message across: communication networks

Cole (1996) described different types of communication networks (Figure 4.2) which may exist in organisations, indicating which are likely to be most effective under different conditions. Which method of communication is used in a school often reflects management style.

In many schools communication is hierarchical, for example, the chain or Y arrangement that permits downward, and, albeit less common, upward communication. The chain and Y networks along with the wheel are all evident in organisations with mechanistic approaches (Cole 1996) (with the wheel allowing some sideways or lateral communication but which has a clear leader in the centre). Information from governors and the SMT usually have an ordered sequence as they move through departments but are not the most effective way of communicating all information. The chain reduces time demands on senior managers. It may not be the most efficient way to deal with serious incidents requiring immediate responses. Under such circumstances a circle or completely connected network within departments is likely to be most efficient since they allow for multidirectional communication.

Teachers dealing with difficult individuals, who know they can communicate a worsening situation quickly to any one of a number of primed individuals, are likely to cope more effectively than teachers who feel they have to communicate to a specific member of staff who may not be available at that time. Whilst a senior manager may have overall operational responsibility for behaviour management in a large split-site school, supporting the interests of all departments simultaneously is not possible. Delegating responsibility to individuals within departments or teams who are available to support directly but who meet as a group with the senior manager to provide feedback on concerns and needs, is one way of overcoming this problem:

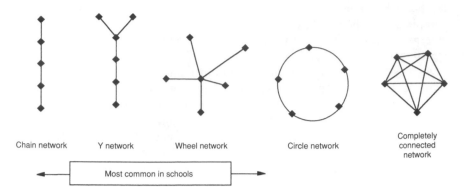

Figure 4.2 Communication networks

- What type of communication network do you have in your organisation?
- Is it effective?
- What are its strengths and weaknesses?
- Is it consistent across the whole school and within departments? If not, how do they differ?
- Do you have established systems for raising issues concerned with behaviour management and for getting help quickly should you need it?
- Do they work?

Communication under pressure: coping with difficult situations

When dealing with difficult students and unpleasant events it is easy to react too quickly and say or write things, when emotions are running high, without due consideration of all the facts. Similarly managers asking staff to deal with a problem whilst they are off guard or already under pressure is unreasonable. The emotional nature of the encounter tends to override problem solving, sometimes with disastrous results as the situation spirals out of control. Organisations expecting their staff to make decisions whilst off guard are not well managed and may result in poor decision-making and dissatisfied or brow-beaten staff.

Much communication in schools is by word of mouth or informal notes. Although both are quick, they are prone to distortion and misinterpretation. I learnt early in my managerial career that recording difficult situations in a written form during or immediately after an event and sending a copy to the person, or people involved as verification of what we both understood to have happened, was a useful safeguard against misinterpretation. Similarly, incidents involving young people or their families should always be recorded in writing at the time or as soon as possible afterwards in case further problems arise. Anyone who has worked with vulnerable young people will be aware of the value of doing so.

If reporting problem encounters, keep the language simple, non-judgemental and to the point. State the facts as you understand them and record the observations of any witnesses to what happened immediately. Where relevant, note any antecedents to the incident, the incident itself and what happened afterwards. It is likely you will want to share your observations with your manager but whatever you do, always keep a copy along with details of what you sent to others and when. Keeping such accurate records is time-consuming and may seem little dramatic, but is an intelligent way of protecting yourself and your school should there be a problem at a later date.

Meetings with parents of difficult children can be quite harrowing. They are often (understandably) defensive if called into school to account for their child's misbehaviour. Part of the defensive reaction results from feeling embarrassed or angry. Parents in this position often feel like a naughty child themselves and may start acting like one, shouting, refusing to listen to the complaint, offering excuses and displacing responsibility for the problem elsewhere (other students or staff). Deflecting attention to other issues allows them to take control of the situation. Only being invited to the school to be told how badly behaved your child is, does not make school a community to which you seek to belong – certainly not in the same way as those parents whose children are behaving well.

Dealing with hostile angry adults is something few people relish. To be successful in such encounters requires the use of complex social skills and maintaining emotional control. Many such encounters are one-on-one, however, the people involved can be supported in a number of ways by using organisational and structural support.

Angry parents should not have direct access to teaching areas and teachers. Stopping them doing so requires looking at procedures for receiving people into the school. Obviously, where staff are expecting a parent under difficult circumstances, advance arrangements can be made; however, some inevitably arrive unexpectedly. The sensible use of time delays can start the diffusion process, allowing people to calm down but not forgetting that keeping people waiting too long can exacerbate the situation. Whilst a good well-briefed and prepared receptionist can usually achieve this, there should be a back-up system which involves a designated member of the teaching/management staff who can be alerted stealthily that their help is required. For instance, if the receptionist feels that the waiting parent is getting more agitated then calling the designated member of staff and saying, 'Mr Hawk called earlier, could you ring back' – Hawk being used as the trigger that their presence is needed at reception. Having a place in school for dealing with visitors away from students and other distractions helps avoid public embarrassment.

Designing feedforward or anticipatory strategies, where a best estimate of what ought to be expected and how to respond when it does not occur, is the most effective way of dealing with difficult behaviour. However, reactive methods are inevitable where things are not going as they should. Being organised in advance for difficult events by developing and rehearsing structures and strategies when not under pressure is the most effective way of being prepared.

Balancing individual and organisational needs

> Every organisation is different. Each school is different from every other school, and schools, as a group, are different from other kinds of organisations. There is something natural and right about that, for organisations are living things, each with its own history and traditions and environment and its own ability to shape its destiny. Nevertheless . . . there are some truths and theories that apply to all organisations, be they schools or hospitals or banks.
>
> (Handy 1988: 107)

In recent years there has been a growing acceptance of the need to pay attention to the contribution that organisation and structures, as opposed to classroom relationships, can make to effective behaviour management. As Duke (1986: 122) pointed out, 'more recently educators have begun to acknowledge the crucial role that organisational factors (in schools) play in shaping behaviour'.

Explanations of behaviour in organisations have traditionally drawn on three groups of theories. The first argue that individual personality traits (e.g. aggressiveness, impulsiveness or anxiety) are relatively stable across all situations. If someone is an extrovert, then he or she is likely to be outgoing in all situations. An organisation represents the combined effects of the qualities of the individuals in it.

The second group place their emphasis on how the situation determines an individual's behaviour. A school's unique nature creates a distinct culture and climate prescribing how staff and students should behave. You will be familiar with how a school 'feels' when you visit for the first time. This feeling results from a combination of what those in the school most value and is conveyed through the physical environment, interpersonal behaviour and a sense of what the school values.

A third group of theories argue that organisational behaviour results from a continuous multidirectional interaction between individuals and their situation. Individuals have idiosyncratic qualities which affect the situation and, at the same time, the situation influences the behaviour of the individual. The situation includes the overall social structure (the whole staff group) and various subgroups (e.g. curriculum groups, friendship groups) plus other influences. An individual joining a school will interact with each at different levels, in various ways and with different outcomes, eventually becoming organisationally socialised.

Several attempts have been made to identify individual and enduring qualities most valued in particular occupations. Teachers, presumably, enjoy human interaction significantly more than a lighthouse keeper. It is not uncommon in commerce and industry to find personality measures being administered during personnel selection – it is a rather less common activity in the teaching profession. Although not without their critics, some personality tests (e.g. Eysenck and Eysenck 1985; Cattell 1971) have been found to yield reliable measures of particular traits considered relevant to particular occupations. As Furnham points out:

> Review studies done in the 90's which have considered the results of a vast amount of research in the area show that personality traits (particularly the Big 5) do significantly predict a wide range of behaviours in the work place. The size of the relationship suggest between 10 and 40% of variance can be accounted for in terms of these traits alone. However, none dispute that other factors such as ability, as well as organisational constraints and method, inevitably affect performance.
>
> (1997: 193)

Another popular explanation of organisational behaviour is in terms of person–organisation fit (Chatman 1989) or the degree to which dispositions, abilities, expectations and performance of an individual match the demands and expectations of the school. Each individual teacher has a set of dispositional characteristics, expectations, skills and experiences which he or she brings to a job. At the same time the school (including governors, SMT, teachers and support staff, students and their parents) will also have expectations and demands of that teacher. The degree to which there is synonymy between what a teacher provides to, and expects from, the school and what the school expects from, and provides to, the teacher, the higher the degree of person–organisation fit (see Figure 4.3). In situations where person–job fit has been identified as poor, a number of negative outcomes have been measured including stress, job dissatisfaction and lower job performance. For instance, teachers who feel that the school's expectations regarding behaviour management are not compatible with their own values and beliefs are unlikely to function well. In contrast, where the person–organisation fit is good, the individual is likely to be more motivated and experience higher levels of job satisfaction. Moving to another school with a different *modus operandi* may significantly change how teachers feel about themselves and how they relate to others:

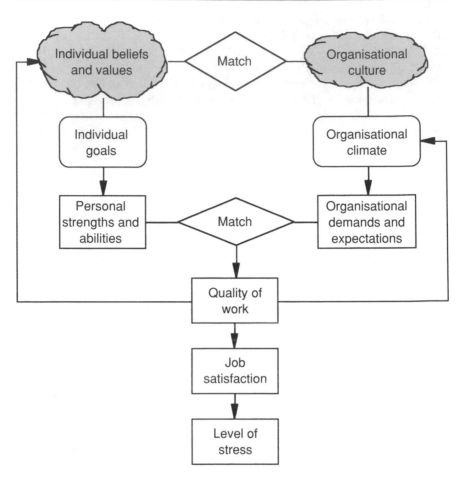

Figure 4.3 Person–environment fit

- Think about your current job or placement and write down the qualities you bring to it (e.g. enthusiasm, bright personality, energy, youth or experience, skills or specific abilities, balance to the curriculum or staff group) plus what you expect from the organisation.
- Next list what you believe the organisation expects from you in terms of knowledge and skills, commitment, responsibility, managing difficult students and what it actually provides you with (good working conditions or atmosphere for instance).
- Compare the two lists – would you say you are enjoying a good person–job fit? If not, where is the imbalance and how changeable are the discrepancies?

Furthermore, whilst you may 'fit well' at one point in time, organisational changes to management (new head), structure (new legislative requirements), the student population (amalgamation of two schools) or you (marriage, divorce, training) can create imbalance at the individual, group or organisational level creating disruption. A new head will inevitably differ from his or her predecessor and will have different expectations or different ways of working with staff which may enhance or inhibit your performance. He or she may want to change the ethos of the school or may have been recruited specifically for that purpose.

Individual and group differences: personal and social identity

Changing a single individual in an organisation can have quite a substantial impact on relationships and group dynamics. A number of competing theories explain the relationship between groups and individuals. Individualist theories argue that groups represent the sum of the parts, that is, a group can be viewed as an amalgamation of the characteristics of its members. Collectivist theories argue that a group has an identity of its own or a social identity, which differs from the individual qualities (Tajfel and Turner 1986). It is not uncommon for people to comment on how differently others behave when in a group compared to when they are alone, for example, a student who works quietly in one class but becomes extremely noisy when with students in another class, or teachers who when alone protest one set of beliefs but respond very differently in their departmental meetings or when with groups of colleagues. Individuals shift from personal to group identity depending on the salience of a particular context in order to maintain a positive image. Monitoring individual student behaviour, alongside how they behave in different groups provides the best way of understanding the changing nature of interpersonal dynamics over time and situations.

The relationship between individuals, groups and the organisation becomes a psychological contract whereby each takes, gives and gradually formulates mutual understanding. Individuals at all levels in a school are 'organisationally socialised', moving through these different stages:

- initial *entry* into the organisation
- becoming *socialised* to the context (coping with the organisational climate)
- achieving *mutual acceptance* and commitment to the organisation.

(Schein 1978)

Understanding organisational behaviour requires consideration of the interactions and interconnections between the thinking, feeling and behaviour of individuals and groups and considering how their different goals and aspirations are empowered or constrained by organisational structures. It also requires attention to how these factors change and develop over time.

Many advertisements for teachers ask for 'a good team player' but what constitutes being a good team player is not universal. Some teams require innovation and management of change whilst others need to maintain or stabilise existing school climates and each require different qualities. Furthermore, as schools develop, different qualities are required to cope with change from new initiatives and demands, which can threaten established group dynamics and expose weaknesses:

- What strengths do you bring to your team?
- Which areas do you feel need developing?
- Is there a mechanism in school for facilitating this development?
- Try doing a SWOT analysis (strengths, weaknesses, opportunities and threats) in your school or department to ascertain the balance between the four qualities.

Suggested further reading

Chaplain, R. (1996) *Pupil Behaviour*, Cambridge: Pearson.

Chapter 5

The role of senior management in facilitating positive behaviour

There is a growing literature regarding the roles of headteachers and senior managers in schools, which connects to an even larger collection concerned with management and organisational behaviour in general. Inevitably, this single chapter is not a review of that literature. Instead, a discussion is offered which seeks to consider the role of the senior management team in respect of producing and maintaining an environment where staff feel supported in the management of students' behaviour. This discussion will be informed by elements of the above research, research into headteachers' and teachers' perceptions of each other, my experience as teacher, deputy, headteacher and researcher.

The central role of the headteacher in the professional leadership of effective schools is well established (Sammons 1999). As Gray (1990: 214) highlights, 'the importance of the headteacher's leadership is one of the clearest of the messages in school effectiveness research'. The head, along with the SMT, are charged with strategic planning, determining the direction of the school (leadership) as well as organising the day-to-day running of the school (management). Both dimensions make important contributions to creating and maintaining a well-behaved school. Being proactive in the development of an effective behaviour policy and ensuring staff have appropriate professional development, support and resources to support the policy at all levels, form part of the leadership component. Monitoring and maintaining the behaviour policy and classroom activity, having a presence around the school (in teaching and recreational areas), being sensitive to the concerns and difficulties of staff and being able to step up a gear when things are not going too well or at critical points in the school's development, are all part of the management function.

At the hub of the SMT is usually the head, who is perceived as being responsible for providing leadership; strategic planning; setting priorities and the tone of the school; safety and security; motivating the staff; plus overall responsibility for students' behaviour. A belief still persists that, in order to achieve these expectations, a head must have particular individual qualities; however, the suggestion that the head or indeed the management team must share some common individual trait-like characteristics is oversimplistic.

Individual differences and management style

The following case study was taken from data collected in a large secondary school and describes three managers who had very different personal characteristics. It describes how, on the one hand, the combined effect of their differences made for an effective management team, and on the other, staff perceived their differences, which qualities they valued and which they failed to recognise.

Stuart, Caren and Phil were all appointed to their posts as head, first and second deputy at the same time when the school Redlands High was newly built. They were all from very different backgrounds. It was Stuart's first appointment as head, whereas both deputies had made lateral moves. Stuart had recently completed a master's degree in educational management and was knowledgeable about recent theories of leadership and school development. Caren was in the process of completing a master's degree in education and was particularly interested in curriculum development. Phil had not taken any recent additional qualifications but was up to scratch with government legislation and local procedures.

What was interesting about the three was how they differed in their attitudes towards management and development. Both Stuart and Caren were keen to try new ideas, whereas Phil preferred to stay with what he knew to have worked in his previous jobs. Caren and Stuart were good at generating new ideas, getting them off the ground and motivating the staff to share their vision, however, both were inefficient at maintaining their projects over time. Thus, a new initiative would enthuse them until the 'honeymoon period' ended, shortly after which their interest in the new system usually fizzled out, and they would move on to something else. One example of this arose following an initiative aimed at reducing bullying around the school, which involved staff checking out particular blind spots in grounds. The initial enthusiasm led to all members of the SMT and staff taking turns to patrol various areas but this started to break down when Caren, Stuart and others did not, for whatever reason, turn up (because of meetings, administration, or they just forgot). At this stage Phil produced a weekly schedule for staff which, although not initially popular, at least offered some structure which could be monitored by him. He also took on the job of reminding his two colleagues when their turn was imminent.

What was noteworthy about these three people was how effective they were as a team despite their different approaches, and how the staff perceived these differences. Phil tended to be seen as the 'weaker' of the three since he was not viewed as creative or linked with generating 'big plans' or new ideas like the other two managers. Yet without his dogged sticking to the rules and maintaining the systems, they invariably failed. Stuart and Caren on the other hand were seen as dynamic with their oversights covered by Phil's (unrecognised) attention to detail.

Anyone who has experience of working with different heads will realise that, whilst individual characteristics are important, different contexts call for different leadership styles and personal qualities, no simple style of management being appropriate for all schools (Bossert et al. 1982). Whilst some leaders may be powerfully charismatic or extrovert, not all are. Headteachers differ substantially at the personal and interpersonal level, as well as in terms of how they organise and lead their schools – characteristics which work well in one situation are not guaranteed to do likewise in another. Behaviour welcomed at one stage of a school's development would be extremely unpopular at a different stage of development. My own experience, as a manager, and in more recent years working with heads as consultant and researcher, has reinforced these beliefs.

Which particular qualities might be needed by a manager to secure a successful school and which, if any, are common to all effective managers? Sammons (1999) suggests three characteristics frequently cited in the research literature: strength of purpose, involving other staff in decision-making and professional authority over teaching and learning. Identifying and developing these qualities are topics for organisational psychology and related disciplines and there is substantial literature examining this area, some of which will be referred to later in this chapter.

Blame it on the boss

What should the headteacher and SMT do in relation to behaviour management and how might this differ from other managerial roles? The simple and most obvious answer to the above question is 'managing the school' but this raises further questions. When I ask groups of teachers what they expect of a headteacher, I usually end up with long lists which include senior teacher, leading professional, manager, leader, supervisor, accountant, troubleshooter, chief executive, politician, ultimate behaviour sanction and facilitator. This diversity is not unlike the list one obtains when asking what is expected of a teacher – educator, social worker, counsellor etc. – it seems that we expect a great deal from those working in education. In practice, any one or all of them could apply at any one time, depending on a range of variables including the climate of the school, its values, stage of development, the perceptions and skills of the staff and the relationships between them – as well as external pressures.

As one head (Jim) recently said to me, 'They expect me to be all things, at all times, when it suits them! Like me to take the flak and lead the way when things aren't so good, but want me out of the way when they are – it's a bit like being a dad really.' Jim went on to say that he sometimes felt put out when, having dealt with something complex and often unpleasant, there seemed few words of praise for him and yet 'it seems staff expect to be told how well they are doing all the time'.

It is not uncommon in any organisation for employees to question the role of, and criticise their managers; schools are no exception.

The process of claiming credit for all things good and externalising failure is known in social psychology as attributional bias (see Chapter 2). Blaming management when things go wrong can be an effective expedient coping strategy, whether or not it is true. Not being seen as responsible for failing to cope limits damage to your (professional) self-esteem – providing the explanation 'appears' credible. Whilst such a coping strategy may be ego-protecting, it is likely to be short-lived. Furthermore, it does not help you to deal directly with the problem since externalising responsibility puts the problem outside of your control (you probably cannot change this 'inefficient manager') and, in situations such as managing student behaviour, it is highly improbable that blame can be ascribed solely to one individual – however convenient that may appear. The head, the students, other colleagues or parents will also be looking for an explanation, which will probably include you! Such misunderstandings and distorted perspectives can create negative cycles of blame which work against developing positive relationships and solving the difficulty.

Low and high profile management: keeping everybody happy

A former headteacher colleague of mine, a man not renowned for sugar-coating his comments, once said: 'A good head should be part of the furniture when things are going well – almost invisible – just tweaking the knobs to keep things running smoothly. But when – as it's bound to at some point in this game – the shit hits the fan, capable of rising to the challenge and grasping the nettle' (John, 20 years' experience as a head). Bouncing between being 'almost invisible' and 'grasping the nettle' is not an unusual experience for many heads and is often expected by staff. Getting the balance right between the two ways of operating is difficult and, if not achieved, can be stressful for both the head and the staff.

What are your expectations of the headteacher and SMT (or if you are a head what do you think is reasonable to expect) in:

- deciding the overall philosophy of the school?
- deciding the content of the behaviour policy?
- deciding the sanctions and rewards for student behaviour?
- supporting staff dealing with disruptive behaviour?
- demonstrating their ability to manage individuals, groups and classes of students?
- providing a screening function from external influences (politicians, inspectors, parents etc.)?
- providing the final sanction for disruptive students?
- being involved in the management of your classroom?
- how much teaching should the head be involved in?

Jones (1988: 42) argued that historically the role of the head was perceived as 'simultaneously loved and hated, revered and ridiculed, powerful and naïve'; she went on to ask whether much had changed following the redefinition of the head as manager and chief executive. It has been long established by the government that leadership is a central component of school management and the new leadership group announced in the Green Paper on Leadership made this clear (Department for Education and Employment (DfEE) 1998). However, the degree to which a good manager also makes a good leader and vice versa is not always as clear.

In recent years, the move towards increased local management of schools and additional responsibilities for the controlled spending of large amounts of money have brought about changes to the general understanding and operation of the head's role. Sid Slater, head of Lymm High School, suggested:

> The role of the head has changed . . . it has taken away things and given other things. . . . Headship has changed from being professional leader to Chief Executive. In my first headship . . . more time was available to work with colleagues on pedagogic techniques, evaluation and review, whole school development planning, professional development, etc. Time was also available to work and meet with children and parents. Now all of that continues with the added responsibilities of managing, at Lymm, a £3 million plus budget, outdoor centre, leisure complex and working more closely with governors.
>
> (Chaplain 1995a: 141)

Whilst not all schools are as big as Lymm High, all have had to cope with perhaps the most turbulent years in education. Substantive changes have occurred to the management structure and function and to the curriculum to name but two. Differences in the size of schools invariably mean wide discrepancies between them in terms of the nature of the relationship between head, SMT, heads of departments, teachers and other staff. It is clearly not possible for a head to spend as much time with staff or students in a school with more than 1,500 students compared to one with fewer than 500, and expectations on the part of head and staff should reflect this. In reality this is not always the case (Chaplain 1995a). Heads often claim that the best part of their job is being with pupils, what Jones (1988: 94) referred to as the 'wistful nostalgia . . . about when they knew how to teach well, and make good relationships with pupils' but in practice have limited amounts of time to do so. The belief that the head should be a super teacher and demonstrate his or her classroom craft to other teachers seems somewhat strange, particularly in larger settings, given the number and diversity of other demands. Nevertheless, heads recognise the popular belief that they must be viewed as experienced teachers 'governing bodies and especially parents on those bodies . . . will want a head who has had a lot of experience as a teacher' (Hustler *et al.* 1995: 127) but there are limits to the amount of time they can spare. As Sid Slater continues, 'you have to be out there making contact' but adds 'I teach less than I did in my previous headships, only a double period at present. Headteachers have been increasingly taken out of the classroom' (Chaplain 1995a: 139). With the best will in the world, headteachers of large or medium-sized secondary schools are going to be limited in the amount of time they can spend working directly with students. Invariably heads step in and fill the gap when there are shortages; however, whilst such activity offers a short-term solution for teachers, it is questionable whether it makes best use of a manager's time.

How might managers contribute to discipline around the school? When things are running well in a school with students behaving appropriately, working on legitimate tasks and causing minimal disruption, low profile monitoring is probably the most useful response. If the going gets tough, or the school is undergoing significant change, then a more visible presence and hands on approach is more usually needed. However, this is clearly an oversimplification for, if the head is spending more time at the chalkface, troubleshooting and making his or her presence felt, then it should not be at the expense of other vital leadership duties. Heads are often likened to the captain of a ship, but, as Gray and Freeman (1988) pointed out, captains of ships do a very different job from the sailors – and furthermore the ship would not get very far if they did not.

People differ quite markedly, and are often diametrically opposed in their perceptions of what constitutes an effective and supportive head and SMT. Nias (1986) offered multiple, and contrasting, accounts from similarly experienced teachers in different schools regarding their positive and negative perceptions of their heads. In many circumstances, these contrasts reflected either loose or tight-coupled organisational management (see Chapter 4).

Some expressed dissatisfaction with 'passive' heads who seemed to respond too quickly to change. Three teachers described their feelings about such headteachers: 'He always seemed to be changing his ideas . . . there was no sense or aim in the school, no philosophy.' 'The general attitude in the school is "you do what you think", and that's not very helpful when you have problems.' 'There was no ultimate purpose in what we did. . . . As long as we didn't annoy the parents or let the kids get too noisy, the head didn't seem interested.'

In contrast, the 'positive' head was often revered for 'setting the direction of the school and leading the way . . . an old-fashioned patriarch . . . *who put them under* . . . quite strong pressure to conform in certain ways . . . *made* . . . the place full of certainties . . . *and* . . . a good place to start in'. Nevertheless there were drawbacks. For example, whilst many wanted the head to lead on formulating aims and policies, 'he should not take this entirely upon himself' nor 'deny staff a part in decision making'; where this was not happening it could lead to major job dissatisfaction and disaffection. As one teacher said: 'all she [head] really wants from the staff and children is obedience. That's really why I'm giving up. I don't feel I have anything to contribute.' Another teacher spoke of 'smouldering in silence' at staff meetings and of the head 'not being interested in anything they had to say'. Many talked of 'mock democracy' and of staff meetings which were 'disguised dictatorships'.

A dilemma for heads, in deciding to extend power sharing and control with others, is the fear of letting go or delegating responsibility. As one head in a recent study confided, 'I need to become more comfortable about delegating tasks to other people . . . I am aware that I will burn myself out if I don't share out the burden' (Chaplain 2001: 208). This can be especially true when a school has gone through a period of difficulty – managing a group of difficult students or major change for example. A head who has maintained a visible presence during a difficult period may find it hard to hand back the reins if he or she perceives doing so might result in a return to the problem situation. The staff will often feel otherwise, wanting autonomy and to regain control of areas of the school they consider theirs. This ongoing conflict between ownership of decision-making and control is common to any organisation.

The dynamics of relationships between heads and staff are multiple and varied. Interpersonal and inter-group relationships vary, contingent on both the individual identities (personal characteristics) of those involved on the one hand, and the social identities (science dept, newly qualified teachers (NQTs), SMT) of the groups on the other. These variations can be in terms of the quality and/or the nature of relationships, irrespective of the size of a school. People categorise themselves as members of groups or as individuals dependent on demands and what is seen as rewarding in the situation. For instance, a head may identify as part of the SMT with overall responsibility for student behaviour in one context but as a competent physics teacher in another; other people should respect that they are different roles with very different meanings for the head.

What makes a good leader?

Prior to 1945, theories about traits focused on identifying the exceptional qualities of leaders, based on the assumption that people fell into one of two groups – leaders and followers – each having distinctly different qualities. For instance, it was believed that leaders had limitless energy, insight, foresight, persuasiveness and creativity. Unfortunately, these studies failed to identify any universal traits that would guarantee success as a leader. Other approaches attempted to identify particular skills of leadership. Katz (1955) for instance identified three developable skills for effective management: conceptual skills (ability to see the organisation as a whole), technical skill (e.g. teaching) and human skill (ability to work as a team member). More recently, changes to research method have enabled researchers to identify relationships between effective leadership, leader behaviour and individual characteristics – most notably motivation and skills. Whilst there is an impressive amount of empirical evidence to inform our understanding of the practice of effective leadership, there are still significant omissions.

Zaleznik (1977) suggested that leaders determined major objectives and strategic courses and brought about major change, whereas managers enforced rules and policies or implemented goals and changes initiated at a higher level. Historically, headteachers have enjoyed varying amounts of each role. On the one hand, more 'power' or responsibility has been given to schools; on the other, government directives have reduced autonomy by controlling key areas such as curriculum content and policies. Leaders engage in behaviour which inspires followers, generate high levels of motivation, beyond what might reasonably be expected, in order to accomplish a collective vision – even if that means forgoing self-interest. In other words they are able to generate conditions in which individuals categorise themselves in terms of their social identity (the organisation) as opposed to their individual identity, and are committed to a common shared vision or aim. Managers, on the other hand, are in a position of formal authority and responsible for the coordination and implementation of strategies and policies and establishing administrative systems. Managers provide the rational-analytic content necessary for the smooth operation of the organisation. One essential difference between the two is that managers are in a position of formal authority, whereas a leader might not be, influencing change because of personal characteristics rather than formal status

The behaviour pattern or style of leadership was first described by Lewin *et al.* (1939) who referred to three styles, *autocratic, laissez-faire* and *democratic*. Since then, dozens of different models have been developed with the number of styles ranging from two to eight. However, there is something of a consensus in support of two styles of leadership – one is person-focused (or person-centred) and based on providing support and participating, whilst the other is task-focused and based on goal setting, direction and appraisal. These two factors were seen as being independent of each other (orthogonal) but could be present at different times and in different amounts, depending on need. Others writers suggested intermediate states or continua between the two extremes. Tannenbaum and Schmidt (1958) identified four sub-categories between the managers concerned with results (task) at one end and relationships (person) at the other. Autocratic and democratic represent the two extreme positions, whilst paternalistic and consultative occupy the middle ground of the model. Later research demonstrated the need for both extremes to be present. For example, Cox and Cooper (1988) in their study of managerial 'high-flyers' produced group profiles within which they identified key areas including problem-solving/decision-making ability, vision and people skills – which relate to both 'managerial types'.

Nevertheless, there is a popular, if mistaken, belief that one style is invariably better in generating a positive organisational climate, which facilitates effective behaviour management. The general consensus amongst the many teachers I have worked with over the years has been that, if given the choice, most would prefer the 'person-focused' head. They think that such individuals would be more prepared to listen to what they have to say, be more understanding, caring, take an interest in what their staff are doing and be generally supportive. However, help with problem solving does not necessarily follow listening and being sympathetic. The preference for person-centred managers reflects social motivation. People are attracted to others who are prepared to listen to them and, in addition, infer other qualities about them. The person-focused head is viewed as being 'warm', whereas the business-like 'task-oriented' manager is seen as being 'cold'. The power of assumptions about people based on beliefs about traits such as 'warm' or 'cold' is discussed in Chapter 2.

Whilst the person-centred head may offer support, it is important to remember that social support is multifaceted and people require different types of support to cope with different pressures (Sarason *et al.* 1990). Whilst person-centred heads might more readily be perceived as providing emotional and self-esteem support, they may be less effective in providing instrumental support or help with problem solving or direction during crises. Different combinations and sequences of support are likely to be needed as a situation develops which are unlikely to all come from the same source. For example, suppose you have to deal with an unusual but extreme event, a student becoming physically violent for instance. During and immediately after the event, you are likely to feel shocked and drained and probably need someone to talk to and help you calm down (emotional support). Later, there are decisions to be made about what action to take with the student (instrumental support). Planning how to deal with future encounters with the student and other students who witnessed the event may need reassurance of one's competence (self-esteem support). Each type of support is likely to come from different people, and take a different form, some will be administrative, some instrumental and others emotional. The head is unlikely to provide all, irrespective of his or her leadership style.

Using the head and SMT inappropriately for support can be indicative of structural difficulties and negative routines in a school. As the Office for Standards in Education (OFSTED) pointed out in its report on exclusion:

> In high excluding schools (but not exclusively) year heads and heads of house worked hard but were often overwhelmed by numbers of pupils referred to them for indiscipline by classroom teachers. Frequently such referrals short-circuited established systems and merely reflected the unwillingness of some staff to deal with problems at source. As a result such problems escalated and, although pastoral heads spent much time with difficult pupils, often that time achieved little other than to register concern and pass sentence.
>
> (1996: 19)

The behaviour policy is intended to represent what a school values and to specify hierarchically ordered procedures and sanctions. If these procedures are being short-circuited to pass on the problem to a manager, it suggests that they are weak, inappropriate or being ignored. Such behaviour could result from managers intervening too quickly or staff who are too eager to pass over control of the situation. Managers who intervene too quickly or who regularly get involved with minor behaviours are in danger of undermining both the teachers' status and their own authority should future major problems occur. Empowering teachers by encouraging them to believe they have the power to control difficult behaviour is more likely to encourage practices that result in positive outcomes.

Supporting staff with behaviour management

It is very difficult to put oneself in another individual's role unless you have experienced it. As a classroom teacher dealing with the daily hassles of keeping students on task, completing student records, preparing lessons, administration and keeping track with developments in your subject may make you feel that the head or SMT has an easy time – particularly in large schools where the head has a small teaching role. There is a sense of reductionism in some schools, that everything is about teaching, when clearly that is not so. In order for a teacher to get on with the job of teaching requires development of various systems. For example, in a school where students are wandering around unchecked or failing to turn up to lessons, classroom management will suffer. Responding to such problems is difficult when you are trying to teach GCSE French to twenty other students. This is not to say the SMT should spend all day as 'sweepers' picking up all wanderers and strays, but may well do at certain strategic points in the day such as break time, lunchtime, lesson changeover etc.

Heads and SMT are under pressure from multiple sources, both internal and external. They have to cope with managing the school, the curriculum, finance, change and also themselves. Interestingly it is usually managing other people which creates the most stress for headteachers (Chaplain 1995a) as is the case in other organisations where managers are responsible for largely autonomous professionals.

What constitutes a difficult-to-teach class will inevitably vary – what is usually common is that students are not on task and the teacher is not using appropriate coping strategies to deal with them. This can occur because the teacher:

- has not learned the appropriate strategies
- finds it difficult to apply them
- lacks confidence or is anxious or both
- finds that the systems available to support him or her are ineffective.

In some schools what is perceived to be supportive by those offering it is not received as such by those needing it. As mentioned earlier, perceiving social support as available is more than it being available; it has to be perceived as appropriate. The following case study illustrates inappropriate support. It relates an account of a teacher appointed to a secondary school and how, in this case, support from management, although well intentioned, failed to help. Following the case study is some analysis of what went wrong:

Julia had been appointed to a post teaching mainly low-achieving students in a medium-sized comprehensive. The school was in an area of low socio-economic status although students were generally well behaved. One class, however, had been something of a problem for several staff since Year 7 and Julia was required to spend a considerable part of her time teaching them, as well as being their tutor.

After an initial honeymoon period, where the students appeared to be enjoying having someone new around, things started to deteriorate. Swearing became fairly commonplace; students would refuse to listen or get on with their work or would leave the classroom without permission. Equipment was being damaged and the situation escalated to a point where one student physically assaulted her.

She was advised by a colleague to try behaviour modification principles and this was effective with some of the students, up to a point, reducing the severity of the swearing, for example. However, because she initially used tangible rewards, several colleagues found this amusing, one commenting that 'the kids receive a treat for telling her to *piss* off rather than *fuck* off'! Whilst the learning support assistant helped administer the programmes and there was some measurable success with individuals, the approach was not successful in changing the whole class.

The head of SEN dept, Mr Mack, was made aware of what was going on through comments from other colleagues who worked in the vicinity of Julia's classroom. These teachers did little, if anything, to actively help her, turning a blind eye to what was going on, since they considered the difficulty to be down to Julia's incompetence and therefore not their problem. However, it became increasingly their concern when the difficulties Julia was experiencing began to have a knock-on effect in their classrooms. Mr Mack initially responded by talking with Julia and suggesting ways of getting attention in class and keeping students on task.

One of the deputies also went into her classroom (at the end of the day when all the students had gone home) and suggested ways of reorganising desks and equipment and removed some of the equipment likely to be damaged, notably the computer. On no occasion did he attend her class during the teaching day, but directed additional learning support for each morning of the week. The headteacher, who considered himself a 'person-centred manager', also spoke with her suggesting she 'stick at it', that 'everybody had problems at some time, especially when moving to a new school' and he 'was there if she needed to talk about anything'.

Needless to say, the situation did not improve, even when three of the ringleaders were suspended, since by then the rest of the class were well versed in creating havoc. Julia left at the end of that term and the class was taken over by a more experienced teacher at the school, who agreed to do so only if a number of students were exchanged with other classes and certain individuals were taught individually for substantive parts of the day – something which Julia would no doubt have appreciated.

- Before reading further, what do you think could or should have been done to support Julia?
- What role should management and teaching colleagues have had in helping her to cope?

Whilst we can never be certain of exactly what led to Julia's problems, the following points highlight some contributory factors:

- Whilst the school had an induction programme, there was little support beyond the standard package for anyone other than NQTs. As Julia had previous experience as a teacher, it was assumed that she would cope.
- The SMT were largely preoccupied with the many other difficulties around the school, trying to overcome lack of resources, staff absence and preparing for inspection, which meant there was less time to spend supporting Julia. What they offered was little more than a token gesture.
- Whilst a behaviour policy did exist, it lacked any real detail or clear direction and was based largely on reactive strategies for dealing with difficult classes or individuals.
- Nothing had been done about this particular class during Years 8 and 9, despite people being aware that there was no improvement in their behaviour. They had found themselves with a succession of teachers on short-term contracts or supply teachers. The school's coping strategy seemed to be passive and indirect, one of containment, based on the premise that these individuals would eventually leave and ignoring the additional problems being generated.
- There was a core of very competent teachers who had generated a culture of 'sink or swim' (Wallace 1996) and sadly, even those teachers who thought more should have been done, did nothing themselves beyond simple suggestions.
- One or two teachers commented that, in the past, they had suggested to the SMT that the group should be reformed but that the head had insisted they could be better dealt with if kept together rather than disrupting other groups and extending the problem.
- Whilst the head saw himself as a person-centred manager, many of the staff felt this was not the case but were not inclined to challenge his decisions.
- Julia felt uncomfortable asking for help, since she thought it would reinforce other people's view of her as incompetent.

Thanks, but no thanks: when is support not support?

Whilst all teachers want to feel secure and supported in their work, and all managers want to facilitate working environments that produce competent teachers and successful students, what constitutes appropriate support is not always agreed. The following illustrate some behaviours that teachers do not appreciate – each accompanied with suggested alternative ways of dealing with the problem:

- Being told publicly theirs is the worst behaved class in school.

Talk to the member of staff in private and develop an action plan for that individual which may include specific management strategies, structural changes to the class or sending the teacher on a course as part of professional development. Make all staff responsible for change:

• Managers walking into their classrooms to discipline students then walking out.

The problem with this strategy is twofold. First, *if* it is effective (i.e. the students make less noise) it usually works only whilst the manager is there, and shortly after he or she leaves, the noise levels rise again. Second, it can make the teacher appear to be sharing the identity of the group being disciplined, since control has clearly been taken away from the teacher because he or she was seen as unable to control the group themselves.

Whilst walking into a noisy classroom may be a welcome intrusion, the management taking an interest, care should be taken to ensure the teacher is seen to be in control. Offering to look after the class, allowing the teacher to remove individuals or small groups to deal with the problem is one way of doing this. Alternatively, having spoken with the teacher first, acting as advocate at a later meeting between the teacher and the students concerned, thereby maintaining teacher control. These strategies clearly benefit from proactive planning, mutual understanding and consistent application:

• Offering simple or fix it quick solutions to complex problems.

The case of Julia exemplified this. The deputy, on that occasion, was aware that the situation was complicated and required attention to a number of structural, interpersonal and personal issues. Given other pressures, he considered that there was insufficient time available to deal with the situation properly, but felt he had to offer Julia something. Unfortunately, it was inadequate, inappropriate and resulted in further difficulties for both the school and the teachers:

• Letting struggling teachers get on with it.

Unfortunately the 'Throw them in at the deep end' philosophy is nothing new. As Wallace (1996: 83) pointed out, 'there is still a tendency to leave teachers to "sink or swim" in the time-honoured professional fashion!' She goes on to identify the personal qualities of those who manage to 'swim to calmer waters' which were concerned with building effective relationships with students and having clear and consistent expectations. Being too busy or having other difficulties is a poor excuse for not supporting colleagues. It also has a payback, as Julia's colleagues found out. Shutting their doors kept it at bay, but only for a time. The degree to which staff pull together is an indicator of the school's organisational climate:

- Taking control of the class without first discussing it with the teacher.

A colleague of mine was recently reminiscing about his first experiences as a deputy head, saying how, on reflection, his enthusiasm in the early days was counterproductive. Whenever he heard staff having difficulty with a student or group, he would intervene and 'support' the teacher, or so he thought, by engaging difficult students, perhaps removing them from class or reprimanding them. Over time he became aware that staff relied on him for increasingly trivial issues, either sending students directly to him or sending a student to get him to come to the class to help. He eventually realised that, far from supporting the staff, he was generating a culture of dependency where staff used him as a first-level response to discipline problems: he had unwittingly made them externalise control. Furthermore, involving himself at this level undermined any notion of hierarchical responses to disruptive behaviour. If students were seeing the deputy for minor issues, what happened if things got worse?

On the surface, the process appeared to be workable except, of course, if he was absent, something that occurred increasingly as his duties changed over time. Moreover, and ironically, whilst staff were happy to regularly refer students to him, they would often complain afterwards that his reprimands were not severe enough!

He gradually withdrew from this approach, making staff take responsibility for coping with the behaviour themselves and supporting them in other ways, including covering a class whilst a teacher dealt with an individual, being available to discuss difficulties and setting up professional development sessions on behaviour management. This was done through a series of school-based problem-solving workshops which were supported with inputs from outside trainers.

The job of managing secondary schools is complex and often difficult. It requires quite exceptional qualities and skills to keep abreast of a rapidly changing, often loose-coupled organisation. It can be equally difficult for others working in the organisation to realise this, given the pressures and demands on professionals who have to work largely autonomously. Making time to listen and take on board each other's perspective, being aware of limitations and responsibilities, and having reasonable expectations is a starting point for developing more effective ways of working.

Suggested further reading

Ainscow, M., Hopkins, D., Southworth, G. and West, M. (1999) *Creating the Conditions for School Improvement: A Handbook of Staff Development Activities*, London: David Fulton.

Part III

Classroom management

Chapter 6

Classroom environment and climate

Teachers expect students to make what Wehlage *et al.* (1989: 177) called a 'psychological investment', measured by how students 'demonstrate attention to and involvement with their schoolwork'. This investment is facilitated by teachers producing a positive atmosphere in their classrooms, through making lessons interesting and stimulating, providing a safe and stimulating environment and appropriate support for learning. Classrooms are represented in a number of ways including social, psychological and physical dimensions. What constitutes an appropriate learning atmosphere will be different from teacher to teacher and subject to subject, and influenced by layout, seating, temperature and smell as well as the quality of student–teacher interaction. This chapter examines the influence of selected physical, social and psychological aspects of classroom environment and climate on the thinking and behaviour of students.

Chapter 4 highlighted the role of school organisation in managing student behaviour. In this chapter, the emphasis moves to analysis at the classroom level. Whilst we are continually reminded of how the quality of interpersonal relationships between student and teacher is at the heart of managing behaviour, the physical environment can also exert significant influence. The combined effects of the physical and social environment are perhaps the strongest forces in shaping the thoughts, feelings, motivation and behaviour of students (see Figure 6.1).

The physical environment: organising the behavioural setting

Classrooms come in a wide range of shapes and sizes. Some are purpose built, whilst others are converted broom cupboards – neither is a guarantee of quality teaching, good behaviour or high standards of learning. Physical characteristics like heating, ventilation, insulation and lighting contribute to the level of physical comfort experienced by students and teachers; however, these are health and safety issues and, if problematic, often require structural changes to the building. Teachers can change other aspects of the physical

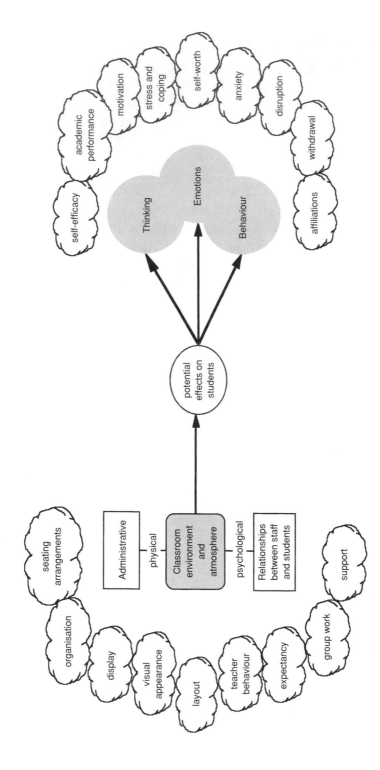

Figure 6.1 Potential influences of classroom environment and atmosphere on the thinking, emotions and behaviour of students

environment more regularly and readily. Paying attention to and manipulating layout, decor and other physical factors can make teaching and learning enjoyable and profitable. I have observed badly managed lessons in purpose-built, newly equipped rooms and some excellent ones take place in corridors and offices. It is the climate generated by the setting and its occupants that matters and, in this respect, the teacher holds centre stage. So what is the best way of laying out a classroom?

Clearly the room's function should be reflected in its decor and organisation, and should transmit what you expect to be going on in there and what is most valued. Posters or three-dimensional objects on display are useful in getting across good examples of what is expected. Piles of paper and junk do not suggest an organised and efficient workplace.

Next time you walk into a classroom in which you teach, have a good look around and ask yourself:

- How does it look and feel?
- Is it an inviting and stimulating environment?
- What do you think of the decor, the materials on show, your desk, students' desks and other furniture?
- Do you think it is well laid out?
- Could it be improved?
- What is good about it?
- What is lacking?

Do you think a stranger would agree with your assessment?

Make a drawing of the room and how furniture and students are organised during a lesson. Identify where there are any bottlenecks, restricting the movement of students around the room. Make a note of your movements around the class and note them on the diagram. Are changes needed?

Industry and commerce devote large amounts of time and energy to making sure the correct image is presented to consumers and using layout of equipment to maximise efficiency. Schools should think likewise. Given that teachers in secondary schools have to change classes quite often, it is difficult to ascribe ownership of a workspace to one individual. As a result, rooms can be in danger of becoming bland, looking unloved and less than cared for. However, the best teaching is not necessarily done in the tidiest rooms and students are also aware of this, as the following quotes indicate:

> Her room is always very tidy and always smells nice, but she's always losing people's coursework ... and their marks ... and she can't control the class.
>
> (Amy, Year 10)

Thus, whilst this student (and many of her classmates, it turned out) appreciated the teacher's equipment being where it should be, they were less than satisfied with what was more important to them.

Another student concluded, on the basis of which teachers he most valued, that tidiness was definitely not correlated with good teaching:

> There are worksheets and stuff all over, so he keeps stuff for his lesson in his drawer – he's a good teacher, people get on with their work . . . Mr B brings all his stuff to class in a box.
>
> (Tim, Year 11)

Tim went on to conclude that 'all the best teachers have messy rooms'.

A learning environment that looks good is no substitute for good teaching – a familiar rather than novel observation. Teachers vary in their levels of tidiness and that is invariably reflected in how they present and operate their classrooms. Whilst it is neither necessary nor desirable for a classroom to be a showroom and look unlived in, there are obvious benefits to keeping a grip on classroom layout and location of equipment: there's nothing worse than planning a lesson, only to arrive and find your overhead projector or retort stands have migrated.

You may be a competent, inspired and highly motivated teacher, but also untidy, so you need to develop systems to keep things in check. Having a layout map for the rooms you use is one way of helping with this problem. Without one, trying to remember how you previously organised seating arrangements and the location of resources is likely to create problems. Keeping a written record of equipment needs and who sat where takes a few minutes but is a valuable and accurate reminder of what you did previously and why. It helps avoid the problem of 'John, sit where you were last time, over there' followed by 'But I didn't sit here last time, Sir – I was over here next to Clive . . . wasn't I Clive?', 'Yes, he was Sir' and so on. Annotating the diagram pointing out difficulties is further useful information.

Anyone who has attended a teaching training course will no doubt have been informed of the need to prepare well for their lessons, to be there in plenty of time, to have necessary and sufficient equipment ready and waiting for their students to maximise their time on task. Ensuring sufficient time to complete the lesson and put equipment away safely and correctly is similarly important. Timing in a lesson is everything, be it related to the speed at which you speak, when equipment is given out or when students are asked to start work on their own. Not knowing where equipment is in the classroom or not taking the time to make sure materials are there and working is not acceptable – assume nothing! Not having the right equipment or insufficient available is a potential recipe for management difficulties – waiting for a student to go and get the textbooks you assumed were still in the classroom creates a vacuum – 'Just read the notes again whilst Gloria gets the textbooks from Mr Muntz!' does not inspire confidence amongst your audience. As a dissatisfied student in Derbyshire pointed out to me:

> You'd think teachers would have textbooks in the classroom before you started the lesson – not sending people out to go and find them . . . he gives us a right going over if we forget things . . . and the other teachers look at you as if it's your fault!
>
> (Joe, Year 9)

As Joe says, teachers are often less than tolerant of students who forget their equipment and should lead by example.

Supporting professional social skills

In Chapter 3 I talked at some length about the value of developing professional social skills. Whilst social skills are human qualities, there are a number of ways that the physical environment can be manipulated to enhance them. Key components of effective communication (eye contact, social distance, posture and gesture) can all be enhanced by attention to layout. Talking to the back of someone's head does little to aid communication. In large, spacious classrooms, with sufficient distance between desks allowing easy movement, teachers are probably best placed to spend equal, or similar, amounts of time with all of their students – provided they monitor that they are doing so. However, many classrooms are smaller and class sizes larger than ideal. Even when this is the case, there are various options available to improve the learning environment. Paying attention to where students are sitting, how they are grouped, their proximity to the teaching 'hub', how often you interact with them, the nature of the interaction and so on. Placing students permanently at a point furthest from your desk, whiteboard, or where you tend to stand most when teaching implies that they are not valued members of your group. Reflecting on who is sitting where, and the reason for doing so, can provide the basis for thinking of how to develop positive relationships with students who are at risk of social exclusion.

How you organise your classroom or behavioural setting (as psychologists call it) will directly influence both the nature of the interaction and your style of teaching and furthermore, should match your behavioural goals. Changing layouts seems to present a problem for some teachers. For example, I am always amazed how difficult many trainee teachers find asking their mentors if they can rearrange classroom furniture. It is almost as if the desks are welded to the floor, or moving them might release the Golem. The issue of being a visitor in the school is perhaps understandable, but I have yet to find a teacher who objected to trainee teachers rearranging the furniture. In fact, most are just as surprised as I am.

The two key questions in deciding what type of seating arrangement to use are how much interaction do you want students to have, and how big is your audience. Let's assume, for the sake of illustration, that the room is big enough for the group, and furniture available is adequate. The usual arrangement for maximum interaction between students is to have groups around a table, whilst the more classical row arrangement minimises group interaction. However, these two options represent a continuum with various other arrangements between and within the two extremes; the following are some examples of variations on the two themes.

Organising students in rows

Traditional classroom

The traditional classroom allows for more interaction between audience and teacher but not between students (see Figure 6.2). For presenting information, facts and rules to the whole class where textbooks represent the key learning tool (Phillips 1983), this arrangement is appropriate. This layout can also prove intimidating to some students, since they are required to respond to teachers' questions or ask questions with the whole class as witness – as opposed to the more private possibilities of group settings. Students who lack confidence, or who are self-worth protecting, are less inclined to ask questions under such conditions, since it can pose a threat to them. Should you wish for students to be engaged in collaborative activity and find yourself in a room organised in this manner, and it cannot be easily changed, putting the desks into pairs or groups of four helps facilitate working with immediate neighbours.

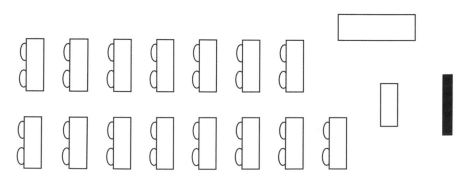

Figure 6.2 Traditional classroom

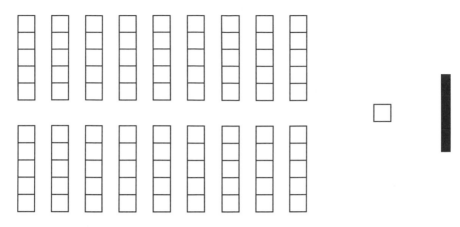

Figure 6.3 Lecture theatre

Lecture theatre

The lecture theatre offers unilateral communication to large groups but does not usually facilitate interaction with the audience – except those in the front row (see Figure 6.3). It is an efficient way of communicating a framework, to use in further discussion, with smaller groups. The lack of a two-way channel means paying particular attention to acoustics, voice projection and quality of visual displays to sustain audience attention when delivering material to large groups.

Small group work

In recent years it has been widely accepted that group work inevitably enhances student learning. However, as with many other areas of education, whilst empirical evidence has shown that group-based activity, in some circumstances, is educationally sound (Rogers and Kutnick 1992), it is not established that it is always so. Merely placing students in small groups is no guarantee that either their performance will be any more enhanced than if they were to work alone, or that all students are capable of working collaboratively in groups. Some classrooms, where students are arranged in groups, occur more by default than design. Physical limitations, room availability or making the best use of space, rather than sound educational or classroom management principles may be the real reason for students being organised this way. Sometimes group work is dictated by the numbers of books or amount of equipment available and does not represent the optimum conditions for learning or collaboration. There is also evidence to demonstrate that the level of academic work increases when students are arranged in rows, as opposed to groups (Wheldall and Lam 1987).

Think of a classroom you currently use and ask yourself:

- Why is it organised in this way?
- Is it the best way to teach this subject or this particular topic?
- How do I know (trial and error, read it somewhere, etc.)?
- Do I feel comfortable teaching this class organised this way?
- Have I tried teaching this subject any other way?
- Could I gain anything by changing the groups or from repositioning or reorganising the tables?
- How do I decide where students will sit?

You might try monitoring output and behaviour with the same class organised in different ways:

- What works best for you?

You should also pay attention to the size of the groups, considering what are the optimum numbers of students to engage in particular activities – sharing a computer, solving a complex problem or making a collage for instance?

Decisions about group membership should be guided by objective information. Who you are putting with whom and why, for which topics, and for how long, are important not just for making behaviour management easier but also for academic and social reasons. Making sure that students are *able* to collaborate with each other, that is they have the appropriate level of social competence, as well as academic competence, should be a fundamental consideration. Organising classes where all SEN students are in a single group may ease resource use and administration, but may also reduce the positive effects of peer-supported learning (Vygotsky 1987):

- What systems exist in your department or school to support students who have difficulty relating to each other in learning and social situations?
- Does they merely focus on those with behaviour difficulties or is there an active programme across all student groups?

Organising students in groups

Although there are numerous ways of organising groups in the classroom I will discuss three arrangements and highlight their suitability for different types of teaching and learning scenarios.

Coffee bar

In the coffee bar arrangement, students sit in small groups around tables facing each other; this is a familiar sight in most schools (see Figure 6.4).

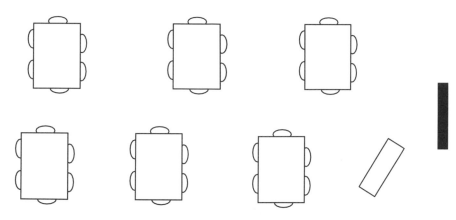

Figure 6.4 Coffee bar

This arrangement maximises interaction and encourages talk, sharing and spontaneity. It also facilitates group problem-solving activity or project work, and invites interpersonal communication. Such an arrangement also enables the teacher to circulate and talk with each group. Whilst this layout allows the teacher to lead the session, it is not the best way to make a presentation to the class, since not all students are able to see the teacher. Furthermore, whilst whole class discussion is possible, it is not the best way of doing so, as some students will have their lines of communication obstructed.

Nightclub

The nightclub allows more multidirectional communication than some arrangements, but is also more 'untidy' than any of the previous arrangements (see Figure 6.5). It represents a halfway house between the traditional classroom and group arrangement and enables more varied small group interaction, but is more hectic because students are not facing each other. However, it also offers a better setting for teacher input to the whole class because no students have their back to the teacher. In this arrangement, tables tend to be bigger or put together to make a larger surface area than in the coffee bar setting, thus enabling students to move themselves and their work around more freely. It also makes adjustment of group sizes more easy during a lesson. However, changing group composition in this way requires caution to avoid creating behaviour management problems and off-task activity. A variation on this theme is to organise the tables so that the overall pattern of the students is semicircular, which helps the teacher present to the whole class.

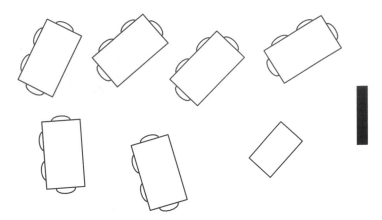

Figure 6.5 Nightclub

Committee table

The committee table arrangement allows for discussion with groups of between fifteen and thirty sitting around a large single table or group of smaller tables (see Figure 6.6). It is the standard setting for seminars, business meetings and case conferences, since it allows interaction between all members, and allows written material or objects to be shared amongst or viewed by the group. Addressing a large group in this way can be intimidating for some students and it can be helpful to note who contributes, who is a wallflower and who needs support – you can do this using sociogram or flow-chart techniques (Hobart and Frankel 1994).

Figure 6.6 Committee table

Open circle

The open circle allows for most interactions between group members and the teacher usually forms part of the circle as a group member (see Figure 6.7). It is a useful format for discussion, provided paperwork or

Figure 6.7 Open circle

writing are not required, as there are no tables or desks: it is the usual format for circle time activities. As group members do not have a table or barrier between them and other students, this arrangement can be very threatening, since those involved are fully exposed and visible to each other.

The psychological environment: influencing students' self-perception and motivation

In Chapter 2, I discussed a range of factors which influence the way in which we perceive and form expectations of students, and how these might affect our behaviour towards them both positively and negatively. The teacher expectancy cycle has the potential to enhance or impair the performance, motivation and social behaviour of students and has been demonstrated, with varying levels of success, on many occasions. The expression or mediation of expectancy comes from interpersonal behaviours plus structural and organisational aspects of the school and classrooms. Where individuals are invited or told to sit, the nature of the work they are asked to undertake, the degree to which they feel empowered to ask a question in class, and the emotional warmth of the classroom environment are all potential influences on how students think, learn and feel about their selves and how they subsequently behave. It is not easy to demonstrate which factors are most important at any one time, since they are subject to individual evaluation and interpretation.

Attribution theory and student motivation

Attribution theory (see also Chapter 2) concerns the explanations that people (individuals and groups) hold or manufacture about the causes of behaviour – both their own and those of other people. We seldom know, for sure, the real causes so base our decisions on what we *perceive* to be the causes. The process is common to everybody, since it is the means by which people make sense of their worlds and affects the way they behave and how they feel. People can be biased in their judgements, distorting reality to maintain consistency and predictability, and making fundamental errors in their explanations. Making judgements and causal analyses can occur at two levels. At the first level they are 'automatic', rely on rapid cognitive processing and are usually based on experience and routine. At the second level they are deliberate and time-consuming activities, implying that one might expect more accurate and just judgements to be made, but this is not always the case, for instance, when making case conference decisions about placements for students with difficulties (Chaplain and Freeman 1994).

People carry out analyses about the reasons for other people's behaviour and also about their own, seeking to understand events occurring in their own lives. Students, for example, may seek to explain their successes and failures (academic and social), which affects their subsequent behaviour. A number of factors can influence this process, one of which is the classroom environment.

A number of contemporary theories of student motivation have been influenced by attribution theories. One theory in particular (see Weiner 1992) has provided the impetus for the development of explanations as to why some students, when faced with new or difficult tasks, engage and persist whilst others just give up at the first sign of difficulty. Weiner (1992) argued that thought processes, as opposed to emotional anticipation, were the principal agents in guiding achievement. A central premise of modern theories of motivation is that individual differences are qualitative and not quantitative, as suggested by earlier drive theories. In other words, people do not just have more or less motivation, they differ in the way they think about their successes and failures. These differences reflect various motivational styles, some of which are adaptive and functional, and others maladaptive and which lead to disaffection and disengagement with learning. It follows that appropriate interventions can be identified only by differentiating between the various types of motivational style of failing students and those at risk of failing. Since these theories argue that it is *how* students think about themselves and their learning, then the potential for teacher behaviour effects becomes immediately apparent.

How students think about themselves and their abilities and what they think teachers think about their ability and motivation, influence whether or not they choose to engage or disengage with academic learning or become involved in disruptive activities. Instances which are not successful in motivating students to engage in academic work include:

- when messages from significant others are interpreted as suggesting you are stupid

- when you find yourself spoken to by the teacher less frequently than others
- when the questions you are asked appear more simple than everybody else's
- when you get printed worksheets and others have textbooks
- when you are seated right at the back, out of the way, or inches away from the teacher, so they can 'keep an eye on you'
- when the teacher visits your desk less frequently than others or does so to give you what you consider negative feedback
- when you receive inappropriate help with simple tasks.

Over time these behaviours can become routine or ritualised and, as a result, some students will:

- feel unable to succeed
- assume they are helpless
- resent their treatment and respond negatively toward the teacher
- work to protect their self-worth often at the cost of academic learning.

Weiner's (1992) model of achievement motivation provides several significant insights into the consequences of students attributing particular causes to their successes and failures in learning or social contexts. He does this with reference to three dimensions – locus, stability and controllability. The first of these – locus of control – relates to whether you attribute your success or failure to factors within yourself (e.g. ability) or factors external to you, such as the situation, other people or good or bad teaching. Thus, students who fail on a test might conclude that they lack ability (internal locus) or alternatively that they had a lousy teacher (external locus).

However, according to Weiner (1992), this single dimension is insufficient explanation, for, whilst some causes are *internal* and others *external*, they differ in terms of their permanence or stability. Ability and effort are both seen as internal qualities but the former is a fairly *stable* quality compared with effort, which is changeable and hence *unstable*. Similar comparisons can be made for external factors, with luck being *unstable* and level of task difficulty being *stable*. To these two dimensions Weiner added a third, controllability. He argued that, whilst a factor could have an internal or external locus of control, some could be controlled whilst others could not. For example, ability is usually viewed as *uncontrollable*, whereas effort is *controllable*.

Table 6.1 gives examples of some possible attributional explanations to success and failure in relation to the three dimensions. Attributing failure to not having made enough effort (internal, controllable, unstable) will have different consequences than attributing failure to teacher bias (external, stable, controllable). Concluding your teacher has it in for you and will negatively affect your future, and that you have no control over it, is not the recipe for

Table 6.1 Explaining success and failure

Controllability	Internal locus		External locus	
	Stable	Unstable	Stable	Unstable
Controllable	Usual effort level	Temporary effort level	Teacher doesn't like me	Unusual help from others
Uncontrollable	Ability	Mood	Task difficulty	Luck

Source: based on Weiner (1992).
Note: Examples of possible explanations a student might use to explain success or failure, based on three dimensions – locus, stability and controllability.

positive teacher–student relationships, nor an incentive to be well behaved. Why would you want to respond positively to someone whom you felt was treating you unjustly? Furthermore, the emotional consequences are also likely to be different, the first example feeling guilty or ashamed, the second feeling hopeless or angry.

Adaptive and maladaptive motivational styles

Attributing causes in one direction or another leads, over time, to the development of motivational styles distinguished on the basis of whether an individual's goals are directed towards performance or mastery. Performance-oriented students are concerned with image, whereas mastery-oriented students are concerned with gaining knowledge and understanding. As Dweck argues, 'with performance goals, an individual aims to look smart, whereas with learning goals the individual aims at becoming smarter' (1985: 91).

Beliefs about ability are central to understanding differences between adaptive and maladaptive motivational styles. Students, who attribute their success to internal, stable factors (e.g. ability) and their failures to lack of effort (internal unstable and controllable), are likely to develop an adaptive style referred to as mastery orientation (Dweck 1990). In contrast, students who attribute their successes to luck and their failures to lack of ability are likely to develop maladaptive motivational styles. Beliefs about intelligence and ability also discriminate between the two behaviour patterns. Some individuals believe that ability is fixed and unchangeable, whereas others believe it is malleable, as a result of the level of effort applied. Teaching students how to think develops in them a view that ability is expandable through experience and practice, what Dweck (1990) called an 'incremental' view of intelligence, which is adaptive.

Individuals who are performance-oriented, and who perceive others as making positive judgements of their ability, are likely to persevere. If, on the other hand, they perceive that they are negatively judged by others, their self-efficacy will be lower and they are likely to experience helplessness. In contrast, learning-oriented students consider ability to be changeable. Should they fail, it is likely to be seen as a challenge or an incentive to solve the problem or to search for alternative approaches. The key difference between the two is the degree to which individuals acknowledge the role of effort above ability. If being smart or having ability is what really counts above all else, and students believe they lack ability, what is the point of making an effort since they are likely to fail anyway? If, on the other hand, students believe that success is more to do with effort, they are more likely to engage with and persevere with a task. This is not to suggest that ability is not important; nonetheless even if students are not gifted, effort can make a big difference. Although it is improbable that any teacher would tell students that they are 'thick', students may interpret their teacher's behaviour towards them as implying that is what they are thinking, based on how they read verbal, nonverbal and organisational messages from the teacher (where they are told to sit, how the teacher talks to them and their body language). If this behaviour also occurs outside the classroom, at home for instance, then the student is more likely to accept it as accurate.

People also make attributions about their social successes and failures. Imagine a student invites someone to go out with her but is rejected; she may well look for a causal explanation. Again, the three above-mentioned dimensions come into effect. She may believe she was rejected because she is ugly (an internal, stable, uncontrollable factor) or alternatively may conclude it was because the person she asked had to attend a family function (an external, unstable, uncontrollable factor).

The two different explanations have the potential to influence what the student thinks about herself and her emotional reaction in different ways. According to Weiner's (1992) theory, this experience occurs at two levels. First, she is likely to feel sad or disappointed at being rejected, at not having achieved her goal. Second, if the goal was an important one (she really liked this person and thought he or she liked her), then she is likely to seek to further explain why she *believes* she was rejected and, as a result, feel either hopeless or hopeful about future success. If she thinks she was rejected because she is ugly – something beyond her volitional control – she is likely to experience hopelessness, because the cause is down to her (internal locus), it is not likely to change over time (stable) and is something she cannot control (uncontrollable). Alternatively, if she puts rejection down to the other person being busy with a family reunion (external locus), which is not likely to happen continually (unstable), she will be more hopeful of success in the future.

Thus, making attributions to explain events can influence how you think about yourself, how you feel about yourself and how you behave, affecting both your self and social identity. The likelihood of being motivated to repeat a behaviour depends on the direction of the causal explanation.

Students who conclude, from their interpretation of teacher behaviour, that they do not fit into a class or the teacher does not like them, eventually incorporate this thinking into their self-schema. Changing such negative self-perceptions is difficult.

Maladaptive styles: coping with threatened identities

Those who repeatedly attribute their failures to internal, stable, uncontrollable factors (e.g. ability) and successes to external, unstable, uncontrollable factors (e.g. luck) develop maladaptive motivational styles.

Two types of maladaptive styles have been identified – self-worth protection and learned helplessness. Whilst on the surface the behaviour of students with maladaptive motivational styles may appear similar – both make minimal effort or give up prematurely, or cannot be bothered to complete work – the two styles are qualitatively different. It is to these differences I now turn.

Self-worth protection

Ability is a highly valued personal quality in the educational system, perceiving you lack it affects various aspects of the self including self-regulation, self-efficacy and self-esteem. As Covington put it:

> It is not surprising that the pupil's sense of esteem often becomes equated with ability – to be able is to be valued as a human being but to do poorly is evidence of inability, and reason to despair of one's worth.
>
> (1992: 6)

Individuals who develop a self-worth protecting style are *unsure* of their own ability, believing they *may* have sufficient competence to be successful. However, they also recognise that ability is negatively correlated with effort (high ability = low effort) consequently, those seen to make more effort in order to gain success must lack ability – an observation which presents them with a dilemma. Success with minimum effort is an indicator of *having* ability, which is far more important than being successful. Making more effort than your peers means you will be perceived as lacking ability, and particularly so if the additional effort results in failure (Kun 1977). The emotional consequences are feelings of shame and humiliation and lowered self-worth (Covington 1998). Whilst being seen as competent is the best way to protect one's self-worth, the risks involved in trying to do so may be too great, making it better not to try than to try and fail. To suggest these students are not motivated would be wrong – they are highly motivated – to avoid the implications of failure. They are also motivated to protect their self-worth and will risk all rather than being seen as lacking ability, employing various tactics to avoid being exposed, refusing to complete school work, for instance. By not bothering to try or trying with excuses, students can minimise information about their ability. Tactics include procrastination, task avoidance and refusal to compete work, the lasting consequence of which is underachievement (Thompson 1994). Whilst in the short term, such strategies may be effective, their life-span is usually short since other people eventually see through the veneer, making any doubt that students have about their competence a certainty.

This negative thinking can also pervade the emotional experiences of the student, changing hope to hopelessness. After all what is the point of working hard if failure is the inevitable outcome? Despairing of one's worth can lead to acquiescence or resentment towards those who are perceived to have contributed to the difficulty – teachers for example.

In a study (Chaplain 1996a) of engaged and disengaged students in three Derbyshire comprehensives, this feeling was made clear. Disengaged students were represented by teachers in terms of students' personal qualities and disposition such as having antisocial tendencies, lacking ability and not making an effort, or having personality or developmental problems. The disengaged students admitted to behaving in ways not conducive to success in school, such as giving up easily with their school work, impulsiveness, difficulties understanding their work and feeling embarrassed if asked questions in public or singled out for special attention. Being seen to fail in public reinforces lack of ability and lowers self-worth. Hence, well-meaning teachers, who believe they are being supportive, are in fact perceived by the students as doing the opposite.

Teachers attempting to support students by offering uncalled-for help or unwarranted praise serve as cues to their low ability, especially with secondary-aged students (Barker and Graham 1987; Graham and Barker 1990) contributing to the development of maladaptive motivational styles. The disengaged students in Derbyshire also considered teachers to be unfair, especially to them, felt that they expressed negativity toward them both verbally and non-verbally, and considered teachers to be largely responsible for their failure at school.

Determining who is responsible for the problem is far from straightforward and perhaps, in some ways, of little value since it detracts from thinking about how to provide an environment which is positive and provides motivational equity to all students regardless of ability. Sadly, students who float on the border of failure, disengagement and disaffection – those at risk – are perhaps the least well attended to in terms of resources – in contrast to students who are receiving special measures or those considered able. The prognosis for the borderline group is especially poor in the latter years of secondary education, since access to credentialled examinations becomes increasingly unlikely because of missed work and their limited problem-solving and task orientation skills limiting their immediate options.

Learned helplessness

Learned helplessness (Smiley and Dweck 1994) is a maladaptive style characterised by a general belief, by students, that they lack ability and without doubt will fail, no matter how hard they try. So, if faced with a difficult task, they give up rather than make extra effort because they believe changes to ability are beyond their control and do not recognise a link between effort and success. Students who are learned helpless feel a global lack of control over their lives and tend to externalise responsibility for important events to others, including even their successes. As a result, their success is not rewarding, nor does it increase their pride and confidence because they do not feel responsible. Help from teachers reinforces their beliefs in their own lack of competence. Once this motivational style is established, it is difficult to change. In some cases, beliefs about the inevitability of failure are so strong that attempting to convince them of the value of making more effort, of encouraging learned industriousness, is like telling someone who is clinically depressed to pull themselves together. Indeed there is a relationship between learned helplessness and acute depression.

Thinking about ways in which students' motivation differs is a useful starting point for developing ways of nurturing a positive psychological climate in the classroom. Classroom environments are teachers' territory, within which students' learning is on teachers' terms, placing them in probably the best position to positively influence students' beliefs about success and failure. Unfortunately, as Thompson (1994: 266) points out, 'there is evidence that the potential is either largely unexploited or (more seriously) distorted in its application'.

Helping students to break maladaptive behaviour patterns requires getting them to rethink their reasons for failure and offering direction to help make changes.

Successes have been recorded with learned helpless students by encouraging them to gain control of their outcomes through changing their attributions from external uncontrollable (luck) to internal controllable (effort) (Perry and Struthers 1994; Craske 1988; Wilson and Linville 1985). Whilst there have been positive results from this approach, not everyone agrees that merely providing effort feedback for success and failure is inevitably successful. Praising students for working hard can produce positive results but telling them that they are not working hard enough or need to work harder is, according to Nicholls (1989), almost as useless as doing nothing. The relationship between effort and ability is complex. Whilst teachers might praise and reward effort in teaching situations the prediction of future success relies heavily on estimates of ability (Kaplan and Swant 1973). According to Schunk (1987), awareness of both is important, success is achieved by encouraging students to attribute success to effort with new tasks but moving to attributing success to ability as they develop their skills and understanding.

One approach to changing the behaviour of students who are self-worth motivated is to make them challenge their own self-deception and fears by, first, getting them to identify goals and, second, to face up to the reasons behind their excuses for not achieving them (Mandel and Marcus 1995). Having an excuse for not having achieved anything or being able to organise your life, because it is not your fault that other people have not done as they should, or taught you the wrong syllabus, removes the need to take responsibility for your own actions.

The focus throughout this book is on designing multilevel approaches to behaviour management and this continues here. The behaviour management of students with maladaptive motivational styles, by helping them to overcome their difficulties, is best facilitated by incorporating different approaches at different organisational levels, ranging from whole school level to student level. Covington (1998) advocates a rethinking of educational systems with a dampening of obsession with ability to one orientated to students' future survival, developing a set of marketable skills, willingness to become engaged and preparation for the inevitability of change. Likewise, at the student level, teachers provide cooperative learning environments in which motivation, strategic thinking skills and how to learn from failure are developed and positively valued. The current pressures on improving performance in British schools are largely based on quantitative models of motivation. Government demands for more exams, more hours and more passes reflect a theory-driven approach to education which lacks imagination particularly when laid alongside other concerns about student behaviour, school attendance and stress, particularly for the failure-prone student.

Suggested further reading

Covington, M.V. (1998) *The Will to Learn: A Guide for Motivating Young People*, Cambridge: Cambridge University Press.

Chapter 7

Classroom structures

The role of rules, routines and rituals in behaviour management

All aspects of our lives require us to operate within rules or boundaries of some sort, whether self-imposed or determined by others. Some rules seem clear, rational and reasonable – others seem petty and irritating. It is not uncommon to hear people grumbling about not being allowed to do what they want, even though it is (to them) perfectly fair and reasonable

Rules can be interpreted literally or in spirit, so care has to be taken with wording to avoid unintended consequences. You will probably be aware of the minute attention to detail some adolescents have when it comes to the interpretation of school rules, in respect of what constitutes 'appropriate footwear' and 'jewellery', or how 'long' a skirt really is; an unwary teacher can be drawn into a protracted discussion of these details. Such discussions are excellent tactics for avoiding schoolwork, provide the class with light entertainment and stop you from doing your job.

The functions of rules

In the classroom it is the teacher who should be in control. Disruptive behaviour, refusing to work, insults, backchat and other attention-seeking tactics are attempts by students to take control. Intelligently constructed rules can help establish teacher control and facilitate learning, provided that their meaning is clear, they are supported by relevant rewards and sanctions, and the teacher behaves assertively. The main function of classroom rules is to set limits to students' behaviour and to make them aware of the conditions required for success (Charles 1999). They operate in a preventive or feedforward way to establish and maintain order and momentum. This does not mean that students are not treated warmly or that humour and developing relationships and mutual respect are not important. Indeed, a principal objective of having rules is to create a safe and warm environment through making clear what the teacher values as important to ensure students' success and to develop positive working relationships.

One common mistake when making rules is to focus on telling students what they cannot do, rather than telling them what they can. Telling students where they are *not* permitted to go creates more difficulties than telling them where they *are* allowed to go, since the former arouses curiosity – why can't we go there? What are they trying to hide? A cupboard or storeroom designated 'staff use only' often fires students' imagination. Perhaps it contains some dark secret, something tasty or embarrassing, holiday snaps, love letters from the head, exam papers, chocolate (when, in reality, it contains photocopy paper and worn trainers!).

Rules can promote appropriate behaviour in three different ways, first, by helping individuals (teachers and students) to cope, second, by framing interpersonal relationships, and third, by supporting whole school behaviour policies. Effective rules, linked to specific and appropriate consequences, establish the boundaries of behaviour. Where rules are effective, they provide a safe environment in which teacher and students can get on with their work.

Rules operate at both the classroom level and whole school level, the latter representing the core behavioural expectations for the school to provide consistency and predictability for both staff and students. Classroom rules, whilst guided by the school rules, will differ and reflect the personal aims, concerns and expectations of the teacher in charge of the class. What one teacher considers 'quiet' will be considered noisy by another, and what constitutes acceptable levels of student movement during a lesson is unlikely to be universally accepted. Provided classroom variations are not in conflict with the core school rules, they personalise the context, offering a slightly different angle on things and, in this way, are healthy. The object of having, and publicising, core rules is not to produce a group of robots, but to make overall shared expectations clear, providing consistency, predictability and a solid framework on which the school can achieve its aims. Balancing whole school and classroom-based rules provides the school community with both consistency and distinctiveness.

Where the behaviour of a teacher, or group of teachers, differs significantly from the overall agreed policy, it leads to ambiguity for both students and colleagues. When discussing school placements with trainee teachers I always direct them to obtain copies of the school's behaviour policy and suggest that they read it in detail, before they commence their practice. I also suggest that, on their initial visits, they try to match what they have read with what they observe, to determine how the rules are being interpreted and applied, and how sanctions and rewards are used. It is not uncommon for students to return and say that a teacher or department seems to do their own thing, something that the trainees, who are being assessed on their placements, can find hard to cope with.

In schools experiencing difficulty, perhaps as a result of change, or those in which colleagues do not work together, there can be a tendency for individual teachers to rely solely on their own strengths. If the school behaviour plan is not agreed by all, or is perceived as having become weak and ineffectual, teachers may feel the need to defend their own domain more than usual. After all, even if there are problems around the school, provided you can hold your class together things will be OK – won't they? The answer is, highly unlikely. If there are problems around the school, an individual teacher will eventually feel the effects, no matter how competent he or she is.

Rules are hierarchical and have different levels of permanency. At the 'highest' level there is government legislation, which usually takes time to change. At the opposite extreme are the rules that a supply teacher might use if covering a class they do not know for a single lesson. In the latter case the teacher will try to establish order quickly, in a context he or she is not familiar with. How an individual achieves this will vary somewhat and should be guided by three basic principles, that they are legally, professionally and morally acceptable.

Classroom rules have various functions. In practice, they should all focus on making a classroom safe, keeping students on legitimate tasks and promoting appropriate social behaviour. One obvious reason for having rules relates to safety. Rules to avoid the dangers of running in class, wandering around or messing about in a laboratory or workshop whilst others are working, not checking gym equipment before it is used or not warming up before vigorous exercise are clearly necessary and need little, if any, qualification.

In addition to physical safety, rules provide psychological safety at both cognitive and emotional levels. If students and teachers do not feel safe and secure in school or classroom, they will be unable to think about learning. Disruption in class interferes with the learning process in various ways; cognitively by disturbing concentration, attention and remembering information (Dalgleish 1995) and emotionally, making people feel anxious or worried (Ellis and Ashbrook 1989). Learning becomes impaired when excessive demands result in limited cognitive resources being redirected to control emotions (Ellis *et al.* 1995). Classrooms with unruly students whom other students *perceive* that their teacher cannot control, provide ideal conditions for generating anxiety amongst other students who, in turn, will use whatever behaviour they feel necessary in order to cope – some acting up, others withdrawing.

Rules and psychological safety

Maslow (1970 [1954]) developed a model which provides a useful basis for understanding the relationship between perceived safety and learning. The starting point for Maslow and others such as Rogers (1951) is that human beings are basically good and striving to achieve all that they wish to be (self-actualisation). For Maslow self-actualisation sits at the pinnacle of a hierarchy of needs, where upward movement requires satisfaction of lower level needs, *at least in part*. As one level is satisfied, the next highest level need then becomes the target of our energies. There are seven levels to this hierarchy of needs. Cognitive needs (e.g. learning) appear at the fifth level and are preceded by physiological, safety, belongingness and esteem needs. One implication of this is that, before students can devote their energies towards their cognitive needs (learning) or belongingness needs (feel part of the class) or their self-esteem needs, they will first have to satisfy some of their physiological and safety needs.

At the lowest level of the hierarchy, the needs are physiological. The most basic needs required for survival include eating, drinking, keeping warm and resting. Although considered basic, not all students arrive at school having eaten or rested, so it is hardly surprising that they find it difficult to move on to a higher motivational target. The 'recent' practice of providing breakfast in some schools stands as testament to the concerns of some teachers in this respect.

Immediately above physiological needs are safety needs, which is where rules and routines have a particular significance. It is worth noting here that feeling safe and secure is an individual perception. Telling and demonstrating to someone that they are safe and have nothing to worry about counts for nothing if the individual does not perceive the situation is safe. Anyone who has taught mountain climbing will know that informing someone that an abseiling rope meets safety standards, and could support the weight of a large elephant, does not necessarily convince the anxious participant that it will not snap when they are on it. Whilst it may be scientifically proven and statistically improbable that the worst might happen, some individuals remain unconvinced. Safety and security are not just about physical factors; for students in a classroom they can come from:

- knowing what behaviour is expected of them and other students, coupled with what will happen if they do not meet those expectations
- believing that their teacher and other responsible adults are capable of protecting them from harm (physical or psychological) and if necessary will do so
- that their teachers have their best interests at heart and will do their utmost to ensure they succeed.

I reiterate my point that it is the student's *perception* that matters, not necessarily the actuality. The law might insist that a teacher has a duty of care to provide the above but that means nothing to students, if they suspect their teacher might not be capable of doing so if under pressure.

When this uncertainty is sensed, students are likely to move from attending to their learning needs and turning their energies towards satisfying their safety needs. It is when, for instance, they observe other students refusing to conform to behavioural expectations and teachers are perceived as reluctant, or unable, to stop them, that a lack of belongingness and insecurity become apparent. When I worked with students who had behaviour difficulties and who had often made their teachers' lives hell, very few ever said they had enjoyed doing so (although many of their teachers disagreed). During interviews with these students, many talked of reacting to not feeling part of the class, to being made to feel different or given 'baby' work or teachers not making them work or just having a laugh with their mates. For many normally attentive students, not considered to have behaviour difficulties, observing other students failing to conform, challenging authority and getting away with it, can make them question the teacher's ability to do their job and control the situation, making them feel unsafe and anxious, as the following quote illustrates:

> Well we were having a lesson in Q12 and Mrs C was teaching us, yeah
> . . . and then these three Year 10's walked in and one hit Danny . . . then
> they walked out laughing and she never did anything. She just said 'Get
> on with your work just ignore them' but that was when they'd already
> left! It wasn't the first time, they are always wandering about and she's
> scared of them yeah – so are most people – but it shouldn't be allowed.
> Nothing ever happens to them though.
>
> (Billy, Year 8)

Students also feel unfairly treated and angry when they are subjected to inappropriate block sanctions because teachers cannot control individuals who are misbehaving:

> He can be a good teacher but when the others start messing about he
> refuses to teach anybody . . . he doesn't sort them out, he punishes us all
> by not teaching. Half the time he jokes with them, then when they go
> too far he gets angry. We asked him if we could go and work some-
> where else or if they could be sent out but he won't do anything about
> it. He just says 'I am not prepared to teach you lot if you will not do as
> you are told. You are the worst class in the school. If you want to spoil
> your exam chances that's your decision.' But we haven't done anything
> and the exams are getting closer and we have to get this coursework and
> revision done but it's noisy so we can't. It's well out of order!
>
> (Sophie, Year 11)

Under such circumstances, sharing a social identity with the group perceived as 'weak' (in this case those getting on with their work) is less appealing than being seen as on the side of the 'strong' (deviant group) so there may be a strong temptation to join in – not because they dislike the teacher as such, but because the alternative provides either a more effective way of coping at the time or because they are swept along with the group:

she's quite nice really but too soft. When the boys at the back start burping and that, she just looks at them in disgust – then everybody starts laughing and then you laugh as well – it's hard not to when everyone else is – but we like her really. Then she looks like she's going to cry and usually goes and gets Mr W and he sorts them out.

(Amy, Year 9)

According to Maslow's formulation, it is only when students feel safe and secure that they can move on to satisfying their belongingness or affiliation needs. Forming a cohesive class or group is central to teaching in schools but unlikely to happen if students feel unsafe and insecure. Furthermore, if the 'legitimate' group does not provide these necessary components, then an alternative is likely to be sought, an option which may be less desirable from a classroom management point of view.

When students feel that their physiological safety and belongingness are addressed (partially at least), then they can focus on their esteem needs, that is, liking themselves and being liked and respected by others. Maslow's hierarchy offers a different slant on trying to understand why some students have low self-esteem and underperform. If satisfying their esteem needs requires first taking care of lower-level needs such as feeling safe, secure and part of a group (class) that cares about them, and students perceive this is not happening, then it is hardly surprising that they have low self-esteem, which may contribute to underachievement. Clearly, this is an oversimplification, as there are a range of other reasons why individuals may have difficulty liking themselves or feeling that others like them, or why they fail, but paying attention to these subordinate needs is one way of eliminating some of them.

Maslow's theory has been questioned as to its worth in offering a complete explanation of human motivation. One criticism relates to the fact that some people appear to focus on higher-level needs ignoring lower-order needs, for instance, sacrificing personal safety to protect a loved one or comrade or doing without food and rest to complete a painting or book. Nevertheless, the model provides an explanation of how most people operate in most conditions. From a behaviour management perspective it offers a sequential framework on which to build a discipline strategy, illustrates what to concentrate on and in what order, and encourages teachers to monitor that all basic elements have been addressed before moving to higher-level aims.

Figure 7.1 also shows how a teacher's behaviour towards a class might support students' needs moving from early encounters (e.g. week 1, Year 7) to later in the year. Early stages focus on defining expectations and boundaries and high levels of direction, whereas in later stages students are given differentiated levels of responsibility and diversity in learning, informed by performance feedback. Thus, in addition to signalling the rights and

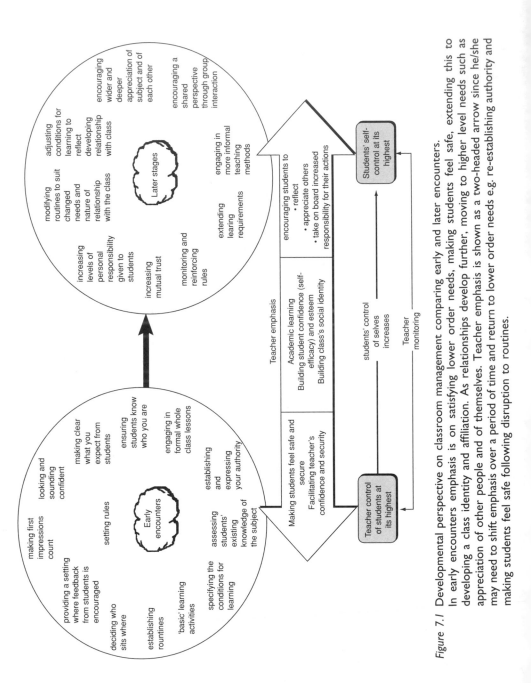

Figure 7.1 Developmental perspective on classroom management comparing early and later encounters.

In early encounters emphasis is on satisfying lower order needs, making students feel safe, extending this to developing a class identity and affiliation. As relationships develop further, moving to higher level needs such as appreciation of other people and of themselves. Teacher emphasis is shown as a two-headed arrow since he/she may need to shift emphasis over a period of time and return to lower order needs e.g. re-establishing authority and making students feel safe following disruption to routines.

responsibilities of students, rules are also an essential component of the conditions for learning (Rudduck *et al.*. 1996a):

- Can you identify how students causing you concern might not be satisfying lower-order needs?
- How might you help them to move on to higher-level needs?
- How do you ensure that your students feel safe?

Determining the basis for your rules

So far, I have discussed the role and function of rules, without saying much about the rules themselves. There are a number of questions to consider in this respect, including: How many rules should there be? How should they be worded? How do you go about setting rules? Who should be involved in deciding which rules to have?

Essentially, there are rules agreed upon for the whole school behaviour plan, those specific to departments (e.g. laboratories, gym, computer rooms) and those used by teachers, as part of their individual discipline plans, all of which must reflect the context. There are some obvious 'core rules' which might be found in any school behaviour policy (treating others with respect, not putting others down, responsibility for the community, for instance), which provide the baseline for classroom rules:

- Think about core rules or behavioural expectations in your school: are they listed in your school literature?
- Do they reflect your personal beliefs about the most important and universal expectations? If not, what would you include?
- When were the school rules last discussed?

Merely writing down rules does not mean that they will be communicated to those for whom they are intended, so attention needs to be given to how the community is made aware of expectations. To do this requires answers to questions, such as, Who needs to be told (e.g. students, teaching and ancillary staff, parents, governors, visitors)? How often do they need reminding? Should core rules be publicly displayed and if so, where and in what form? How do you monitor their effectiveness and relevance?

There are a number of ways of setting rules and which is used depends, to a large extent, on your beliefs about human behaviour. For instance, do you believe that students of secondary age:

- should be treated with respect and hence rules should be negotiated with them from the start?
- know how to behave so should not need rules spelling out?

- are strongly influenced by context and group dynamics, so it is important to let them find boundaries which are acceptable to you and the school and then respond to them?
- will always try to push the boundaries, so need them spelling out clearly at the beginning and reminding along the way?

Which approach you favour will reflect a combination of your previous experience and personality, how you feel about the individuals or groups you work with, what you consider acceptable behaviour, along with what the school or department expects. There is no single correct approach because none fit all individuals and contexts. Your confidence in your ability (self-efficacy) to deliver and enforce a particular approach, along with your knowledge and experience of the school and class, will be important determinants.

It would be unwise, for instance, to opt for negotiating rules with a new class if you were not sure of your ability to negotiate with that particular group, at that stage – however much you subscribe to democratic principles. New teachers dealing with new classes are unlikely to know the dynamics of the group, nor individual personalities. If the students are not used to dealing with that level of responsibility and given that they do not know you, suggesting negotiation at that stage may be problematic.

Whilst young people are aware of standards and rules from an early age (Stipek *et al.* 1992), assuming they 'know' how to behave in your class can be unwise, since each teacher has his or her personal expectations.

Similarly, getting on with teaching and waiting for students to do something wrong before correcting them is not advisable, since case law approaches rely too much on being reactive as opposed to proactive.

This leaves us with the final 'limit-setting' approach, that is the teacher spelling out boundaries in advance. This approach has several advantages, particularly when establishing authority with a new group, assuming that the rules have been well thought out, are appropriate and achievable by the group. A limit-setting approach is an effective method because:

- it provides students with a predictable and safe environment
- unlike case law or negotiated approaches, it gives a relatively fixed point of reference for the teacher, since the rules will have been considered and rehearsed in advance rather than having to think on your feet
- quickly projects the teacher's control of the situation
- enables the teacher to consider the content and likely consequences of making specific rules before going into action, thereby being proactive.

However, this does not mean that inevitably students will not be involved in updating or renegotiating rules, as classroom relationships develop. The objective in setting limits, in the early stages, is to establish control and provide a usable and predictable structure reflecting the safety and security needs identified by Maslow. Over time the teacher can engage in negotiating new rules, should existing ones become redundant and he or she feels that the students are sufficiently responsible and able to do so.

Early in their careers, or often when starting a new job, a teacher's primary concerns are likely to be self-orientated and focused on survival and adjustment to the school, so prescribing rules at this stage is more likely to minimise threat to self and satisfy these concerns. As time progresses, the teacher's self-efficacy, relationships with students, knowledge of the group and its dynamics and individual students develop, and the teacher's concerns shift from survival towards wider developmental issues. Attention moves to increasing student autonomy and preparing them for transition to the next stage of their development and producing the conditions under which negotiation about expectations is more appropriate.

Making rules work for you

Relying solely on word of mouth to communicate behavioural expectations is likely to be problematic and lead to unwanted modifications (we are all familiar with the game of Chinese whispers). Likewise, merely recording them on a document that is given out on the first day of school, half-read then put away, is also not a good idea. Whilst publishing classroom rules on the wall is a popular tradition in primary schools, it is less so in secondary schools (except for health and safety rules) for various reasons. First, there is an expectation that older students will be able to remember the rules and how to behave more easily than younger ones. Second, unless teaching in a very specialised room *all* the time, you will be moving around from classroom to classroom. Having a set of rules posted in the classroom would necessitate carrying a large card or similar around all day with you and setting it up at each lesson. Furthermore, given rules are associated not only with teachers but also with rooms, changing lists every forty minutes would probably not be wise.

To have a set of rules to cover all possible situations would result in a rather long, unmemorable and unmanageable list, so the number of rules should be kept to a minimum. I recommend a maximum of five simply worded and easy to remember rules. Hargreaves *et al.* (1975) recommend five types of rules which relate to movement, talking, time, teacher–student relationships and student–student relationships. Although there are clear overlaps between them, Canter and Canter (1992) suggest four generally applicable rules:

- follow directions
- keep hands, feet and objects to yourself
- no teasing or name-calling
- no swearing.

Glasser (1998) also recommends a minimum number of rules but suggests they be negotiated with students and based on what constitutes courteous behaviour.

When designing rules, consideration must be given to consequences (rewards and sanctions) for students who behave appropriately or inappropriately. Making it pay to be good, as well as indicating what happens to those who misbehave needs careful consideration, must be organised hierarchically and be transparent and fair. Rules supported by rewards and sanctions which demonstrate a clear cause and effect relationship remove ambiguity for staff and students. When deciding on which rewards and sanctions to use, it pays to carry out a consequence analysis to help clarify the likely value of rewards and sanctions to students. This allows you to consider the possible unintended consequences, for instance, selecting a sanction you would not be able to enforce.

Rewards for completing tasks might range from the abstract (praise) to the concrete (a pen). Behavioural approaches (see Chapter 8) inform us that without some form of contingency reinforcement (i.e. reward for behaving in a particular way), the behaviour is not likely to continue. This is not to suggest that rewards must be tangible – for many people the personal satisfaction of competing or persevering with a task is sufficient reward in itself. For others, some form of concrete reinforcer is necessary but only usually in the early stages.

Sanctions should equally be predictable and hierarchical. Fuzzy sanctions or threats, those broadcast with an accompanying note of uncertainty and those that are threatened and not carried through are a waste of time. Being clear about what sanctions are available in school and which are appropriate for particular types of misdemeanour, how they are organised, who has the authority to issue and carry them through, helps to remove ambiguity and allows teacher and class to focus on the task in hand, that is, teaching and learning.

The higher the level of sanction, the more likely it is to undermine relationships. Once you have reached the stage of involving other parties, parents, police or others, consideration has to be given to how relationships can be repaired afterwards.

When threatening a sanction, where possible, offer an alternative course of action at each stage of the hierarchy. Offering an alternative gives students the opportunity to engage in their own consequence analysis, to re-examine causes and outcomes (usually prompted by a teacher) and consider vicariously the potential outcomes of their behaviour. In doing so, they are likely to make a more rational decision, assuming there is sufficient space and time for those who are angry and feel unjustly treated to regain emotional control. Forcing them into a corner is less likely to achieve this. However, this does not mean failing to carry out the proposed course of action, but offering student an alternative course of action is more likely to help when rebuilding relationships at a later time. Don't lose sight of the object of the exercise – managing students' behaviour to keep them on legitimate learning tasks and maintaining positive relationships between teacher and student. Offering students a choice not only helps save face for both sides, a win-win situation, but also provides space for damage limitation in teacher–student relationships.

Should rules be enforced all the time? In principle, yes, is the answer to this question. If you have taken time to produce a small number of important expectations that you believe are necessary to ensure the smooth running of the lesson or school day, then not enforcing them is usually unwise. However, breaking the flow of the lesson to deal with a clear, but not serious, breach of the rules is not always the best strategy. Depending on how well you know the class or the individual involved, or whether you are dealing with other more serious behaviour at the time, you may choose not to respond immediately, preferring to use deflection strategies. There are several techniques that can be used to deal with such problems. You might choose to defer your response until later, deliberately ignoring it or defusing the situation with humour.

Rules about rules

Whilst people differ in their beliefs about how to introduce and sustain rules, there are five basic principles which I advise people to consider when deciding how to develop rules:

- *Keep 'em positive:* the wording of a rule can make or break it. Rules should reflect what you value and want to encourage in your classroom. Negative rules encourage a negative climate for both students and teacher. Negative rules, such as 'don't talk' or 'stop wandering around', although sometimes successful in terminating behaviour briefly, do not tend to have lasting effects, nor do they encourage positive behaviours. Becker *et al.* (1975) argued that such rules might be successful in the short term; they are likely to increase the frequency of the misbehaviour over time.
- *Keep 'em brief:* rules should include only key concerns. Make sure they are kept brief as this makes them easier to remember.
- *Keep 'em realistic:* set rules which reflect expectations that are appropriate and achievable by you or the class.
- *Keep 'em focused:* the overall objective for having rules is self-regulation, which is enabled through helping students to internalise those qualities necessary to facilitate their development. Qualities such as rights, responsibilities, safety and respect for self and others create the conditions for learning. Rules should therefore concentrate on key issues, including being aware of personal safety and the safety of others, being considerate,

cooperative, honest, friendly as well as attending to legitimate classroom activity and maintaining appropriate noise levels for specific
contexts.

- *Keep 'em:* if the rule is worth having in the first place, then it needs to
be regularly reinforced. If you find it is not working or has lost its
relevance, then either modify it or drop it.

Do not make rules ineffective by applying them one minute and letting them
slide the next; if they are worth having, they need to be applied consistently.
If you cannot make your rules work for you, ask why. Are you unable to
enforce them? Are they inappropriate or unreasonable?

- What rules do you currently have in your classroom?
- How do they promote positive behaviour?
- What concerns are they designed to address?
- How did you communicate them?
- Were they negotiated with students or presented to them by you?
- What are the rewards for behaving well?
- Do your sanctions work?

Routines and rituals: adding meat to the bone

The primary function of school rules is to develop harmonious relationships amongst the school community, whereas in the classroom their primary purpose is to maximise engaged learning time (Savage 1991). To be
successful, rules must be few in number and reflect general concerns, for
example, being polite to others. But how does a teacher regulate the multi-
tude of activities taking place in a classroom with four or five rules? Rules
do not take into account the many ways one might demonstrate politeness
for instance. Being polite in the school dining hall is likely to have a different meaning from sharing a takeaway in front of the television. In order
to match the rule to the diverse range of situations in school and ensure its
safe and efficient operation, an additional system to translate expectations
into actions is needed. This is achieved by developing an array of routines
and rituals which add detail to the rule and are responsive to culture and
context.

Routines are procedural supports, used to manage everyday social behaviour around school and in class, as well as supporting teaching and learning.
They are often organised around a particular time (e.g. start of a lesson), a
place (classroom) or context (group work). Their object is to add meaning
to rules and to translate their spirit into action. If being polite is an important rule, then the routines established for greeting students and staff when
they arrive in school or class, how equipment is shared, and empowering
people to have their thoughts and feelings heard, should reflect this. If not

disturbing other students while working is a rule, then a routine for checking or marking students' work, distributing materials and movement around the classroom should ensure that disruption to students is minimalised. Well-thought-out and communicated routines facilitate the smooth running of lessons, keep students on task and ensure the efficient and well-ordered operation of your classroom.

Some routines operate at the school level (lunchtime, school buses), others at the classroom level (getting work out, changing activities). There are a great many routines roughly similar to all schools, whilst others vary significantly between schools to reflect different cultures and contexts, as well as the values and beliefs of those responsible for running the schools. Common routines include those used to control movement around school, entering classrooms, getting work out, issuing materials, asking questions, putting things away and so on.

Different teachers and subjects require different routines, but there are some common examples such as:

- entering the classroom
- getting the attention of the class
- getting out materials
- marking work
- changing activities
- going to the toilet
- dealing with interruptions
- dealing with latecomers
- keeping students on task
- finishing the lesson.

Non-teaching activities such as getting students ready to learn, distributing materials and marking work, whilst necessary, can take up substantial amounts of teaching time – up to 50 per cent of some lessons (Jones and Jones 1990) but well-thought-out routines can streamline these activities, increasing the time available for learning. Routines are usually more flexible than rules, so are more receptive to changing needs. Whilst the expectation for students to be polite in social encounters is an ongoing expectation, the way in which politeness is represented (routine and ritual) changes over time. Routines usually incorporate a number of rules.

Efficient routines provide you with more time to teach, and students with more time to learn. Spending time planning and reviewing routines beforehand pays dividends, since it provides students with a sense of organisation and order. Emmer *et al.* (1994) found that competent and effective teachers spend considerable time in their early encounters with students teaching them routines. This is not to suggest that routines are only important in early encounters, spending time establishing and practising routines results in them becoming automatic and can be triggered by simple ritualised behaviours – clapping the hands, a stare, folding arms, for example.

Routines and rituals offer a very powerful form of demonstrating authority to all members of the school community; they give shape to and facilitate the smooth running of the school day. A ritual, such as assembly, requires participants to behave in a formalised way and includes particular actions, words and movements, and a series of routines occurring in a particular sequence. How students enter assembly often reflects how they are expected to enter other formal areas, such as classrooms, but may be modified to give the assembly more status, such as playing music when people enter. The rules about who is expected or permitted to speak, and in what order, are usually fairly easily understood. These routines and procedures are usually learnt, at first by instruction and prompting, and later by internalising the various routines involved. The formality of the occasion encourages conformity and those who fail to conform are often masked in large gatherings by the contributions of others. Singing 'alternative' words to hymns and sniggering are usually localised. The power of such rituals is so great that, even when people feel unwell, they are reluctant to leave, even if the result is suffering the embarrassment and teasing from being sick where they sit. Rituals reinforce the status of the members of the community, often represented by who sits on chairs and who sits on the floor (or who has the comfy chairs and who does not), who stands up for whom as a mark of respect and so on.

However, rituals also provide a sense of community, incorporating feelings of belonging and security which can be emotionally uplifting and within which personal development can take place. In doing so, they help satisfy what Maslow (1970 [1954]) identified as second and third level needs. These thoughts and feelings are experienced by both staff and students since such rituals publicly reinforce their position in the organisation and help them to psychologically accept that position. Assemblies are events which promote the social identity of the school and are used as a vehicle for reminding students of what is valued, for example giving prizes for positive behaviour or publicly admonishing unacceptable behaviour. Similar processes operate in the classroom but with less formality.

In the classroom, a rule (e.g. respecting others) will be supported with routines (e.g. students raising their hands before asking questions) and often triggered by a teacher's ritual of moving to a particular place and use of gesture (e.g. a raised finger to forewarn an individual eager to shout out an answer). Other rituals include standing or sitting in particular places in the classroom, clapping hands or folding arms in order to elicit particular behaviour such as gaining attention:

> we always know when the school was in for a telling off because he [the head] takes his glasses off and folds them up then he glares at everybody – that's when you know.
>
> (Mark, Year 8)

she folds her arms and just looks out of the window, sometimes tapping her arm if she's really not pleased – she doesn't say anything. Then everyone shuts up and she starts talking again.

(Jean, Year 9)

So what's the big deal if these rituals are well known in school and all teachers use them? Problems can occur when teachers fail to evaluate the effectiveness of their rituals or do not develop new ones to respond to changing contexts. One example of this is what I call the '*ssh*' and '*erm*' ritual. These two sounds are commonly associated with expecting people to be quiet (*ssh*) and indicating disapproval (*erm*) and not uncommon generally (e.g. library and cinema). If they act as a trigger or reminder of a rule (e.g. you are expected to complete written work without talking), they are OK. Unfortunately, I have witnessed many teachers over the years using these two sounds repeatedly but having no effect. They have become automaticised – an EMPLOYEE strategy which has been overlearned (see Chapter 1) but is no longer effective nor contextually appropriate. Whilst the teacher is busy '*sshing*' and '*erming*' the noise level remains unchanged and worse, he or she is seldom aware either of doing it or that it is ineffective – it has become ritualised and beyond the teacher's conscious awareness. I have videotaped lessons and it is only when these teachers see the video that they realise what is happening. However, acknowledging the ineffectiveness of the behaviour is the easy part, breaking the habit is usually harder since it has become so automatic. Changing to a new strategy requires deliberate conscious effort and practice over a sustained period. Because it is so automatic, when we are under pressure we are more likely to use it than the new, improved version, initially at least. As pointed out in Chapter 1, identifying and overlearning a replacement strategy is sensible, economic and to be encouraged – the continued use of redundant or ineffective ritualised behaviour is not.

Ineffective rituals often begin when new or trainee teachers attempt to replicate the behaviour of a teacher they observed and considered competent. A teacher perhaps by merely coughing or folding her arms, tapping a pencil or similar behavioural cue, might well trigger instant silence, gain the attention of the class or bring a halt to a squabble over who has the next turn on a computer. Unfortunately, as seductive as copying the behaviour might be, a new teacher is in no way guaranteed the same response if they do so. Whilst modelling behaviour is a powerful learning technique, appreciation of the personal qualities of the teacher and the situation is needed. Merely copying one seemingly 'magical' aspect of behaviour, without reference to the personalised nature of the encounter, is rarely sufficient. In Chapter 3 I discussed how being socially competent requires the selection, use and integration of appropriate social skills (posture, gesture) with personal idiosyncratic features (physical appearance, age, sex). One person's effective use of '*ssh*' or arm folding is another's potential disaster. In addition to social skills, other factors that influence the authority of rituals include time, control of space, objects and setting, power and leadership.

How effective are your rules and routines?

To determine the effectiveness of your rules and routines requires monitoring and evaluation. You can do this using a form similar to that shown in Table 7.1. Self-evaluation in this way will give you some insight as to whether or not particular routines are working, need updating or replacing. If they are working, well, that's fine: as the old saying goes, 'if it ain't broke don't fix it!' Nevertheless, it is worth remembering my comments in Chapters 1 and 3 about the inherent difficulties of self-evaluation, and how its shortcomings can be overcome with the assistance of a trusted colleague or use of audiovisual equipment, to identify what automatic behaviours are accompanying your instructions, which may be undermining their effectiveness unbeknown to you.

Evaluate your routines

In Table 7.1 an example of the routines which might be used to introduce a lesson is given, and alongside each is a grid for evaluation of their effectiveness in achieving the required objective. This can be used to highlight problems and what is working well, and to identify priorities for change:

Table 7.1 Evaluating classroom routines

Routine	Behaviour	Works well	Usually works	Not working	Action
Getting the class ready for work	Children walk quietly into room		x		
	They go to their desks	x			
	I check students are sitting where I want them to be			x	Will produce a seating plan and direct students on arrival at class
	I ask them to get out the appropriate equipment	x			
	I get their attention		x		
Exchange greetings	I say hello	x			
	They respond		x		
Commencing the lesson	I introduce the topic	x			
	They are invited to ask questions	x			
	I reinforce what they have to do	x			

- Have you established what routines you need?
- How do they differ for different rooms or for different year groups/ classes?
- Do your routines reinforce the rules and generate the climate you want to promote in your classroom?
- Which of your routines work well?
- Why is that?
- Which of your routines are problematic?
- Can you identify a reason why that might be the case?

Rules and routines are not an alternative to good teaching, nor will they be successful if they are not well thought out, or if a teacher is not sufficiently assertive to enforce them. Along with other mechanisms discussed in this book, they do have the potential to ensure a smooth-running classroom, providing a key component of a teacher's classroom management plan. When carefully considered, planned and monitored, rules, routines and rituals are money in the bank for a teacher managing student behaviour

Suggested further reading

Chaplain, R. (1996) *Pupil Behaviour*, Cambridge: Pearson.

Part IV

Coping with emotional and behavioural difficulties

Managing students with emotional and behavioural difficulties

When the going gets tough

Of all the students in school, those with emotional and behavioural difficulties (EBD) are probably responsible for the highest levels of stress amongst teachers (Travers and Cooper 1996). Students with EBD are a heterogeneous group which includes those who internalise their behaviour and are withdrawn, as well as those who externalise their behaviour and act in confrontational ways. The latter tend to receive the most attention, both in terms of teacher time and in the literature, since they are very difficult, if not impossible to avoid.

In this chapter I will focus on the following areas:

*   what behavioural difficulties are
*   defining behavioural difficulties
*   assessment issues
*   intervention.

If not already aware, you should be in no doubt that the long-term effective management of these students is hard work. Whilst bringing about change can be very rewarding, it is often frustrating, unpredictable and draining both emotionally and physically. Various intervention techniques have been developed to support students with EBD based on different psychological perspectives on human behaviour.

Deciding which technique to use depends on:

*   your beliefs about the causes of behavioural difficulties
*   your school's ethos and behaviour policy
*   the nature of the behavioural difficulty causing concern
*   resources available to you.

I shall discuss three popular and contrasting approaches: behavioural, cognitive-behavioural and humanistic, all of which have proved effective in changing the behaviour of students with EBD.

- List what you consider to be the main causes of EBD.
- How many of the causes on your list are located within the child and how many the result of the environment (e.g. schooling, parenting, low socio-economic status)?
- What are the possible teaching implications of attributing causes to the child as opposed to the environment?

What are behavioural difficulties?

Emotional and behavioural difficulties are wide-ranging and are, at one level, classified as a special educational need. Teachers 'know' what they mean by the term, but their student with behavioural difficulties may be very different when with other teachers and it is seldom the case that students exhibit behavioural difficulties with all teachers. Defining EBD and related terms (such as maladjustment, disturbed, disturbing) has a long and often complicated history that is exacerbated by the relationship inferred between behavioural difficulties in school and antisocial behaviour in the wider community. Many of the terms used to describe these students are used in a way which implies a common unproblematic understanding when, in practice, this is not the case. Images of students with EBD can stir strong emotions amongst teachers and other professionals, negatively affecting the expectations and social behaviours of those involved, destabilising relationships. So what is it about EBD that creates such concern? Difficulties can be identified in terms of the challenges that they present: personal and interpersonal challenges and organisational and structural challenges.

Personal and interpersonal challenges

Teaching students with EBD can be complicated for the following reasons:

- They present a challenge to teachers' perceived competence – because some students with behavioural difficulties relentlessly test teachers' ability to manage them and wear them down in the process.
- Where the difficulty is held to be caused by something within the student, for example, she is psychologically dysfunctional or he is genetically different, then the prognosis is poor and will probably need intervention by specialists outside school.
- If the difficulty in school is seen as emerging from dysfunctional relationships in the family home, then there is little, if anything, that can be done by teachers to bring about change.
- Many students with behavioural difficulties are unpredictable and there are various reasons for this. One is that many lack social competence, which can make social encounters difficult for them to interpret and

stressful. As a result, the student uses inappropriate strategies in order to cope, including angry outbursts, sulking or destructive behaviour, making matters worse.

- Students who externalise their difficulties (acting up, aggression or violence) can be frightening, making it difficult to build positive teacher–student relationships.
- Many students with behavioural difficulties underperform academically, which can be frustrating when a teacher is convinced that the student has ability. Some deliberately destroy good pieces of work, just to gain attention, albeit negative.
- It is commonly held that behavioural difficulties in young children (tantrums, aggression, defiance) are predictive of bigger problems to come (e.g. criminality), something which is not necessarily the case. Chazan *et al.* (1994) also argued that aggressive behaviour in young children is often a precursor to developing assertiveness. Interpretations of other behaviours can be contradictory, for example, one student's 'behaviour difficulty' is another's 'high spirits'. Many predictions and explanations draw on information which is way beyond the behaviour itself. Social class, context, dress, sex and ethnicity are all factors which can affect the interpretation put on behaviour and subsequent beliefs about future outcomes for a student.

We have all borne witness to the screaming 4 year old in the supermarket, demanding a new toy or chocolate bar, and probably heard comments from 'spectators' such as 'what she needs is . . .' or 'if he's like that now he will be a right one when he gets older' or 'the poor woman having to put up with that' and so on.

Ask yourself to what extent context is important – is this type of behaviour more acceptable in the supermarket than in a restaurant? Is the age of the adult in charge of the child important? Would you think differently if the woman with the child appeared to be 17 or 33 years of age? What does this tell you about interpreting behaviour?

Supporting children with behavioural difficulties earlier, rather than later, is usually preferable since the behaviours will be less well established and therefore require less intrusive interventions. However, care must be taken not to overreact and misinterpret normal developmental behaviour as predictive of a future catastrophe.

Organisational and structural challenges

Not all concerns about students with behavioural difficulties are related to personal and interpersonal issues; there are equally issues which are inherent in the structure and organisation of education because:

- There is a wide range of differing definitions and understandings of what constitutes behavioural difficulties both within education and other services. These occur because of different beliefs about the causes of human behaviour and about how to intervene.
- Behavioural difficulties, unlike other learning difficulties, suffer from a lack of normative data. Measuring reading or maths competence is far 'easier' than trying to measure the degree to which someone's behaviour deviates from the 'norm'.
- Whilst there are a number of different interventions available (everything from anger management classes to the use of a therapeutic milieu), one endearing problem is how, and when, to measure outcomes. Unlike interventions focused on academic skills, where improved performance is readily measured using *largely* trusted tests, similar confidence is often not shared with social behaviour. Whereas $9 \times 9 = 81$ anywhere, improved behaviour in one class may not be repeated in others. Nor is there any guarantee that it will be sustained over time. The problem of reliably measuring behavioural outcomes has been discussed in detail elsewhere (Chaplain and Freeman 1994).
- Many students experiencing behavioural difficulties are involved with more than one human service agency, such as social services, medical professionals and the police. Whilst on the surface, multi-agency involvement may sound like a good idea, since it involves the mobilisation of more resources, the opposite can frequently be the case. Lack of a shared philosophy, professional ethics and practice can unwittingly work against the students' and their families' interests. Of all the professionals involved, it is usually teachers who have the most contact with the student, but that is no guarantee that they will be kept informed of what professionals outside education are doing because of regulations governing practice and access to information (Chaplain and Freeman 1994).

Defining behavioural difficulties

So what exactly are behavioural difficulties? The Department for Education (DfE 1994) offered an official catch-all definition in *Circular 9/94 – Pupils with Problems: The Education of Children with Emotional and Behavioural Difficulties*:

> Children with EBD are on a continuum. Their problems are clearer and greater than sporadic naughtiness or moodiness and yet not so great as to be classed as mental illness. . . . Emotional and behavioural difficulties range from social maladaptation to abnormal emotional stresses. They are persistent (if not necessarily permanent) and constitute learning difficulties.

(DfE 1994: 7)

When a student's behaviour is close to the 'mental illness' end of the continuum, identification can be made with some confidence. However, being specific about what point 'sporadic naughtiness' or 'moodiness' translate into EBD can be somewhat more difficult. Determining the cut-off point depends on a number of issues, which range from individual beliefs through whole school policy to legislation. The tolerance level of a school and its staff will influence the point at which outside support is invited to become involved or the statementing process started. This variation can result in the different treatment of students, exhibiting very similar behaviour, between schools only a short distance away from each other.

> EBD may show through withdrawn, depressive, aggressive or self-injurious tendencies. There may be one or several causes. Family environments or physical or sensory impairments may be associated.
>
> (DfE 1994: 4)

This part of the definition raises another issue, the extended complexity of the difficulties. Family environments may contribute to the difficulties, to a lesser or greater extent, but these are contexts over which teachers have no control. In some cases, where there are family difficulties, other agencies such as social services may well be involved, which may be helpful if they are prepared to support the school and provide an extended support system for the student.

> Whether the child is judged to have EBD will depend on the nature, frequency and persistence, severity, *abnormality* or cumulative effect of the behaviour compared with *normal* expectations of a child of the age concerned.
> There is no absolute definition.
>
> (DfE 1994: 4, added emphases)

References to normal and abnormal are problematic – the age-old question of what is 'normal' generally and what is normal in the particular context persists.

Being labelled as having 'abnormal' behavioural difficulties is unlikely to make you popular, 'But EBD is often engendered or worsened by the environment including schools' or teachers' responses' (ibid.: 4).

This final quote recognises the potential of teachers to influence behavioural difficulties in either direction – improvement or exacerbation.

Assessing behavioural difficulties

Assessment is the keystone to teaching; without it, teaching could not occur. Teachers are continually engaged in making assessments about the social and academic behaviour of their students. These assessments include formal and informal components, as well as making judgements about existing and predicted behaviour of students.

As I mentioned earlier, there are a number of instruments available designed to measure social behaviour and behaviour causing concern. Coping with students who have EBD can be a very emotional experience. Feeling anxious, angry, humiliated and even hopeless is not uncommon, particularly in circumstances where there are public challenges to professional competence. Such encounters can lead staff to seek solutions which may include using measures to confirm that the student is different and hence in need of special attention. Directing attention to the 'student's problem' takes the pressure away from the teacher. It can, however, result in a desperate search for *fix-it-quick* solutions, to ease the pressure and lower the temperature in a fraught situation. It may also result in the student being removed from school, which, whilst offering a short-term solution for staff, is not always the case for the student – or even for the staff in the long term. Unfortunately, some assessment tools serve to make matters worse, uncovering more complex problems and resorting to such strategies when under pressure can be counterproductive.

It is all too easy to become prematurely focused on which measure to use, just because one exists, rather than first determining how much information already exists. Will the results of a short inventory really tell you any more than what is already known and recorded? To avoid rushing into assessing a student I recommend first seeking answers to six questions:

- Why are we assessing this student?
- What behaviour do we need to assess?
- How should we assess this behaviour?
- Who should carry out the assessment?
- Where should the assessment be carried out?
- When should the assessment be carried out?

Why are we assessing this student?

Asking why a student needs additional assessment is an important first stage and should be considered together with who is seeking the data and for what purpose? Another issue is whether the assessment is to explore the student's difficulties in more depth or to confirm what you already know. The two questions can mean very different things – the former appearing more diagnostic – a search for the causes of a difficulty or to perhaps obtain baseline data, on which to base future observations. The second is often used to seek 'formal' evidence to support existing knowledge, insight or intuitive beliefs about an individual. Test results are often perceived as more official and scientific than other data collected by other means, even if they are not. However, it is salient to ask, where there are gaps in existing records and also what, if any additional or useful knowledge can be acquired through engaging in further data collection. In other words, do not get drawn into the process of collecting data just because it can be collected; ask why it is needed.

What behaviour do we need to assess?

Having determined why we need to assess, the next question is, what do we need to know and how might this influence how we collect the information? The identification of gaps or inconsistencies in existing information helps decide what additional information is required.

Select a student's file at random. Read through it. What do you think about the quality of information recorded? How much is factual information and how much is inference? Is your recording of student behaviour informative and in what way?

You should not set out to collect information which merely confirms what you already think. I discussed bias in teacher expectancy in Chapter 2, a process to be especially aware of when assessing young people with EBD. If data gathering is to be valid, it should be done in as detached a manner as possible, to minimise bias. Keeping an open mind about what is happening offers a greater chance to redefine the situation and change our perceptions of what is in fact happening, a process familiar to those involved in counselling.

So what might be asked and are all key players in agreement? There are a number of possibilities, some relating to the student, others to the situation; the following offer some possibilities:

- the student's qualities (disposition, learning or motivational style, social skills)
- interpersonal relationships (relationships with peers and with teachers in and out of class, ancillary staff)
- organisational factors (classroom environment, teaching styles, curriculum focus, learning resources, staffing)
- social behaviour, academic competence or both (levels of academic performance, social competence)
- information from outside the school (family, other agencies).

How should we assess this behaviour?

Having established there is a need to assess, and agreed what you want to assess, there follows the more commonly asked question, how do you set about doing so? Possibilities include the following:

- Has the student been assessed previously? When did it take place?
- What was discovered? What can we gain from the findings of previous attempts?
- Where is the shortfall in our knowledge of this student?
- If more information is needed, what is the most effective and relevant way to do so (bearing in mind costs, staff availability and training in assessment techniques)?
- *Scales and checklists:* there are a number of measures on the market, some are available to teachers (e.g. Elander and Rutter 1996), others require specialist knowledge or training. You could design your own but need to be aware of reliability and validity issues.
- *Open recording:* this approach includes a range of methods, ranging from recording everything that goes on to focusing on specific events (such as temper tantrums, refusal to work). You might, for example, employ audio or visual recording techniques or get a colleague to observe what is going on. Alternatively, a diary approach might be useful in recording behaviour from lesson to lesson, over a fixed period to map changes in different situations. This approach usually requires more time to collect data than closed scales, but the data is usually more detailed.

The two approaches differ principally in the type of data recorded. In scales and checklists, the lists used determine what behaviour is recorded, which may mean 'fitting' an observation to a particular category. In open recording, data are recorded in a more open-ended manner, which has implications for how they are analysed. With the checklist there is often a scoring key that provides a numeric score, which is usually linked to a category, or level of behaviour, and often comes with details of how the general population is distributed on the scale. Open data are more qualitative and interpretation is down to the individual or group carrying out the analysis.

Who should carry out the assessment?

Those directly involved with the student are usually a good source of data. However, it is not always wise for those working directly with a student to be involved in all aspects of the assessment, because the relationship may undermine objectivity or provoke ritualised responses.

People who know the student may help him or her feel comfortable but because they are part of the same system, the student may view them as having a vested interest, or feel that their knowledge of the situation might unduly influence the outcome. Alternatively, someone the student does not know might be perceived as being less likely to have a vested interest, but then the student may find a stranger more difficult to talk to. Who should interview or observe a student depends on what data are being collected, and under what circumstances. There is no simple answer.

Where should the assessment be carried out?

In order to understand behaviour, it should be contextualised. Shouting in a mathematics class may sound abhorrent, but less so in a drama production. The administration of scales or observation of behaviour should be carried out in the least inappropriate environment. If a student is exhibiting behavioural difficulties in a science laboratory, then recording his or her behaviour in a geography room may provide an interesting comparison, but is unlikely to offer much to the understanding of what happens in science. However, the science laboratory may be considered too dangerous.

There may be other safety concerns and observing some behavioural difficulties may be ethically unsound. For example, recording the behaviour of a student who is physically aggressive, in a busy classroom, can put other students and the teacher at risk. There are a number of things to consider in deciding where to assess a student. Has the behavioural difficulty occurred only in one subject or classroom or area of the school or has location not appeared to matter? *And in support of this*, have all staff, including ancillary staff, been asked for their observations? Does the behaviour change when you manipulate the environment, changing teacher, group or room for example?

If it is considered inappropriate or unsafe to observe particular behaviour in certain contexts, you could do so in a more controlled environment, perhaps with fewer students present. However, under such conditions, account needs to be taken of how this 'alien' environment might influence the student's behaviour when analysing the results. Similarly, taking account of the potential influence of an observer's presence, especially in areas students consider their own (e.g. the playground) is important.

When should the assessment be carried out?

If you are planning to carry out specific data collection, you will need to decide when is the most appropriate time to do this (during lessons, after school, in recreation periods) and over what period of time the behaviour should be observed. This decision depends on what you have identified to observe. How long or how often to observe particular behaviour, and how many observations are necessary to provide a representative sample need careful consideration. Staff time and training, the needs of other students and reliability are all important considerations in this respect.

Helping students overcome their behavioural difficulties

There are a large number of different approaches available designed to help students overcome EBD. Some are designed for used in special environments, whereas others can be used with success in the mainstream classroom. Whilst there are a variety of approaches, all are based on psychological theories of human behaviour and development. To apply them effectively requires some knowledge of these theories.

These methods focus on the students; however, the difficulties may be occurring because of environmental influences. It is assumed, therefore, that possible organisational and structural factors (curriculum, timetable, teaching styles) and interpersonal factors have first been explored and eliminated as major causes, before embarking on these more extreme courses of action with students. These intensive strategies should therefore be considered a last resort. However, it is also important to note that many of the approaches include techniques and ways of working, which are useful for behaviour management and teaching in general. For example, developing helping relationships (humanist approaches), the value of positive reinforcement (behavioural approaches) and developing problem-solving strategies (cognitive behavioural approaches) are all useful to everyday teaching. The explanations and examples offered are necessarily brief in this volume; however, additional references are provided and you are strongly recommended to read widely, before attempting to put these methods into action. Whilst the approaches are different in their understanding of human behaviour, they all share the same goal, to empower the student to control his or her own behaviour, but differ in the ways they achieve this aim. None of these or any other approaches is magical, each requires attention to detail for them to be effective.

I will discuss examples of:

• behavioural approaches
• cognitive behavioural approaches
• humanistic approaches.

The three approaches differ in terms of focus, in their premises about the causes of EBD and the role of the helper (teacher) in addressing those difficulties. Table 8.1 contrasts the main features of each approach.

Behavioural approaches

Behaviourists are (unsurprisingly) concerned with overt behaviour. Whilst thinking (or covert behaviours) are recognised (Skinner 1989) because they cannot be observed, they are seen as less relevant. The central principle of behaviourism is that all behaviour is learned and thus can be unlearned and replaced by alternative behaviour, by offering the right reward. Behavioural approaches represent a family of approaches not just one. Historically these approaches owe much to the work of Watson (1913), Pavlov (1927) and B.F. Skinner (1953). Behaviourists argue that we are born with a blank sheet, except for some instinctive behaviour. The fundamental difference between a child and an adult's knowledge is quantitative and relates to the

Table 8.1 Comparison of the key differences between three approaches to intervening with behavioural difficulties

Approach	Role of helper	Object	Assumptions	Method
Behavioural	Directive	To make student self-reinforcing	Behaviour is the result of stimulus–response chains	Behaviour analysis and modification
Cognitive-behavioural	Directive	To get student to self-regulate and think rationally	Behaviour results from internal causes – thinking and emotions	Cognitive restructuring
Humanistic	Non-directive	To empower student toward self-actualisation	Behaviour results from balance between self-regard and regard from others	Warm and genuine relationships

amount of learning each has been exposed to. We tend to learn (repeat) things for which we receive a reward.

Learning is explained in terms of the relationship between stimulus, response and reinforcement. If a child smiles (stimulus) and the mother responds by smiling back and giving him or her a hug (reward), the child is likely to repeat the behaviour. Praising (reward) a student for making an effort in class (stimulus) may motivate that student to work harder, in order to gain more praise. However, of equal importance is the degree to which a student considers the reward as appropriate. Being praised publicly may not be seen as rewarding to some students, who would rather just have a note in their exercise book. Some students need more tangible rewards, a prize or gift for their efforts. Others are self-reinforcing and, in effect, reward themselves for their successes. Behavioural difficulties result from students being inappropriately rewarded for their behaviour or rewarded for unacceptable behaviour as in the following case study.

From an early age, Tommy had never enjoyed maths nor had he been successful in the subject. When he attended maths lessons he often 'forgot' equipment, did not do his homework, disturbed other students and did not pay attention to Miss Warwick, his teacher. When his behaviour became unacceptable to Miss Warwick, she would send him to Mr Anderson, who was Head of Year and Head of Physical Education (PE), where he would stay until the end of the lesson. As Mr Anderson inevitably had things to do, he would give Tommy jobs such as tidying the PE store, which for Tommy was much better than maths. The misbehaving in maths and sending to the Head of Year became ritualised behaviour for all involved and proved hard to break.

There are four points to make about the case study. First, it is not acceptable for a student to be spending time off legitimate learning tasks (however important the PE cupboard might be). Second, what constituted an appropriate reinforcer in this case (PE cupboard) was preferable to having to spend time wrestling with maths, despite teachers informing Tommy of the importance of maths to his future. Third, the ritual provided a coping strategy for all three individuals, since each was operating away from the other. Fourth, the habitual nature of the process made it difficult for people to stand back and think out alternative ways of dealing with the problem.

Negative cycles can be self-reinforcing, destructive and students locked into them can feel helpless. Many rituals develop by chance and often none of the parties involved are aware of it. A class observing a negative cycle developing between a teacher and a student frequently collude to focus attention away from their own misbehaviour. Students regularly in trouble are blamed automatically; sometimes even in their absence.

Think of a class or an individual with whom you may have fallen into ritualised negative behaviour:

- How do you greet them?
- What sort of conversations do you have with them?
- Do you feel tense when you are with them?

Making a conscious effort to change what has become a negative ritual can have significant effects. Making a conscious effort to be more polite when you think the group is rude and ignorant, or using humour when you would routinely use a reprimand, can produce positive effects. Changing the ritual is, in effect, changing part of the chain between stimulus and reinforcer.

It is clear that applying behavioural approaches to the classroom places the teacher in control of behaviour change. Many behaviourists believe that this is the only way to maintain control over students' learning (Alberto and Troutman 1999). It is the teacher who manipulates the environment to bring about changes in the behaviour of the student (Wheldall and Merrett 1984). However, it is now more common for students to be consulted and involved in the process, making for a more even distribution of power and control. As a technique, it is most relevant for individual students but many of the processes involved are used for managing groups.

Phase I Behaviour analysis

The behavioural approach has two phases (see Figure 8.1). The first is behaviour analysis and the second is behaviour change – both are essential components and require users to apply them systematically. Behaviour analysis

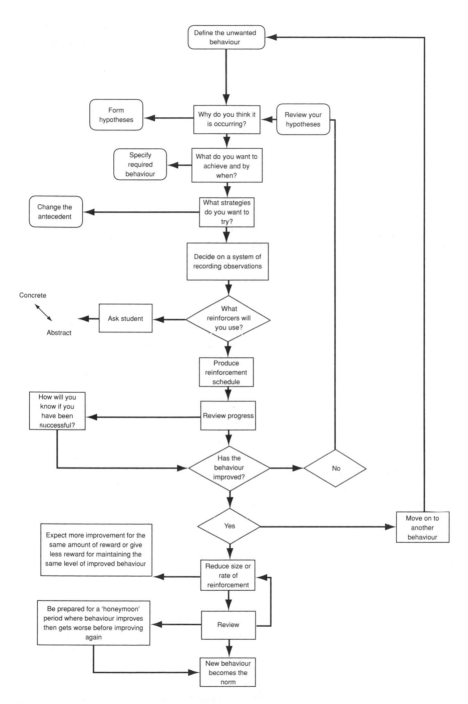

Figure 8.1 Behaviour change cycle

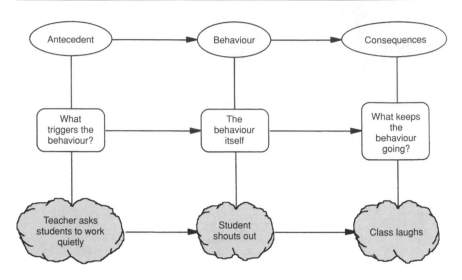

Figure 8.2 An A-B-C model of behaviour

is the systematic collection of data about three areas of activity: defining the behaviour giving concern, identifying what initiates this behaviour (antecedent) and establishing what keeps it going (reinforcer): see Figure 8.2.

The first step in the process is to define the behaviour. This usually requires observation over a period of time to establish a baseline of what is happening, who is involved, when it occurs and under what conditions. This information provides the *baseline* against which any changes in behaviour can be compared. Data regarding the frequency (number of times it occurs), rate (frequency within a fixed time period) or intensity (duration) of the behaviour are often summarised in the form of a graph (see Figure 8.3).

Many students with behavioural difficulties have a number of behaviours giving concern, the problem is deciding in what order to tackle them. Decisions about which behaviours to focus on first should be influenced by the degree to which it proves a threat to the health and welfare of the student, his or her peers and the staff. Highest priority should be given to behaviours which threaten the safety of students or staff (e.g. physical violence) whereas lower priority should be given to behaviours such as refusal to work (see Table 8.2 for other examples).

The examples of priorities are notional. Whilst physical violence is usually at the top of most people's list of most extreme behavioural difficulties, it may never occur in your school. It could be that what I have described as intermediate priority would be considered high priority in your school. In responding to these behaviours, where students pose a danger to themselves or others, immediate action is required, which may necessitate removal from school and the involvement of outside agencies.

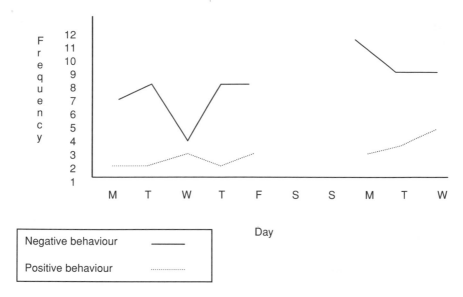

F r e q u e n c y

Day

Negative behaviour ——

Positive behaviour ·················

Figure 8.3 Frequency graph showing number of occurrences of negative and positive behaviours recorded by day of the week

Table 8.2 Relative seriousness of antisocial behaviours

Priority	Example
High	Physical assault on students or staff; self-injurious behaviour; dangerous or reckless behaviour (setting fires, being irresponsible in high-risk areas such as laboratories)
Intermediate	Verbal abuse, refusing to attend class; disrupting other classrooms and refusing to leave; refusing to leave school premises when told to do so; damaging property; foul language
Low	Refusing to work in class; being out of seat without permission; continually failing to bring equipment or homework; shouting out in class; refusing to obey class rules

Dealing with extreme behaviour, such as aggression, takes time. Do not expect quick results. In the early stages of intervention, when people are teaching a student how to cope in a more socially valued way, contingency arrangements to deal with outbursts (staff being available to restrain a student if necessary or a time out room) are required. Such arrangements need to reflect procedures agreed by all staff and usually other students and based on the principles contained in the school's behaviour policy, legislation and official guidance.

Using behavioural methods competently requires attention to detail and practice. Whilst high priority behaviour warrants a speedy response, it is perhaps not a good starting point for the inexperienced. As a first step, I would suggest concentrating initially on low priority behaviours until you feel sufficiently confident to move up a gear.

The second step, in behaviour analysis, is to determine what initiates the behaviour (antecedent), which requires observation of what occurs before the unwanted behaviour and which may be the trigger. This may be the start of a particular lesson or activity, the presence of certain staff or students, a time of day or day of the week and so on. However, it may also be that what you think is responsible is not so. In other words, you make hypotheses (intelligent guesses) about what might be the trigger – hypotheses which you will later test with your programme.

The third step is to identify what keeps the behaviour going – what is reinforcing it. The reinforcer may be the actions of the teacher (attention), other students (laughing) or factors outside the classroom (being sent to a time out room or other staff).

In the fourth step, you must decide what behaviour you wish to replace, that which is unwanted. It is not possible to merely extinguish unwanted behaviour, it needs to be replaced with a more desirable alternative. Attention needs to be directed to precisely what appropriate behaviour you want the student to be doing instead, the conditions under which they should be doing it and how much has to be completed successfully to be acceptable (Wolery *et al*. 1988). For instance, 'Getting on with their work' is insufficient whereas 'Successfully completing all questions in Exercise 4.3 in English For Today Level 4' is more appropriate.

There is a danger in becoming preoccupied with negative behaviour and ignoring any positive behaviour on the part of the student. Taking time to record and encourage positive behaviour is worthwhile at all stages and can contribute to constructive change.

Finally, you should set a timeframe against which you will measure the effectiveness of your behaviour programme.

Phase 2 Modifying behaviour

Having carried out the above analysis of the unwanted behaviour, its antecedents and consequences and what you wish to replace it with, you can move on to considering how to change it and how to make the changes permanent. The two main considerations are:

- how to teach what replacement behaviour is required
- how to reward the wanted behaviour.

First, there are a number of different methods to convey what behaviour is required. These include methods where the whole behaviour is modelled on another student's or the teacher's behaviour. Modelling is a form of vicarious reinforcement, whereby watching someone else behave in a particular way, and seeing them being rewarded for it, is likely to make the observer copy it. Where the behaviour is very complex, it may have to be broken down into elements, which are arranged sequentially and learned separately. The required behaviour is shaped through a series of small developmental stages, gradually increasing in size and complexity, until the final required behaviour is achieved. Contracts between a student and teachers involved in a programme are a useful means of clarifying precisely what is expected, over what time period and the rewards and sanctions to be used in order to minimise ambiguity and stress.

Second, rewarding or reinforcing behaviour appropriately leads to its repetition, so choosing the most appropriate reinforcer needs careful thought. Reinforcers vary widely and include concrete rewards (food, pens, magazines), access to alternative activities (sports or computer) or self-concept enhancing (praise, positive climate and feedback). Selecting the right reinforcer for a particular student depends upon your knowledge of what interests them, what is appropriate for the situation and school policy. The use of external rewards is to engage students in the required behaviour just long enough for it to become valued for its own sake – or self-rewarded. When a reward is given for *completing* a task it is said to be *positive reinforcement* (e.g. allowing someone to join a football team for having completed a task). In contrast, the *removal* of something unattractive to increase required behaviour is called *negative reinforcement* (e.g. giving students a night free of homework for having completed work in class).

Reinforcement must be dependent (contingent) on completing the required behaviour and not given if the behaviour is not completed. However, in the early days of reshaping the behaviour of a student, you may reward attempts at task completion, which are not quite up to scratch. Whilst *reinforcement* increases the likelihood of a behaviour being carried out, *punishment* reduces it. For example, failure to complete a task may be punished by detention or preventing a student from attending a football match. Often different forms of reinforcement and punishment are used to establish and strengthen wanted behaviour, whilst at the same time, decreasing unwanted behaviour.

How do you know if the programme was successful? The programme should be reviewed by recording the behaviour after a predetermined period of time and comparing it with the baseline data (see Figure 8.1).

If the programme has been successful, that is, the behaviour has improved, you should next plan to reduce the size or frequency of reward given (for example, shorter periods of time on the computer for having completed a written task) or expect more for the same level of reinforcement (for example, increasing the expected time spent on task or disturbing other students less frequently). Remember, the object of the exercise is for the student to become self-reinforcing as soon as possible and not to be giving out concrete awards (above what is given to all students) *ad infinitum*.

What if it does not work? Either your hypothesis was incorrect or you chose the wrong reinforcer. You should revisit your original hypotheses about why the behaviour is occurring or what is keeping it going – and ask, what alternative stimuli or reinforcers are there? Are your contingent reinforcers the right ones? Are you sure what you are offering is seen as valuable to the student?

In short, behavioural approaches offer a practical and usable solution for use in the classroom. They do, however, require you to follow the procedures carefully and pay attention to detail, systematically recording data and evaluation.

Suggested further reading

Alberto, P.A. and Troutman, A.C. (1999) *Applied Behavior Analysis for Teachers*, 5th edn, Upper Saddle River, NJ: Merrill.

Cognitive behavioural approaches

Cognitive behavioural approaches are on a continuum, with methods close to behaviourism at one end and cognitive approaches at the other. In many ways, they represent an extension of behavioural approaches, treating thoughts as behaviours which will respond to restructuring using behavioural principles.

Cognitivists argue that people construct mental models about their worlds, which they use to decide how, or how not to interact with others. They also recognise the important influence that emotions (e.g. anxiety, anger and self-esteem) can have on thinking. You will, no doubt, be able to recall occasions when you had to complain about something, or had to attend a difficult meeting. In preparation, you probably rehearsed, in your mind, what you would say and how others would respond, which may have been very different from what happened in reality. Emotions often intervene with carefully rehearsed plans to stand up for yourself. The student who does not trust teachers, because of previous experiences, expects future encounters to be similarly unpleasant. This can influence his or her thinking, motivation, emotions and behaviour, and result in defensive behaviour and putting up a barrier.

The above examples highlight the four processes involved in cognition:

*   The basic thinking processes: perception, memory, appraisal and reasoning.
*   Imagery: when you think about somebody you can usually generate a picture of the person in your head.
*   Inner speech: rehearsing what you plan to say to a shopkeeper in your head is an example of the third component, some of which takes place below the level of conscious awareness.

- The process of thinking about what you are thinking, or regulating your thoughts, referred to as metacognition, which allows us to review our effectiveness at coping or problem solving.

Cognitive-behaviourists argue that thinking, emotions and behaviour are interlinked and that our thoughts and feelings about events, even events that have not occurred, can have a profound influence upon our functioning, more so than the event itself. Whilst a behaviourist would manipulate the environment to effect change in a student's behaviour, cognitivists seek to change the way in which students perceive or interpret events which subsequently influences their behaviour.

As with all the approaches discussed in this chapter, cognitive behaviourism represents a family of methods that share a fundamental premise which is, that to change an individual's behaviour involves changing the way they think and feel about their worlds. Albert Ellis (1962) developed a procedure known as rational emotive therapy, which is based on a few simple principles:

- people are responsible for their own emotions and actions
- harmful emotions and dysfunctional behaviours are the product of irrational thinking
- people can learn more realistic views and, with practice, make them a part of their everyday behaviour
- people will experience a deeper acceptance of themselves and greater satisfaction in life if they develop a reality-based perspective.

Ellis emphasised the relationship between the degree to which we are 'rational' or 'irrational' in our thinking about an event, and the resultant positive or negative emotional experience. Where the thinking is irrational, not only will it trigger unwanted negative emotion, but also it is often overly dramatic – what he referred to as catastrophising. This reaction may lead to pathological anxiety. Irrational thinking for Ellis (1962) concerns beliefs that things 'must', 'ought' or 'should' be so, otherwise life will be awful. There are three categories of must statements, personal, interpersonal and situational, any or all of which can cause dysfunctional thinking. To contextualise 'must' statements I will use a teacher example:

- *Personal, or demands on yourself:* 'I must be able to control any class at any time; if I cannot, it is awful and means I am a worthless teacher.' This demand causes anxiety, depression, lack of assertiveness and feelings of incompetence.
- *Interpersonal, or demands on others:* 'I must be liked and respected by all of my students; if they don't, they are horrible and do not deserve to be taught by me.' This 'must' leads to resentment, hostility and disaffection.

- *Situational, or demands on situations:* life must be fair and hassle free, if not it would be awful – 'I must have all the necessary resources in order to teach properly and if I haven't it is unfair and dreadful.' This thinking is associated with hopelessness, procrastination and addictions.

If a teacher thinks that all his or her students must behave impeccably at all times, or that all must like him or her, then this is irrational. A rational thinker may wish or would prefer the class always to be well behaved, and while preferring to be liked by all the students all the time, is more flexible and tolerant of the likelihood of this not always being the case. Teachers who think that *all* members of their class 'must' like them, and 'must' behave well because that is fair and just, are likely to be disappointed.

The emphasis in cognitive behavioural approaches is getting students to self-regulate by restructuring their thinking, moving from irrational to more rational alternatives. To do this a helper challenges irrational thinking by asking:

- What evidence is there to support your (irrational) thoughts?
- What is another way of looking at the situation?
- So what if this terrible thing does happen?

There are various ways of responding to the answers to these questions, each tending to follow a sequence. When working with a student the sequence might be:

- information gathering from existing sources
- identifying areas of difficulty such as getting angry and lashing out when provoked
- getting the student and others close to him or her to list the student's strengths and weaknesses – emphasising her or his strengths and challenging self-deprecating thoughts such as 'I have always been useless at school so what's the point?'
- making clear those areas of the student's life where he or she can take control
- guiding the student toward rational explanations for his or her thinking and emotions
- setting a baseline and agreeing new specific targets and a time frame.

There are also several strategies that can be employed to help students identify, challenge and restructure the sources of their difficulties:

- challenging irrational beliefs by pinpointing their source and questioning established negative statements – 'I cannot control my anger'

- putting things into perspective by challenging attributions which result in self-blame for things over which they have no control – 'I only get things right when I am lucky'
- looking for evidence of negative self-talk and put-downs – 'I can't do it' or 'I'll never be able to cope'
- getting the student to challenge the evidence and validity of his or her negative beliefs – 'Teachers never give me a chance to put things right'.

To make these strategies work requires a positive relationship between helper and student made possible by having the 'core conditions' of warmth, genuineness, empathy and unconditional regard (described in more detail later). However, cognitive behavioural approaches are structured and the helper adopts a strongly directive approach, which distinguishes them from humanistic approaches. A teacher using this or behavioural approaches, which are similarly structured and directive, would need to feel comfortable with these requirements in order to achieve success.

Suggested further reading

Feindler, E. (1991) 'Cognitive strategies in anger control interventions for children and adolescents', in P.C. Kendall (ed.) *Child and Adolescent Therapy: Cognitive Behaviour Procedures*, London: Guilford Press.

Humanistic approaches

In contrast to behavioural and cognitive-behavioural approaches, humanistic approaches are anti-technique. Humanists consider the most effective means of overcoming behaviour difficulties lies in attention to attitudes and providing a psychological growth-promoting climate. The central tenet is that humans are basically good; rational in the things they do; capable of directing their own lives and destinies; and strive to achieve their self-perceived potential; and become all they might wish to be (self-actualisation). These strivings are best facilitated in a climate of positive self-regard and positive regard from others and it is maintaining a balance between these two objectives that ensures functionality. Some people sacrifice their own needs and self-regard in their efforts to be socially accepted, whereas other individuals are preoccupied with themselves to the exclusion and ignoring of others – both extremes lead to dysfunctional behaviour. Behavioural difficulties arise when movement towards self-actualisation is prevented or thwarted or an individual has a low self-esteem, as a result of not valuing him or herself or not feeling valued by others.

Carl Rogers (1951) developed a form of counselling known as the person-centred approach, which is the type of counselling most commonly encountered in schools. The role of the helper (teacher, for example) in this approach is to build a positive relationship with the client (student). This relationship is used to facilitate the student's understanding of himself or herself, to enable exploration of his or her difficulties and access parts of the self which are usually kept hidden away from others. To do this requires the teacher to possess four 'core' qualities:

* Have *unconditional positive regard* for the student with no strings attached, that is accepting the student as a worthwhile young person who is capable of changing the way he or she acts. This does not mean that you approve of any previous behaviour. This can be difficult to do with students who have exhibited extreme behaviour.
* Express a genuine *warmth* towards the student – again despite whatever he or she may have done. Warmth fosters the conditions for development without stifling him or her.
* Be comfortable in your dealings with the student to enjoy a *congruence* which permits you to be your real self when with him or her, rather than putting on an act.
* To work toward seeing the world how the student sees it (not how you see it) and what it means to them, more commonly known as *empathy*.

Unlike the two previously described approaches, humanistic approaches are non-directive and do not have structured procedures. The teacher acts as a mirror, helping the student to frame and reframe his or her life so as to cope more effectively with his or her difficulties. The relationship between teacher and student is characterised by warmth – behaviour likely to be criticised by some cognitive-behaviourists if it encourages dependency.

Central to humanistic approaches is the self-concept, which is a multi-faceted construct, influenced both by how individuals perceive themselves and how they believe others view them. The self has both global (overall) and domain-specific components (physical, social, academic for example) whose salience varies over time and context.

The self-concept is commonly described with reference to three components:

* *ideal self:* how you would like to be
* *self-image:* how you see yourself
* *self-esteem:* the difference between ideal self and self-image.

Hence, where the self-image is significantly short of the ideal self, then self-esteem is likely to be low. Where self-image matches the ideal self, it is likely to be high – you are what you are striving to be. Levels of self-esteem will vary from one aspect of the self to another, again dependent on the balance between self-image and ideal self measured against different components. Self-esteem, or the degree to which you like yourself, is fed by both your own thoughts about yourself plus feedback from others

Humanistic approaches have been popular with many teachers because of the emphasis on warmth and enhancing self-esteem. However, merely enhancing self-esteem alone, without reference to competence, is no guarantee that students will have a higher self-efficacy and feel capable of success. As Mruk (1999) highlighted, the problems connected with self-esteem education in the USA arose from an emphasis on raising perceived worthiness, without recognising its interdependence with competence. Understanding the complex nature of the self, along with the interrelatedness of self-esteem and perceived competence, is a prerequisite for the effective support of an individual's development. However, as Bandura (1997) points out, whilst certain specific categories of self-esteem may be more influential on global self-esteem than others, inability in one domain may have little, if any, effect on overall (global) self-esteem. Overall self-esteem is maintained despite fluctuations in the different aspects of the self (social self, academic self and so on).

Those working with students who experience behavioural difficulties who opt to use this approach should remember that it is the student who has control of the encounter and not them. Meetings should be dedicated to exploring what the students think about themselves and their environment, to the exclusion of all else. The importance of being non-directive cannot be overemphasised, since this approach rejects the desire for power and control over others. Thus, meetings should not be used as a front for telling the student what he or she should do, nor what the school wants. Whilst people do mix and match approaches (sometimes disastrously), if the intention is to direct a student to a particular course of action, then other approaches are more suitable.

Given the absence of technique, how might teachers use a humanistic approach effectively to deal with a student with behavioural difficulties? The primary consideration is the personal qualities of individual teachers, who should be aware of their attitudes, strengths, weaknesses, quirks, needs, feelings and predispositions. Humanists emphasise the power that individuals have to resolve their own difficulties inside themselves, so teachers planning to use this method should first attend to their own thinking – something which I have been emphasising throughout this text. Whilst self-analysis is often alien in circumstances where we feel we are coping admirably, reflection can provide some useful insights as to what we are taking as read, but which would benefit from attention. The ritualised behaviour referred to above is one example of this (pp170–1).

The cornerstone of this approach is building relationships, which in turn relies upon having a positive attitude about the process partnered with a high level of social competence. This includes the ability to read social cues, to be sensitive to motivational intent, and to interpret verbal and nonverbal signs in a student beyond what is actually being said. All are essential qualities and effective listening skills, which were discussed in more detail in Chapter 3 so are not developed here.

Suggested further reading

Gartrell, D. (1998) *A Guidance Approach to Discipline for the Encouraging Classroom*, 2nd edn, Albany, NY: Delmar.

Suggested further reading about emotional and behavioural difficulties

Chaplain, R. and Freeman, A. (1998) *Coping with Difficult Children: Emotional and Behavioural Difficulties*, Cambridge: Pearson.
Cooper, P. (1999) *Understanding and Supporting Children with Emotional and Behavioural Difficulties*, London: Jessica Kingsley.

Bibliography

Abelson, R.P. (1981) *Constraint, Construal, and Cognitive Science*, Proceedings of the Third Annual Cognitive Science Society Conference, Berkeley, CA, Hillsdale, NJ: Erlbaum.

Abrams, D. and Hogg, M.A. (1999) *Social Identity and Social Cognition*, Oxford: Blackwell.

Adler, R.B., Rosenfeld, L.B. and Towne, N. (1995) *Interplay: The Process of Interpersonal Communication*, Fort Worth, TX: Harcourt Brace.

Alberto, P.A. and Troutman, A.C. (1999) *Applied Behavior Analysis for Teachers*, 5th edn, Upper Saddle River, NJ: Merrill.

Anderson, N.H. (1981) *Foundations of Information Integration Theory*, New York: Academic Press.

Argyle, M. (1975) *Bodily Communication*, London: Methuen.

Argyle, M. (1981) *Social Skills and Health*, London: Methuen.

Asch, S.E. (1946) 'Forming impressions of personality', *Journal of Abnormal and Social Psychology*, 42: 1230–1240.

Babad, E., Inbar, J. and Rosenthal, R. (1982) 'Pygmalion, Galatea and the Golem: investigations of biased and unbiased teachers', *Journal of Educational Psychology*, 74: 459–474.

Bacharach, S.B., Bauer, S.C. and Conley, S. (1986) 'Organisational analysis of stress: the case of elementary and secondary schools', *Work and Occupations*, 13: 7–32.

Bandura, A. (1981) 'Self-referent thought: a developmental analysis of self-efficacy', in J. Flavell and L. Ross (eds) *Social Cognitive Development: Frontiers and Possible Futures*, Cambridge: Cambridge University Press.

Bandura, A. (1995) *Self-efficacy in Changing Societies*, New York: Cambridge University Press.

Bandura, A. (1997) *Self-Efficacy: The Exercise of Control*, New York: Freeman.

Barker, G.P. and Graham, S. (1987) 'Developmental study of praise and blame as attributional cues', *Journal of Educational Psychology*, 79(1): 62–66.

Bartlett, D. (1998) *Stress: Perspectives and Processes*, Buckingham: Open University Press.

Baxter, J.C., Winter, E.P. and Hammer, R.E. (1968) 'Gestural behavior during a brief interview as a function of cognitive variables', *Journal of Personality and Social Psychology*, 8: 303–307.

Becker, W.C., Englemann, S. and Thomas, D.R. (1975) *Classroom Management*, Henley-on-Thames: Science Research Associates.

Bossert, S., Dwyer, D., Rowan, B. and Lee, G. (1982) 'The instructional management role of the principal', *Educational Administration Quarterly*, 18: 34–63.

Bower, S.A. and Bower, G.H. (1976) *Asserting Your Self*, Reading, MA: Addison-Wesley.

Braun, L.M. (1989) 'Predicting adaptational outcomes from hassles and other measures', *Journal of Social Behaviour and Personality*, 4(4): 363–376.

Brewer, M.B. (1988) 'A dual process model of impression formation', in T.K. Srull and R.S. Wyer, Jr (eds) *Advances in Social Cognition*, vol. 1, Hillsdale, NJ: Erlbaum.

Brockner, J. (1988) *Self-esteem at Work: Research, Theory and Practice*, Lexington, MA: Lexington Books.

Bronfenbrenner, U. (1979) *The Ecology of Human Development: Experiments by Nature and Design*, Cambridge, MA: Harvard University Press.

Brookover, W.B., Beady, C., Flood, P., Schweitzer, J. and Wisenbaker, J. (1979) *Schools, Social Systems and Student Achievement: Schools Can Make a Difference*, New York: Praeger.

Bryk, A.S. and Driscoll, M.E. (1988) *An Empirical Investigation of the School as a Community*, Chicago: School of Education, University of Chicago.

Buck, R. (1988) *Human Motivation and Emotion*, 2nd edn, New York: Wiley.

Burchfield, S.R. (1985) *Stress: Psychological and Philosophical Interactions*, London: Hemisphere.

Calder, B.J. and Gruder, C.L. (1988) 'A network activation theory of attitudinal affect', unpublished manuscript, Kellogg School of Management, Northwestern University.

Canter, L. and Canter, M. (1976) *Assertive Discipline: A Take Charge Approach for Today's Educator*, Los Angeles: Lee Canter & Associates.

Canter, L. and Canter, M. (1992) *Assertive Discipline: Positive Behavior Management for Today's Classroom*, Santa Monica, CA: Lee Canter & Associates.

Cantor, N. and Mischel, W. (1979) 'Prototypes in person perception', in L. Berkowitz (ed.) *Advances in Experimental Social Psychology*, vol. 12, New York: Academic Press.

Carver, C.S. and Scheier, M.F. (1988) 'A control-process perspective on anxiety', *Anxiety Research*, 1: 17–22.

Carver, C.S. and Scheier, M.F. (2001) *On the Self-Regulation of Behavior*, Cambridge: Cambridge University Press.

Cassidy, T. (1999) *Stress, Cognition and Health*, London: Routledge.

Cattell, R.B. (1971) *The Scientific Analysis of Personality*, Harmondsworth: Penguin.

Cattell, R.B. and Eber, M.T. (1970) *Handbook for the 16PF Questionnaire*, Champaign, IL: Institute for Personality and Ability Testing (IPAT).

Chaplain, R. (1995a) 'Leading under pressure: headteacher stress and coping', in D. Hustler, T. Brighouse and J. Rudduck (eds) *Heeding Heads: Secondary Heads and Educational Commentators in Dialogue*, London: David Fulton.

Chaplain, R. (1995b) 'Stress and job satisfaction', *Educational Psychology*, 15: 473–89.

Chaplain, R. (1996a) 'Making a strategic withdrawal: disengagement and self-worth protection in male pupils', in J. Rudduck, R. Chaplain and G. Wallace (eds) *School Improvement: What Can Pupils Tell Us?*, London: David Fulton.

Chaplain, R. (1996b) 'Pupils under pressure: coping with stress at school', in J. Rudduck, R. Chaplain and G. Wallace (eds) *School Improvement: What Can Pupils Tell Us?*, London: David Fulton.

Chaplain, R. (1996c) *Pupil Behaviour*, Cambridge: Pearson.

Chaplain, R. (2000a) 'Beyond exam results? Differences in the social and psychological perceptions of young males and females at school', *Educational Studies*, 26(2): 177–190.

Chaplain, R. (2000b) 'Helping children to persevere and be well motivated', in D. Whitebread (ed.) *The Psychology of Teaching and Learning in the Primary School*, London: Routledge.

Chaplain, R. (2001) 'Stress and job satisfaction among primary headteachers: a question of balance?', *Educational Management and Administration*, 29(2) 197–215.

Chaplain, R. and Freeman, A. (1994) *Caring under Pressure*, London: David Fulton.

Chaplain, R. and Freeman, A. (1996) *Stress and Coping*, Cambridge: Pearson.

Chaplain, R. and Freeman, A. (1998) *Coping with Difficult Children: Emotional and Behavioural Difficulties*, Cambridge: Pearson.

Charles, C.M. (1999) *Building Classroom Discipline: From Models to Practice*, 6th edn, New York: Longman.

Chatman, H. (1989) 'Improving organizational research: a model of person–organization fit', *Academy of Management Review*, 14: 333–349.

Chazan, M., Laing, A.F. and Davies, D. (1994) *Emotional and Behavioural Difficulties in Middle Childhood*, London: Falmer Press.

Cinelli, L.A. and Ziegler, J. (1990) 'Cognitive appraisal of daily hassles in college students showing type A or type B behaviour patterns', *Psychological Reports*, 67: 83–88.

Coates, T.J. and Thoresen, C.E. (1976) 'Teacher anxiety: a review and recommendations', *Review of Educational Research*, 46(2): 159–184.

Cobb, S. (1976) 'Social support as a moderator of life stress', *Psychosomatic Medicine*, 38: 301–314.

Cohen, S. and Wills, T. (1985) 'Stress, social support and the buffering hypothesis', *Psychological Bulletin*, 98: 310–357.

Cole, G.A. (1996) *Management Theory and Practice*, London: Letts.

Cooper, H.M. (1979) 'Pygmalion grows up: a mode for teacher expectation, communication and performance influence', *Review of Educational Research*, 49: 389–410.

Cooper, H.M. and Good, T.L. (1983) *Pygmalion Grows Up: Studies in the Expectation Communication Process*, White Plains, NY: Longman.

Covington, M.V. (1992) *Making the Grade: A Self-worth Perspective on Motivation and School Reform*, Cambridge: Cambridge University Press.

Covington, M.V. (1998) *The Will to Learn: A Guide for Motivating Young People*, Cambridge: Cambridge University Press.

Cox, C. and Cooper, L. (1988) *High Flyers: An Anatomy of Managerial Success*, Oxford: Blackwell.

Craske, M.L. (1988) 'Learned helplessness, self-worth motivation and attribution retraining for primary school children', *British Journal of Educational Psychology*, 58: 152–164.

Creemers, B.P.M. and Reezigt, G.J. (1996) 'School level conditions affecting the effectiveness of instruction', *School Effectiveness and School Improvement*, 7(3): 197–228.

Dalgleish, T. (1995) 'Performance of the emotional Stroop task in groups of anxious expert, and control participants: a comparison of computer and card presentation formats', *Cognition and Emotion*, 9: 326–340.

Darley, J.M. and Fazio, R.H. (1980) 'Expectancy confirmation process arising in the social interaction sequence', *American Psychologist*, 35: 867–881.

Darley, J.M. and Gross, P.H. (1983) 'A hypothesis-confirming bias in labelling effects', *Journal of Personality and Social Psychology*, 44: 20–33.

DES (1989) *Discipline in Schools: Report of the Committee of Enquiry Chaired by Lord Elton*, 'The Elton Report', London: HMSO.

DfE (1994) *Circular 9/94 – Pupils with Problems: The Education of Children with Emotional and Behavioural Difficulties*, London: HMSO.

DfEE (1998) *Teachers Meeting the Challenge of Change*, Green Paper, London: The Stationery Office.

Duke, L.D. (1986) 'School discipline plans and the quest for order in American schools', in D.P. Tattum (ed.) *Management of Disruptive Pupil Behaviour in Schools*, New York: Wiley.

Dunham, J. and Varma, V. (eds) (1998) *Stress in Teachers: Past, Present and Future*, London: Whurr.

Dweck, C. (1985) 'Intrinsic motivation, perceived control and self-evaluation maintenance: an achievement goal analysis', in C. Ames and R. Ames (eds) *Research in Motivation in Education*, vol. 2, *The Classroom Milieu*, London: Academic Press.

Dweck, C. (1990) 'Self-theories and goals: their role in motivation, personality and development', in R. Dienstbier (ed.) *Nebraska Symposium on Motivation*, vol. 38, Lincoln, NE: University of Nebraska Press.

Ekman, P. and Friesen, W.V. (1975) *Unmasking the Face*, Englewood Cliffs, NJ: Prentice-Hall.

Ekman, P. and Friesen, W.V. (1978) *Facial Action Coding System: A Technique for the Measurement of Facial Movement*, Palo Alto, CA: Consulting Psychologists Press.

Ekman, P., Levenson, R.W. and Friesen, W.V. (1983) 'Autonomic nervous system activity distinguishes among emotions', *Science*, 221: 1208–1210.

Elander, J. and Rutter, M. (1996) 'An update of the status of the Rutter Parents' and Teachers' Scales', *Child Psychology and Psychiatry Review*, 1: 31–35.

Elashoff, J.D. and Snow, R.E. (eds) (1971) *Pygmalion Reconsidered*, Worthington, OH: Charles A. Jones.

Elliot, G.R. and Eisdorfer, C. (eds) (1982) *Stress and Human Health: Analysis and Implications of Research*, New York: Springer.

Ellis, A. (1962) *Reason and Emotion in Psychotherapy*, Secaucus, NJ: Lyle Stuart.

Ellis, A. and Dryden, W. (1987) *The Practice of Rational-emotive Therapy*, New York: Springer.

Ellis, H.C. and Ashbrook, P.K. (1989) 'The "state" mood and memory research: a selective view', in D. Kuiken (ed.) *Mood and Memory: Theory, Research and Applications*, special issue of *Journal of Social Behaviour and Personality*, 4: 1–21.

Ellis, H.C., Seibert, P.S. and Varner, L.J. (1995) 'Emotion and memory: effects of mood states on immediate and unexpected delayed recall', *Journal of Social Behaviour and Personality*, 10: 349–362.

Ellis, R.A.F. and Whittington, D. (1981) *A Guide to Social Skill Training*, London: Croom Helm.

Emmer, E.T., Evertson, C.M., Clements, B.S. and Worsham, M.E. (1994) *Classroom Management for Secondary Teachers*, 3rd edn, Englewood Cliffs, NJ: Prentice-Hall.

Eysenck, H. and Eysenck, M. (1985) *Personality and Individual Differences: A Natural Science Approach*, London: Plenum.

Feldman, S.S. (1959) *Mannerisms of Speech and Gestures in Everyday Life*, New York: International University Press.

Fiske, S.T. and Neuberg, S.L. (1990) 'A continuum of impression formation, from category-based to individuating processes: influences of information and motivation on attention and interpretation', in M.P. Zanna (ed.) *Advances in Experimental Social Psychology*, vol. 23, New York: Academic Press.

Fiske, S.T. and Taylor, S.E. (1991) *Social Cognition*, New York: McGraw-Hill.

Fosterling, F. and Rudolph, U. (1988) 'Situations, attributions and the evaluation of reactions', *Journal of Personality and Social Psychology*, 54: 225–232.

Freedman, N. and Hoffman, S.P. (1967) 'Kinetic behavior in altered clinical states: approach to objective analysis of motor behavior during clinical interviews', *Perceptual and Motor Skills*, 24: 527–539.

Freeman, A. (1987) 'Stress and coping: the idea of threshold', *Child and Educational Psychology*, 5(1): 37–40.

Fullan, M. (1988) 'Change processes in secondary schools: towards a more fundamental agenda', mimeo, University of Toronto.

Fuller, F.F. (1969) 'Concerns of teachers: a developmental conceptualisation', *American Educational Research Journal*, 6: 207–226.

Funk, S.C. (1992) 'Hardiness: a review of theory and research', *Health Psychology*, 11(5): 335–345.

Furnham, A. (1997) *The Psychology of Behaviour at Work: The Individual in the Organisation*, Hove, East Sussex: Psychology Press.

Gage, N.L. and Berliner, D.C. (1988) *Educational Psychology*, Boston, MA: Houghton Mifflin.

Galloway, D., Boswell, K., Panckhurst, F., Boswell, C. and Green, K. (1985) 'Sources of satisfaction and dissatisfaction for New Zealand primary school teachers', *Educational Research*, 27: 44–51.

Gibson, S. and Dembo, M.H. (1984) 'Teacher efficacy: a construct validation', *Journal of Educational Psychology*, 76: 569–582.

Glasser, W. (1969) *Schools without Failure*, New York: Harper & Row.

Glasser, W. (1998) *Choice Theory in the Classroom*, rev. edn, New York: Harper Perennial.

Goldstein, H. (1995) *Multilevel Statistical Models*, 2nd edn, London: Edward Arnold; New York: Halsted Press.

Good, T.L. and Brophy, J.E. (1991) *Looking in Classrooms*, New York: Harper & Row.

Graham, J.A. and Heywood, S. (1975) 'The effects of elimination of hand gestures and of verbal codability on speech performance', *European Journal of Social Psychology*, 5: 189–195.

Graham, S. and Barker, G.P. (1990) 'The down side of help: attributional-developmental analysis of helping behaviour as a low-ability cue', *Journal of Educational Psychology*, 82(1): 7–14.

Gray, H. and Freeman, A. (1988) *Teaching without Stress*, London: Paul Chapman.

Gray, J. (1990) 'The quality of schooling: frameworks for judgement', *British Journal of Educational Studies*, 38(3): 204–223.

Gray, J., Jesson, D. and Reynolds, D. (1996) 'The challenges of school improvement: preparing for the long haul', in J. Gray, D. Reynolds, C. Fitzgibbons and D. Jesson (eds) *Merging Traditions: The Future of Research on School Effectiveness and School Improvement*, London: Cassell.

Gray, J. and Wilcox, B. (1994) 'The challenge of turning round ineffective schools', paper presented to the ESRC seminar series on School Effectiveness and School Improvement, Newcastle University, October.

Greenspan, S. (1981) 'Defining childhood social competence: a proposed working model', in B. Keogh (ed.) *Advances in Special Education*, vol. 3, Greenwich, CT: JAI Press.

Halpin, A.W. and Croft, D.B. (1963) *The Organizational Climate of Schools*, Chicago: Midwest Administration Center, University of Chicago.

Hampson, P.J. and Morris, P.E. (1989) 'Imagery, consciousness and cognitive control: the BOSS model reviewed', in P.J. Hampson, D.F. Marks and J.T.E. Richardson (eds) *Imagery: Current Developments*, London: Routledge.

Hampson, P.J. and Morris, P.E. (1996) *Understanding Cognition*, London: Blackwell.

Handy, C. (1988) 'Cultural forces in schools', in R. Glatter, M. Preedy, C. Riches and M. Masterton (eds) *Understanding School Management*, Milton Keynes: Open University Press.

Hargreaves, D.H., Hestor, S. and Mellor, F. (1975) *Deviance in Classrooms*, London: Routledge & Kegan Paul.

Harris, M.J. and Rosenthal, R. (1986) 'Four factors in the mediation of teacher expectancy effects', in R.S. Feldman (ed.) *The Social Psychology of Education: Current Research and Theory*, New York: Cambridge University Press.

Harrison, R.P. (1976) 'The face in face-to-face interaction', in G.R. Miller (ed.) *Explorations in Interpersonal Communication*, London: Sage.

Health and Safety Executive (HSE) (2001) *Tackling Health Related Stress: A Manager's Guide to Improving and Maintaining Employee Health and Well Being*, London: HSE Books.

Heider, F. (1958) *The Psychology of Interpersonal Relations*, New York: Wiley.

Hess, E.H. (1972) 'Pupilometrics', in N.S. Greenfield and R.A. Sternback (eds) *Handbook of Psychophysiology*, New York: Holt, Rinehart & Winston.

Hewstone, M. (1994) *Causal Attribution: From Cognitive Processes to Collective Beliefs*, Oxford: Blackwell.

Hiebert, B. and Farber, I. (1984) 'Teacher stress: a literature review with a few surprises', *Canadian Journal of Education*, 9 (winter): 14–27.

Hills, H. and Norvell, N. (1991) 'An examination of hardiness and neuroticism as potential moderators of stress outcomes', *Behavioural Medicine*, 17(1): 31–38.

Hobart, C. and Frankel, J. (1994) *A Practical Guide to Child Observation*, Cheltenham: Stanley Thorne.

Holmes, T.H. and Rahe, R.H. (1967) 'The Social Readjustment Rating Scale', *Journal of Psychosomatic Research*, 11: 213–218.

Hopkins, D. (1996) 'Towards a theory for school improvement', in J. Gray, D. Reynolds and C. Fitz-Gibbon (eds) *Merging Traditions: The Future of Research on School Effectiveness and School Improvement*, London: Cassell.

Hoy, W.K. and Miskel, C.G. (1991) *Educational Administration: Theory, Research and Practice*, 4th edn, New York: McGraw-Hill.

Hoy, W.K., Tarter, C.S. and Kottkamp, R.P. (1991) *Open Schools: Healthy Schools*, London: Sage.

Hustler, D., Brighouse, T. and Rudduck, J. (eds) (1995) *Heeding Heads: Secondary Heads and Educational Commentators in Dialogue*, London: David Fulton.

International Labour Organisation (ILO) (1982) *Employment and Conditions of Work of Teachers*, Geneva: ILO.

Jakubowski, P. and Lange, A. (1978) *The Assertive Option: Your Rights and Responsibilities*, Champaign, IL: Research Press.

James, W. (1884) 'What is emotion?', *Mind*, 9: 188–205.

Jerusalem, M. (1993) 'Personal resources, environmental constraints, and adaptational processes: the predictive power of a theoretical stress mode', *Personality and Individual Differences*, 14: 15–24.

Johnstone, M. (1989) *Stress in Teaching: An Overview of Research*, Edinburgh: Scottish Council for Research in Education.

Jones, A. (1988) *Leadership for Tomorrow's Schools,* Oxford: Blackwell.

Jones, E.E. and Davis, K.E. (1965) 'From acts to dispositions: the attribution process in person perception', in L. Berkowitz (ed.) *Advances in Experimental Social Psychology*, vol. 2, New York: Academic Press.

Jones, V.F. and Jones, L.S. (1990) *Comprehensive Classroom Management*, 3rd edn, Needham, MA: Allyn & Bacon.

Jussim, L. (1986) 'Self-fulfilling prophecies: a theoretical and integrative review', *Psychological Review*, 93: 429–445.

Kahn, R. and Antonucci, T. (1980) 'Convoys over the life course: attachments, roles and social support', in P. Baltes and O. Brim (eds) *Lifespan Development and Behaviour*, vol. 3, New York: Academic Press.

Kalker, P. (1984) 'Teacher stress and burnout: causes and coping strategies', *Contemporary Education*, 56(1): 16–19.

Kanner, A.D. and Feldman, S.S. (1991) 'Control over uplifts and hassles and its relationship to adaptational outcomes', *Journal of Behavioural Medicine*, 14(2): 187–201.

Kaplan, R.M. and Swant, S.G. (1973) 'Reward characteristics in appraisal of achievement behaviour', *Research in Social Psychology*, 4: 11–17.

Katz, R.L. (1955) 'Skills of an effective administrator', *Harvard Business Review*, January–February: 33–42.

Katz, Y. (1998) 'Dealing with stress in the elementary school', in P. Lang, Y. Katz and I. Mene (eds) *Affective Education*, London: Cassell.

Kelley, H.H. (1967) 'Attribution theory in social psychology', in D. Levine (ed.) *Nebraska Symposium on Motivation*, vol. 15, Lincoln, NE: University of Nebraska Press.

Kihlstrom, J.F. (1999) 'Conscious and unconscious cognition', in R.J. Sternberg (ed.) *The Concept of Cognition*, Cambridge, MA: MIT Press.

Kun, A. (1977) 'Development of the magnitude-covariation and compensation schemata in ability and effort attributions of performance', *Child Development*, 48: 862–873.

Kyriacou, C. (1997) *Effective Teaching in Schools*, 2nd edn, Cheltenham: Stanley Thorne.

Kyriacou, C. (1998) 'Teacher stress: past and present', in J. Dunham and V. Varma (eds) *Stress in Teachers: Past, Present and Future*, London: Whurr.

Laird, J.D. (1974) 'Self-attribution of emotion: the effects of expressive behaviour on the quality of emotional experience', *Journal of Personality and Social Psychology*, 29: 475–486.

Lallgee, M., Lamb, R. and Abelson, R.P. (1992) 'The role of event prototypes in categorization and explanation', in W. Stroebe and M. Hewstone (eds) *European Review of Social Psychology*, vol. 3, Chichester: Wiley.

Laughlin, A. (1984) 'Teacher stress in an Australian setting: the role of biographical mediators', *Educational Studies*, 10(1): 7–22.

Lazarus, R.S. (1966) *Psychological Stress and the Coping Process*, New York: McGraw-Hill.

Lazarus, R.S. (1993) 'From psychological stress to the emotions: a history of changing outlooks', *Annual Review of Psychology*, 44: 1–21.

Lazarus, R.S. (1999) *Stress and Emotion: A New Synthesis*, London: Free Association.

Lazarus, R.S. and Folkman, S. (1984) *Stress, Appraisal, and Coping*, New York: Springer.

Lefcourt, H.M. (1976) *Locus of Control: Current Trends in Theory and Research*, Hillsdale, NJ: Erlbaum.

Lewin, K. (1951) *Field Theory in Social Science*, New York: Harper.

Lewin, K., Lippitt, R. and White, R.K. (1939) 'Patterns of aggressive behaviour in experimentally created social climates', *Journal of Social Psychology*, 10: 271–279.

Leyens, J.P., Yzerbyt, V. and Schdron, G. (1994) *Stereotypes and Social Cognition*, London: Sage.

Louis, K. and Miles, M. (1992) *Improving the Urban High School: What Works and Why*, London: Cassell.

McAteer-Early, T. (1992) 'The impact of career self-efficacy on the relationship between career development and health-related complaints', paper presented at the Academy of Management meeting, Las Vegas, August.

Maier, S.F., Laudenslager, M.L. and Ryan, S.M. (1985) 'Stressor controllability, immune function, and endogenous opiates', in F.R. Brush and J.B. Overmier (eds) *Affect, Conditioning, and Cognition: Essays on the Determinants of Behaviour*, Hillsdale, NJ: Erlbaum.

Major, B., Cozzarelli, C., Sciacchitano, A.M., Cooper, M.L., Testa, M. and Mueller, P.M. (1990) 'Perceived social support, self-efficacy, and adjustment to abortion', *Journal of Personality and Social Psychology*, 59: 452–463.

Mandel, H. and Marcus, S. (1995) *The Psychology of Underachievement: Differential Diagnosis and Differential Treatment*, New York: Wiley.

Martin, R.A. and Dobbin, J.P. (1988) 'Sense of humor, hassles and immunoglobulin A: evidence for a stress-moderating effect of humor', *International Journal of Psychiatry in Medicine*, 18(2): 9–105.

Maslow, A.H. (1970 [1954]) *Motivation and Personality*, 2nd edn, New York: Harper & Row.

Meichenbaum, D. (1977) *Cognitive-Behavior Modification*, New York: Plenum.

Millar, K.U., Tesser, A. and Millar, M.G. (1988) 'The effects of a threatening life event on behavior sequences and intrusive thought: a self-disruption explanation', *Cognitive Therapy Research*, 12: 441–458.

Morris, P.E. (1981) 'The cognitive psychology of self-reports', in C. Antaki (ed.) *The Psychology of Ordinary Explanations of Social Behaviour*, London and New York: Academic Press.

Morris, P.E. and Hampson, P.J. (1983) *Imagery and Consciousness*, London: Academic Press.

Mortimore, P., Sammons, P., Stoll, L., Lewis, D. and Ecob, R. (1988) *School Matters: The Junior Years*, Wells, Somerset: Open Books.

Mruk, C. (1999) *Self-esteem: Research Theory and Practice*, London: Free Association.

Murphy, J. (1992) 'School effectiveness and school restructuring: contributions to educational improvement', *School Effectiveness and School Improvement*, 3(2): 90–109.

Nadler, D. and Tushman, M. (1980) 'A model for diagnosing organisational behaviour', *Organisational Dynamics*, 9: 35–51.

National Union of Teachers (NUT) (2000) National Union of Teachers Conference 2000 Resolution on Teachers' Stress and Workplace Bullying, Harrogate, October.

Nias, J. (1986) 'Leadership styles and job-satisfaction in primary schools', in T. Bush, R. Glatter, J. Goodey and C. Riches (eds) *Approaches to School Management*, London: Harper & Row.

Nicholls, J.G. (1989) *The Competitive Ethos and Democratic Education*, London: Harvard University Press.

OFSTED (1996) *Exclusions from Secondary Schools 1995/96* (Nov. 1996), HMI no. 0-11-350087-4, London: The Stationery Office.

Open Systems Group (eds) (1981) *Systems Behaviour*, London: Harper & Row.

Ostrom, T.M. (1984) 'The sovereignty of social cognition', in R.S. Wyer, Jr, and T.K. Srull (eds) *Handbook of Social Cognition*, vol. 1, Hillsdale, NJ: Erlbaum.

Pavlov, I.P. (1927) *Conditioned Reflexes: An Investigation of the Psychological Activity of the Cerebral Cortex*, New York: Dover.

Payne, R.L. (1990) 'Method in our madness: a reply to Jackofsky and Slocum', *Journal of Organizational Behaviour*, 11: 77–80.

Pease, A. (1997) *Body Language: How to Read Others' Thoughts by their Gestures*, London: Sheldon Press.

Perry, R.P. and Struthers, C.W. (1994) 'Attributional retraining in the college classroom: some causes for optimism', paper presented at Sustainable Educational Effects: A Motivational Analysis, American Educational Research Association annual meeting, New Orleans, April.

Phelan, P., Locke-Davidson, A. and Cao, H.T. (1992) 'Speaking up: students' perspectives on school', *Phi Delta Kappa*, May: 695–704.

Phillips, S. (1983) *The Invisible Culture: Communication in Classroom and Community on the Warm Springs Indian Reservation*, New York: Longman.

Power, I. and Dalgleish, T. (1997) *Cognition and Emotion: From Order to Disorder*, Hove, East Sussex: Psychology Press.

Power, M.J. and Brewin, C.R. (1991) 'From Freud to cognitive science: a contemporary account of the unconscious', *British Journal of Clinical Psychology*, 30: 289–310.

Reynolds, D. (1976) 'The delinquent school', in M. Hammersley and P. Woods (eds) *The Process of Schooling*, London: Routledge & Kegan Paul.

Rist, R.G. (1970) 'Student social class and teacher expectation: the self-fulfilling prophecy in Ghetto Education', *Harvard Educational Review*, 40: 441–451.

Rogers, C. and Kutnick, P. (eds) (1992) *The Social Psychology of the Primary School*, London: Routledge.

Rogers, C.G. (1982) *A Social Psychology of Schooling: The Expectancy Effect*, London: Routledge & Kegan Paul.

Rogers, C.G. (1989) 'Early admission: early labelling', *British Journal of Educational Psychology* Special Monograph 4.

Rogers, C.R. (1951) *Client-centred Therapy*, London: Constable.

Rosenthal, R. and Jacobson, L. (1968) *Pygmalion in the Classroom: Teacher Expectation and Pupils' Intellectual Development*, New York: Holt, Rinehart & Winston.

Rosenthal, T.L. and Rosenthal, R.H. (1985) 'Clinical stress management', in D. Barlow (ed.) *Clinical Handbook of Psychological Disorders*, New York: Guilford Press.

Rudduck, J., Chaplain, R. and Wallace, G. (1996a) 'Reviewing the conditions of learning in school', in J. Rudduck, R. Chaplain and G. Wallace (eds) *School Improvement: What Can Pupils Tell Us?*, London: David Fulton.

Rudduck, J., Chaplain, R. and Wallace, G. (1996b) 'Pupil voices and school improvement', in J. Rudduck, R. Chaplain and G. Wallace (eds) *School Improvement: What Can pupils tell us?*, London: David Fulton.

Rutter, M., Mortimer, P., Ouston, J. and Maugham, B. (1979) *Fifteen Thousand Hours: Secondary Schools and their Effects on Children*, Wells, Somerset: Open Books.

Sammons, P. (1999) *School Effectiveness: Coming of Age in the Twenty-First Century*, Lisse: Swets & Zeitlinger.

Sammons, P., Thomas, S., Mortimore, P., Owen, C. and Pennell, H. (1994) *Assessing School Effectiveness: Developing Measures to Put School Performance in Context*, London: Office for Standards in Education (OFSTED).

Sarason, B.R., Sarason, I.G. and Pierce, G.R. (1990) *Social Support: An Interactional View*, New York: Wiley.

Savage, T. (1991) *Discipline for Self-control*, Englewood Cliffs, NJ: Prentice-Hall.

Schaubroeck, J. and Ganster, D.C. (1991) 'Associations among stress-related individual differences', in C.L. Cooper and R. Payne (eds) *Personality and Stress: Individual Differences in the Stress Process*, Chichester: Wiley.

Schein, E. (1978) *Career Dynamics: Matching Individual and Organizational Needs*, Reading, MA: Addison-Wesley.

Schimmel, D. (1976) 'Assertive behavior scales: global or subscale measures', unpublished paper.

Schmuck, R.A. and Schmuck, P.A. (1992) *Group Processes in the Classroom*, Dubuque, IA: William C. Brown.

Schroeder, D.H. and Costa, P.T. (1984) 'Influence of life event stress on physical illness: substantive effects or methodological flaws?', *Journal of Personality and Social Psychology*, 46(4): 853–863.

Schunk, D.H. (1987) 'Self-efficacy and motivated learning', in N.J. Hastings and J.J. Schwieso (eds) *New Directions in Educational Psychology 2: Behaviour and Motivation in the Classroom*, London: Falmer Press.

Schwarzer, R. (1992) 'Self-efficacy in the adoption and maintenance of health behaviours: theoretical approaches and a new model', in R. Schwarzer (ed.) *Self-efficacy: Thought Control of Action*, Washington, DC: Hemisphere.

Selye, H. (1956) *The Stress of Life*, New York: McGraw-Hill.

Skinner, B.F. (1953) *Science and Human Behavior*, New York: Macmillan.

Skinner, B.F. (1989) *Recent Issues in the Analysis of Behavior*, Columbus, OH: Merrill.

Smilansky, J. (1984) 'External and internal correlates of teachers' satisfaction and willingness to report stress', *British Journal of Educational Psychology*, 54(1): 84–92.

Smiley, P.A. and Dweck, C.S. (1994) 'Individual differences in achievement goals among young children', *Child Development*, 65: 1723–1743.

Snyder, M. (1992) 'Motivational foundations of behavioral confirmation', in M.P. Zanna (ed.) *Advances in Experimental Social Psychology*, vol. 25, San Diego, CA: Academic Press.

Snyder, M. and Cantor, N. (1979) 'Testing hypotheses about other people: the use of historical knowledge', *Journal of Experimental Social Psychology*, 15: 330–342.

Spence, S. (1979) *Social Skills Training with Children and Adolescents*, Windsor: National Foundation for Educational Research.

Steil, L.K. (1991) 'Listening training: the key to success in today's organizations', in D. Borisoff and M. Purdy (eds) *Listening in Everyday Life*, Lanham, MD: University Press of America.

Steptoe, A. and Appels, A. (eds) (1989) *Stress, Personal Control and Health*, Chichester: Wiley.

Stern, G.G. (1970) *People in Context*, New York: Wiley.

Stipek, D., Recchia, S. and McClintic, S. (1992) 'Self-evaluation in young children', *Monographs of the Society for Research in Child Development*, 57(1), serial no. 226.

Stoll, L. (1996) 'Linking school effectiveness and school improvement: issues and possibilities', in J. Gray, D. Reynolds and C. Fitz-Gibbon (eds) *Merging Traditions: The Future of Research on School Effectiveness and School Improvement*, London: Cassell.

Sutherland, V.J. and Cooper, C.L. (1991) *Understanding Stress: A Psychological Perspective for Health Professionals*, London: Chapman and Hall.

Swann, W.B., Jr (1990) 'To be adored or to be known? The interplay of self enhancement and self-verification', in E.T. Higgins and R.M. Sorrentino (eds) *Handbook of Motivation and Cognition: Foundations of Social Behavior*, vol. 2, New York: Guilford Press.

Swann, W.B., Jr (1996) *Self-traps: The Elusive Quest for Higher Self-esteem*, New York: Freeman.

Swann, W.B., Jr, Pelham, B.W. and Krull, D.S. (1989) 'Agreeable fancy or disagreeable truth? Reconciling self-enhancement and self-verification', *Journal of Personality and Social Psychology*, 57: 782–791.

Syrotuik, J. and D'Arcy, C. (1984) 'Social support and mental health: direct, protective and compensatory effects', *Social Science and Medicine*, 18: 229–236.

Taguiri, R. (1968) 'The concept of organizational climate', in G. Taguiri and G. Litwin (eds) *Organizational Climate: Explorations of a Concept*, Cambridge, MA: Harvard University Press.

Tajfel, H. and Turner, J.C. (1986) 'The social identity theory of intergroup behaviour', in S. Worchel and W.G. Austin (eds) *Psychology of Intergroup Relations*, Chicago: Nelson Hall.

Tannenbaum, R. and Schmidt, W.H. (1958) 'How to choose a leadership pattern', *Harvard Business Review*, March–April: 95–101.

Taylor, S.E. and Cocker, J. (1981) 'Schematic bases of social information processing', in E.T. Higgins C.P. Herman and M.P. Zanna (eds) *Social Cognition: The Ontario Symposium*, vol. 1, Hillsdale, NJ: Erlbaum.

Thompson, T. (1994) 'Self-worth protection: review and implications for the classroom', *Educational Review*, 46(3): 259–274.

Torrington, D. and Weightman, J. (1989) *The Reality of School Management*, Oxford: Blackwell.

Travers, C.J. and Cooper, C.L. (1996) *Teachers under Pressure*, London: Routledge.

Van Werkhoven, W. (1990) 'The attunement strategy and spelling problems', in A. Van der Ley and K.J. Kappers (eds) *Dyslexie '90*, Lisse: Swets & Zeitlinger.

Vine, I. (1973) 'The role of facial-visual signalling in early social development', in M. von Cranach and I. Vine (eds) *Social Communication and Movement*, New York: Academic Press.

Vygotsky, L.S. (1987) *Thought and Language*, Cambridge, MA: MIT Press.

Wallace, G. (1996) 'Relating to teachers', in J. Rudduck, R. Chaplain and G. Wallace (eds) *School Improvement: What Can Pupils Tell Us?*, London: David Fulton.

Walsh, B. (1998) 'Workplace stress: some findings and strategies', in J. Dunham and V. Varma (eds) *Stress in Teachers: Past, Present and Future*, London: Whurr.

Watson, J.B. (1913) 'Psychology from the standpoint of a behaviourist', *Psychological Review*, 20: 158–177.

Wayson, W.W., deVoss, C.G., Kaeser, S.C., Lasley, T. and Pinnel, G.S. (1982) *Handbook for Developing Schools with Good Discipline*, Bloomington, IN: Phi Delta Kappa.

Wehlage, G.G., Rutter, R.A., Gregory, A., Smith, N.L. and Fernandez, R.R. (1989) *Reducing the Risk: Schools as Communities of Support*, Lewes: Falmer Press.

Weick, K.E. (1976) 'Educational organisations as loosely coupled systems', *Administrative Science Quarterly*, 21: 1–19.

Weiner, B. (1992) *Human Motivation*, London: Sage.

Wheldall, K. and Lam, Y.Y. (1987) 'Rows versus tables II: the effects of classroom seating arrangements on classroom disruption rate, on task behaviour and teacher behaviour in three special school classes', *Educational Psychology*, 7(4): 303–312.

Wheldall, K. and Merrett, F. (1984) *Positive Teaching: The Behavioural Approach*, London: Allen and Unwin.

Wilkinson, C. and Cave, E. (1987) *Teaching and Managing: Inseparable Activities in Schools*, New York: Croom Helm.

Wilson, T.D. and Linville, P.W. (1985) 'Improving the performance of college freshmen with attributional techniques', *Journal of Personality and Social Psychology*, 49: 287–293.

Wolery, M., Bailey, D.B. and Sugai, G.M. (1988) *Effective Teaching: Principles and Procedures of Applied Behavior Analysis with Exceptional Students*, Boston, MA: Allyn & Bacon.

Zaleznik, A. (1977) 'Managers and leaders: are they different?', *Harvard Business Review*, May–June: 47–60.

Zebrowitz, L.A. (1990) *Social Perception*, Buckingham: Open University Press.

Zuckerman, M., DePaulo, B.M. and Rosenthal, R. (1981) 'Verbal and non-verbal communication of deception', in L. Berkowitz (ed.) *Advances in Experimental Social Psychology*, vol. 14, New York: Academic Press.

Author index

Abelson, R.P. 39, 60
Abrams, D. 38
Adler, R.B. 78
Ainscow, M. 116
Alberto, P.A. 171, 177
Anderson, N.H. 45
Antonucci, T. 11
Appels, A. 12
Argyle, M. 56, 59, 64–68
Asch, S.E. 45
Ashbrook, P.K. 141

Babad, E. 38
Bacharach, S.B. 11
Bailey, D.B. 175
Bandura, A. 25–27, 182
Barker, G.P. 136
Bartlett, D. 9
Bauer, S.C. 11
Baxter, J.C. 70
Beady, C. 88
Becker, W.C. 150
Berliner, D.C. 52
Bossert, S. 104
Boswell, C. 11
Boswell, K. 11
Bower, G.H. 73
Bower, S.A. 73
Braun, L.M. 12
Brewer, M.B. 39, 45
Brewin, C.R. 15
Brighouse, T. 107
Brockner, J. 12
Bronfnebrenner, U. 25
Brookover, W.B. 90
Brophy, J.E. 35
Bryk, A.S. 92
Buck, R. 64
Burchfield, S.R. 12

Calder, B.J. 15
Canter, L. 72, 148
Canter, M. 72, 148
Cantor, N. 42
Carver, C.S. 26
Cassidy, T. 24
Caswell, C. 78
Cattell, R. 98
Cave, E. 92
Chaplain, R. 12, 14, 16, 27, 32, 86 87,
    101, 106–108, 112, 131, 136, 146,
    156, 163, 183
Charles, C.M. 139
Chatman, H. 98
Chazan, M. 162
Cinelli, L.A. 12
Clements, B.S. 152
Coates, T.J. 12
Cobb, S. 11
Cocker, J. 40
Cohen, S. 24
Cole, G.A. 94
Conley, S. 11
Cooper, C.L. 9, 14, 56, 160
Cooper, H.M. 34
Cooper, L. 110
Cooper, M.L. 24
Cooper, P. 183
Costa, P.T. 13
Covington, M.V. 135, 138
Cox, C. 110
Cozzarelli, C. 24
Craske, M.L. 137
Creemers, B.P.M. 89
Croft, D.B. 90

D'Arcy, C. 12
Dalgleish, T. 15, 141
Darley, J.M. 38, 52

Davies, D. 162
Davis, K.E. 48
Dembo, M.H. 27
DePaulo, B.M. 66
deVoss, C.G. 86
Dobbin, J.P. 12
Driscoll, M.E. 92
Dryden, W. 58
Duke, L.D. 97
Dweck, C. 133, 137
Dwyer, D. 104

Eisdorfer, C. 10
Ekman, P. 64, 65
Elander, J. 167
Elashoff, J.D. 35
Elliot, G.R. 10
Ellis, A. 58, 178
Ellis, H.C. 141
Ellis, R.A.F. 75, 78
Emmer, E.T. 152
Englemann, S. 150
Evertson, C.M. 152
Eysenck, H. 98
Eysenck, M. 98

Farber, I. 11
Fazio, R.H. 38
Feindler, E. 180
Feldman, S.S. 13
Fernandez, R.R. 120
Fiske, S.T. 42, 45, 48
Flood, P. 88
Folkman, S. 30
Fosterling, F. 48
Frankel, J. 129
Freedman, N. 69
Freeman, A. 12, 14, 16, 18, 27, 32, 107, 131, 163, 183
Friesen, W.V. 64, 65
Fullan, M. 87
Fuller, F.F. 12
Funk, S.C. 12
Furnham, A. 88, 92, 98

Gage, N.L. 52
Galloway, D. 11
Ganster, D.C. 12
Gartrell, D. 183
Gibson, S. 27
Glasser, W. 149
Goldstein, H. 86
Good, T.L. 35

Graham, J.A. 70
Graham, S. 136
Gray, H. 107
Gray, J. 85, 86, 102
Green, K. 11
Greenspan, S. 55
Gregory, A. 120
Gross, P.H. 52
Gruder, C.L. 15

Halpin, A.W. 90
Hammer, R.E. 70
Hampson, P.J. 18
Handy, C. 97
Hargreaves, D.H. 148
Harris, M.J. 35, 38, 52
Harrison, R.P. 64
Heider, F. 45, 47, 49
Hess, E.H. 59
Hestor, S. 148
Hewstone, M. 15, 39
Heywood, S. 70
Hiebert, B. 11
Hills, H. 12
Hobart, C. 129
Hoffman, S.P. 69
Hogg, M.A. 88
Holmes, T.H. 13
Hopkins, D. 86, 117
Hoy, K.W. 89
Hoy, W.K. 88
Hustler, D. 107

Inbar, J. 38

Jacobson, L. 34
James, W. 64
Jerusalem, M. 12
Jesson, D. 86
Johnstone, M. 11
Jones, A. 88, 106, 107
Jones, E.E. 48
Jones, L.S. 152
Jones, V.F. 152
Jussim, L. 38

Kaeser, S.C. 86
Kahn, R. 11
Kalker, P. 11
Kanner, A.D. 13
Kaplan, R.M. 137
Katz, R.L. 109
Kelley, H.H. 48, 50

Kihlstrom, J.F. 15
Kottkamp, R.P. 89
Krull, D.S. 58
Kun, A. 135
Kutnick, P. 126
Kyriacou, C. 9, 11, 14

Laing, A.F. 162
Laird, J.D. 64
Lallgee, M. 60
Lam, Y.Y. 126
Lamb, R. 60
Lasley, T. 86
Laudenslager, M.L. 26
Laughlin, A. 12
Lazarus, R.S. 14, 30
Lee, G. 104
Levenson, R.W. 64
Lewin, K. 34, 109
Leyens, J.P. 39
Linville, P.W. 137
Lippitt, R. 109
Louis, K. 85

Maier, S.F. 26
Major, B. 24
Mandel, H. 138
Marcus, S. 138
Martin, R.A. 12
Maslow, A.H. 141, 144, 148, 153
McAteer-Early, T. 26
McClintic, S. 148
Meichenbaum, D. 58
Mellor, F. 148
Merrett, F. 171
Miles, M. 85
Millar, K.U. 15
Millar, M.G. 15
Mischel, W. 42
Miskel, C.G. 88
Morris, P.E. 18
Mortimore, P. 85, 86, 87, 88
Mruk, C. 182
Mueller, P.M. 24
Murphy, J. 89

Nadler, D. 89
Neil, S. 78
Neuberg, S.L. 45
Nias, J. 107
Nicholls, J.G. 137
Norvell, N. 12
NUT 10

Open Systems Group (ed.) 89
Ostrom, T.M. 39
Owen, C. 86

Panckhurst, F. 11
Pavlov, I.P. 169
Payne, R.L. 90
Pease, A. 65, 66, 67
Pelham, B.W. 58
Pennell, H. 86
Perry, R.P. 137
Phillips, S. 125
Pierce, G.R. 11, 110
Pinnel, G.S. 86
Power, I. 15
Power, M.J. 15

Rahe, R.H. 13
Recchia, S. 148
Reezigt, G.J. 89
Reynolds, D. 85, 86
Rist, R.G. 35
Rogers, C.G. 36, 38, 54, 126
Rogers, C.R. 141, 181
Rosenfeld, L.B. 78
Rosenthal, T.L. 27
Rosenthal, R. 34, 38, 52, 66
Rosenthal, R.H. 27
Rowan, B. 104
Rudduck, J. 87, 107, 146
Rudolph, U. 48
Rutter, M. 85, 88, 167
Rutter, R.A. 120
Ryan, S.M. 26

Sammons, P. 86, 87, 101, 104
Sarason, B.R. 11, 110
Sarason, I.G. 11, 110
Savage, T. 151
Schaubroeck, J. 12
Schdron, G. 39
Scheier, M.F. 26
Schein, E. 100
Schimmel, D. 74
Schmidt, W.H. 110
Schmuck, P.A. 36
Schmuck, R.A. 36
Schroeder, D.H. 13
Schunk, D.H. 137
Schwarzer, R. 12
Schweitzer, J. 88
Sciacchitano, A.M. 24
Seibert, P.S. 141

Selye, H. 13
Skinner, B.F. 169
Smilansky, J. 12
Smiley, P.A. 137
Smith, N.L. 120
Snow, R.E. 35
Snyder, M. 52
Southworth, G. 117
Spence, S. 68
Steil, L.K. 70
Steptoe, A. 12
Stern, G.G. 88, 90
Stipek, D. 148
Stoll, L. 86
Struthers, C.W. 137
Sugai, G.M. 175
Sutherland, V.J. 14
Swann, W.B. 58
Swant, S.G. 137
Syrotuik, J. 12

Taguiri, R. 88
Tajfel, H. 100
Tannenbaum, R. 110
Tarter, C.S. 89
Taylor, S.E. 40, 42, 48
Tesser, A. 15
Testa, M. 25
Thomas, D.R. 150
Thomas, S. 86
Thompson, T. 136, 137
Thoresen, C.E. 12
Torrington, D. 11
Towne, N. 78
Trautmann, A.C. 171, 177

Travers, C.J. 9, 56, 160
Turner, J.C. 100
Tushman, M. 89

Van Werkhoven, W. 69
Varner, L.J. 141
Vine, I. 64
Vygotsky, L.S. 127

Wallace, G. 87, 114, 115, 146
Watson, J.B. 169
Wayson, W.W. 86
Wehlage, G.G. 120
Weick, K.E. 89
Weightman, J. 11
Weiner, B. 131, 132, 133, 134
West, M. 117
Wheldall, K. 126, 171
White, R.K. 109
Whittington, D. 75, 78
Wilcox, B. 85
Wilkinson, C. 92
Wills, T. 24
Wilson, T.D. 137
Winter, E.P. 70
Wisenbaker, J. 88
Wolery, M. 175
Worsham, M.E. 152

Yzerbyt, V. 39

Zaleznik, A. 109
Zebrowitz, L.A. 39, 44
Zeigler, J. 12
Zuckerman, M. 66

Subject index

Achievement motivation 132
Adaptive motivational styles 131, 132, 133
Affiliation needs 144
Aggressive behaviour: as a coping style 30, 62, 70, 72, 74–75, 87, 97; in pupils 59, 162, 164, 168
Anger 15, 66, 72–73, 87, 163, 177–180
Anticipatory: strategies 4, 97; coping 30
Anxiety: 10, 12, 14, 26, 56, 69, 77, 97, 177–178; in pupils 141
Anxiousness 10, 56, 63, 67, 73, 77, 112, 141–143
Appraisal: cognitive 4, 14–15, 22–24, 26, 77, 177; teacher 110
Assault on self 15, 48
Assertive behaviour 72–75, 139, 156
Assertiveness 12, 25, 56, 58, 63, 70, 72, 75, 162, 178
Assessment: issues 160; of behaviour 40, 50, 63, 160, 164–168; of classroom 122; self 58, 89
Atmosphere: classroom 34, 120; school 85, 88, 92, 99; *see also* organisational climate
Attribution: causal 44, 47–48, 50, 132, 134, 180; theory 39, 47–48, 130–131
Attributional: bias 105; errors 49
Authority 74, 82, 84, 149, 153, 155; of Head teachers 104, 109, 111; of teachers 16, 57–58, 63, 68–70, 72, 143, 147
Automaticity 16

Behaviour analysis 171–175
Behaviour modification 175–177
Behaviour policy 2–5, 17, 32, 82–85, 86, 91, 93, 102, 106, 140, 146, 160

Behavioural confirmation effect 36
Behavioural methods 75–76, 149, 160, 169–177
Behavioural setting 120, 124
Belongingness 142–144
Body language 16, 69, 71, 78, 134
Body posture 57–58, 62–63, 68–69, 71, 124, 154
Body-focussed movement 69
BOSS model 17–21

Causal schema 48
Classroom management 3, 34, 83, 88, 112, 126, 144, 156
Co variation model 48–51
Cognitive appraisal SEE APPRAISAL
Cognitive-behavioural approaches 77, 160, 169, 177–180
Communication systems 24
Conditions for learning 5, 126, 146, 150
Configuration of forces 34
Conscious activity 15, 17–21
Controllability (perceived) 132–133
Conveying authority 63
Coping: levels of 15–23; styles 31; teacher 15–17, 20
Counselling 75, 166, 180
Culture 56, 68, 116

Data driven impressions 45–46, 52
Data gathering 166–167
Decision making 82, 95, 108
Delegation of responsibility 92, 94
Depression 14, 24, 53, 137, 178
Difficult students 4, 83, 96, 99, 108, 111
Disengaged students 136

Disposition 12, 36, 98, 136, 166
Disruptive students 11, 15, 41, 46, 53, 106

Effective schools 82, 85–89, 102
Emotions *and*: assertiveness 74; attributions 134–136; control of 95–96, 149, 165; facial expression 44, 64–65; gesture 70; social competence 55–57; stress 15–16, 21–26; students 86; thinking 177–179; warmth 52–53, 130–131
Emotional and behavioural difficulties (EBD), definition of 163–164
Emotional: support 109–110, 153; security 141
Enthusiasm 27, 99, 116
Ethos 1, 87–89, 100, 160, *see also* organisational climate
Event schema 39–41
Exclusion 5, 36, 111, 124
Expectancy confirmation cycle 34–35, 48, 52
Expectations: of headteacher 105, 107; pupils 12, 24, 33, 41, 46, 52–53, 82–85, 120, 140, 142–145, 150; teachers 9–100, 177
Extraversion 12
Eye: contact 39, 52, 57–58, 62, 64–67; movement 67–68, 71

Facial expression 15, 57, 64–65, 71
Fear 57, 59, 66, 72–73, 138
Feedback: to pupils 52–53, 58, 70–71, 132, 137, 144, 176, 181; from others 11, 22, 24, 26, 36, 39, 56, 60, 61, 64, 71, 74–75, 77, 156
Feedforward strategies 97, 139

Gaze (*see* eye contact)
Gesture 51, 57–59, 62–63, 69–70, 124
Golem effect 38
Guilt 15, 56, 133

Headteacher, role of 102–109
Hierarchy of needs 141
Hopelessness 134, 136, 179
Humanistic approaches 160, 169, 180–184
Humour, value of 12, 47, 92, 139, 150, 171

Ideal self 181
Impression formation 39, 44–47, 53
Individual coping analysis (ICAN) 27–32
Individual differences 12–14, 104, 131
Interpersonal relationships 12, 34, 39, 61, 64–66, 93, 120, 140, 166

Job satisfaction 11, 99

Leadership styles 104, 109–111
Learned helplessness 137–138
Listening skills 64, 70–72
Locus of control 12, 131–132
Loose/tight coupled management 89, 108, 116

Memory 16, 40, 42, 177
Mastery orientation 133
Metacognition 178
Metaperception 43
Motivational styles 133–139
Multilevel model of behaviour management 1–4

Non-verbal communication (NVC) 59–65

Open systems approaches 89–91
Organisational climate 5, 82, 87–94, 110, 115, *see also* ethos
Organisational culture 11, 88, 97, 151
Organisational socialisation 100
Organisational support 23

Perception 18, 33, 49, 89–90, 130, 135, 142, 178; social 34–36, 39, 40, 42–44, 58–59, 63, 71, 102–103, 107, 166
Personal agency 25–27, *see also* self-efficacy
Personality 22, 44, 49–50, 88, 98–99, 136, 147
Person-job (environment) fit 98–100
Physical assault 93, 173–174
Posture 51, 57–59, 62, 64, 68–69, 71, 124, 154
Powerlessness 73
Problem solving 18, 73, 95, 110, 116, 127, 169, 178
Procrastination, as a coping strategy 75, 136, 179
Professional self 15, 77

Professional self-efficacy 26–27
Prototype (pupil) 42–43
Psychological safety 141–146
Pygmalion effect 38

Rational emotive therapy (RET) 178
Reactive strategies 4
Reinforcement 149, 169–171, 176–177
Rituals 5, 152–155, 170–171
Routines: classroom 5, 17, 22, 73;
    whole school 183–184, 142, 151–156
Rules: classroom 4–5, 72, 125, 139–151,
    155; limit setting 147–148; school
    (core) 59, 84, 140, 146

Sanctions 4, 24, 53, 72, 82–84, 111,
    139–140, 143, 149–151, 176
Schema 39–41
School improvement 85–87
Seating arrangements (classroom) 4,
    123–130
Self-actualisation 141, 180
Self-efficacy student 53, 134–135, 182;
    teacher 12, 26–27, 147–148, see also
    personal agency
Self-esteem 12, 181
Self-fulfilling prophecy 34–35
Self-image 181
Self-regulation 26, 57, 72, 135
Self-worth protection 135–136
Senior management team (SMT) 5, 83,
    94, 98, 102–108, 111–114

Social categorisation 41–43, 63
Social cognition 38–51
Social competence 41, 55–56, 58, 63,
    70, 75, 127, 161, 166, 182
Social identity 24, 40, 53, 90, 100, 109,
    134, 143, 153
Social intelligence (awareness) 55
Social schema 39–41
Social skills training 75–77
Social support 11–12, 23–25, 28, 91–92,
    110, 112
Special provision 36, 168
Stereotyping 39
Stress, models of 13–14, 16–22; ill
    health and 9
Stressors 11, 13–15, 27–29, 31–32
Student voice 85–87
Systems approach 77

Teacher expectancy (see expectancy
    confirmation)
Threshold, coping 16–19
Traits, personality 45–46, 97–98,
    109–110

Unconditional positive regard
    180–181
Underachievement 34, 136, 144

Vicarious reinforcement 176

Workload 11, 26